R

D0549051

The English House 1860–1914

The English House 1860–1914

The Flowering of English Domestic Architecture

GAVIN STAMP and ANDRÉ GOULANCOURT

THE UNIVERSITY OF CHICAGO PRESS

The University of Chicago Press, Chicago 60637

First published in 1986
by Faber and Faber Limited
Printed in Great Britain

95 94 93 92 91 90 89 88 87 86   5 4 3 2 1

Library of Congress Cataloging-in-Publication Data

Stamp, Gavin.
   The English House, 1860–1914.

   Bibliography: P.
   Includes index.
   1. Architecture, domestic—England.   2. Eclecticism in architecture—England.
I. Goulancourt, André.   II. Title.

NA7328.S84   1986   728′.0942   85–28846

ISBN 0–226–77081–8

CONTENTS

ILLUSTRATIONS

Preface

This book grew out of an exhibition of photographs and drawings sponsored by the Building Centre Trust and Redland Limited and held in 1980 with the title 'The English House 1860–1914'. The exhibition had been itself inspired by the publication in 1979 of the first English translation of Hermann Muthesius's classic study of late-Victorian British domestic architecture, *Das Englische Haus*, published in Berlin in three volumes in 1904–5. Muthesius has been quoted extensively in our book because his judgements were objective and illuminating and because the opinions of a perceptive foreign observer can tell us so much about ourselves.

Perhaps it needs to be pointed out these days that when Muthesius wrote about 'The English House' he meant the *British* House, but as this imprecise use of language was once common – even among Scotsmen – it is sometimes used in this present work. Many of Britain's greatest architects have, of course, been Scots and among the creators of the English/British House, Norman Shaw, J. J. Stevenson, James MacLaren, William Flockhart, George Walton and R. Weir Schultz were all born north of the Border. Nevertheless, with the necessary exception of a house by Charles Rennie Mackintosh, all the houses illustrated here are in England – even that designed by that most distinguished and very Scottish architect, Sir Robert Lorimer.

Most of the architects who interested Muthesius are included, although in several cases different houses have been chosen for illustration because of alterations or demolition. In addition, several architects whose work he did not discuss are included, such as G. F. Bodley and Parker and Unwin. Each architect is represented by at least one characteristic house, usually in the country and occasionally in a suburb, although some town houses have also been included as the development of the 'Queen Anne' town house was an important part of British domestic architecture in the period. The survey begins with John Nash and has been extended beyond the scope of *Das Englische Haus* to 1914, which makes a convenient terminal date even though fine houses continued to be built after the Great War, albeit on a reduced scale. The architects who were responsible for good domestic work in the period are legion and it is sad to have had to omit, amongst others, Herbert Baker, Colonel Robert Edis, Horace Field,

Niven and Wigglesworth, Alfred Powell and Edward Warren.

This is intended to be a book of modern portraits of houses, mellowed by time and weather as their architects probably anticipated. Unless otherwise attributed, all photographs have been taken by André Goulancourt, mostly in 1979–81. There are comparatively few illustrations of the interiors of houses, not because these are thought to be less interesting than photogenic exteriors but because the internal character of so many houses has been changed by alterations or by inappropriate furniture. For such houses, early *Country Life* or other original illustrations are a much more satisfactory guide.

Similarly, not many plans are given of the houses illustrated – a grave offence against the canons of architectural history necessitated by practical considerations and justified by the fact that this book consists primarily of photographs which study external effect: texture and materials, mass and outline, image and style. Outward appearance – as the photographs in estate agents' advertisements testify – is a very important part of the character of the English house. Ground plans were given for most houses in the catalogue to the 1980 exhibition and many can be found in Muthesius's book.

The eighty or so houses illustrated here are arranged according to broad themes and in approximate chronological order. First come the precursors and pioneers, then all the late-Victorian country houses from Shaw to the turn-of-the-century extremes and eccentricities of the Arts and Crafts movement, followed by the more Classical or neo-Georgian houses of the period. Town houses are grouped together, followed by suburban houses, and the book ends with the realisation of architectural and social ideals in garden suburbs.

We are most grateful to all the kind owners who have allowed their houses to be photographed and we owe it to them to point out that these houses are private and, in almost all cases, not normally open to the public.

It would be difficult to enter the vast field of Victorian and Edwardian domestic architecture without the help and advice of Alan Crawford, Roderick Gradidge and Andrew Saint. The following also deserve thanks for their assistance in different ways: Jill Allibone, Clive Aslet, Colin Baylis (for information about Walter Cave), Messrs

Preface

Brierley, Leckenby, Keighley and Groom, D. J. Buckman and P. Kendrick of the London Borough of Barnet (The Leys, Elstree), Peter Howell, Edward Hubbard, Paul Joyce, Mervyn Miller (Parker and Unwin), Stefan Muthesius, David Ottewill (Schultz and Troup), Ken Powell, Peter Reid, Margaret Richardson, the Richmond Fellowship, Rory Spence (Leonard Stokes), Anthony Symondson and Robert Thorne (Bellagio, Surrey). I am also most grateful to Mosette Broderick, authority on the early work of those great American architects, McKim, Mead and White, for the photograph of an unfamiliar example of the Shingle style. Claude Lubroth was responsible for all the organisation for the original Building Centre exhibition.

Southwark 1980 – King's Cross 1984   GAVIN STAMP

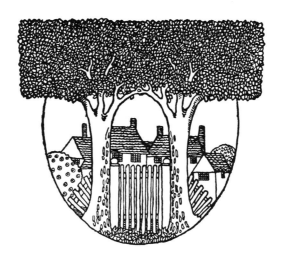

Introduction

Nostalgia can be a creative force. 'I can't think the land will ever be grey with old buildings again,' Philip Webb once sadly remarked,[1] yet that careful and influential house architect did his best to ensure that new buildings had all the sympathetic qualities of the old – and more. His evocative lament beautifully sums up the Romanticism of nineteenth-century Britain, a Romanticism which inspired much excellent and some great architecture: a love of the land, of England; a respect for old ways, old traditions and old buildings in the face of the modern industrialism and materialism which seemed to be destroying both country and society; a reverence for the small house and the cottage, for the roof and the hearth, for the home in the country rather than the house in the town. Webb, his friend William Morris, and so many of their contemporaries cherished a traditional world in which there seemed to be virtue and value and which seemed to be passing away. Morris, in 1879, concluded that 'though many of us love architecture dearly, and believe that it helps the healthiness both of body and soul to live among beautiful things, we of the big towns are mostly compelled to live in houses which have become a by-word of contempt for their ugliness and inconvenience. The stream of civilisation is against us, and we cannot battle against it.'[2]

Yet the remarkable fact about late-Victorian Britain is that the stream of civilisation changed direction, against Progress and things modern and towards the traditional and old. Today few parts of Britain outside the Cotswolds are 'grey with old buildings' but many areas are red and gold and brown, or black and white, with new buildings which might be old: sweeping roofs, tall chimneys and brick or stone walls glimpsed through the trees of Surrey or Sussex, Hampshire or Hertfordshire, Cheshire or Westmorland. Out of the Romanticism of the nineteenth century came a domestic architecture which was popular and successful yet far from vulgar. Like most creative expressions of British art, it was decidedly insular and yet it secured the admiration and provoked the emulation of architects abroad.

This architecture, these houses, are popular still. The Romantic, mellow, picturesque and comfortable smaller houses built in the last three decades of the nineteenth century and the first three of this – a continuous tradition – fill the glossy advertisements of estate agents and remain most ordinary people's dream despite all the rapid changes in architectural fashion over a century and despite the modern dogmas promoted in the architectural schools and imposed by local authorities. The sort of architecture which derives from the Victorian revival of the cottage and the manor house, of vernacular building traditions and styles, has been, in Sir John Summerson's words, 'the only sort (in England) *which has never been laughed at. This is rather significant.*'[3] The reasons for the success of late-Victorian and Edwardian domestic architecture in Britain go far beyond concern with purely architectural qualities, with firmness, commodity and delight – well endowed in all three though such houses usually are; the explanation lies in the history of British culture and society: in snobbery and in nostalgia, in the aspirations of clients as much as the ambitions of architects, in the traditional love of home and sus-

KELMSCOTT MANOR, an old Oxfordshire stone house, built in the sixteenth and seventeenth centuries, which was the home of William Morris from 1871 until his death in 1896 (photo: National Monuments Record).

picion of the big city – in other words, in the complex and paradoxical history of the Industrial Revolution in Britain. Romanticism and revivalism are of the essence of English art and architecture.

Das Englische Haus

The English House has always been much more than a machine for living in. 'Belief in the sacredness of home-life', Ernest Newton told the Architectural Association in 1891, 'is still left to us, and is itself a religion, pure and easy to believe. It requires no elaborate creeds, its worship is the simplest, its discipline the gentlest and its rewards are peace and contentment.'[4] 'The Englishman sees the whole of life embodied in his house.... The Englishman's love of his home has become proverbial', concluded a Continental observer in 1904, who was 'bound to ask whether there is any evidence in the character of the present-day English of the advantages we have extolled in living in private houses'. He had no doubt about the answer: 'I can say for certain ... about the recent revival of the applied arts, that this could never have become as widespread as it is without the practice of living in houses. The work of William Morris, the revival of arts and crafts in England, began quite specifically in the house.'[5]

The Continental observer was, of course, Hermann Muthesius who was attached to the German Embassy in London from 1896 until 1903 and whose principal object of interest was the quality of British domestic architecture. The first volume of his great work, *Das Englische Haus*, was published in 1904. Muthesius had no doubt why his subject would interest his readers in his ambitious, energetic and nationalistic homeland, for 'The end of the nineteenth century saw the remarkable spectacle of a new departure in the tectonic arts that had originated in England and spread across the whole field of our European culture. England, the country without art, the country that until recently had, so to speak, lived on the art of the continent was pointing the way to the world and the world was following – admittedly after some consideration, but all the more decisively and enthusiastically for that. Given this opportunity for the first time to look more closely at English art, one saw that indeed by keeping strictly to her own paths she had repeatedly discovered new artistic ground.'[6]

It is typical of England that this comprehensive study of what was one of the most truly original phases of English architecture should be the work of a foreigner; it is all too typical of England that it should remain unread and untranslated until 1979, accessible only to German readers or to a few *cognoscenti* like W. R. Lethaby, who, in the dark, hating days of the Great War, could write that 'The first thing in the arts which we should learn from Germany is how to appreciate English originality. Up to about twenty years ago there had been a very remarkable development of English art in all kinds. For five or six years, round about the year 1900, the German Government had attached to its Embassy in London an expert architect, Herr Muthesius, who became the historian (in German) of the English free architecture. All the architects who at that time did any building were investigated, sorted, tabulated, and, I must say, understood.'[7]

The influence of the English House abroad is plain to see: in half-timbering and tall brick chimneys from Potsdam to Newport, Rhode

HOUSE FOR HERMANN FREUDENBERG IN NIKOLASSEE, BERLIN. Built in 1907–8, this is an intelligent adaptation of English ideas to German conditions by Hermann Muthesius (photo from *Landhäuser von Hermann Muthesius*, Munich, 1922).

THE CASINO AT GARDEN CITY, LONG ISLAND, NEW YORK, probably designed by Stanford White in 1893, an example of the American Shingle style which was a development of Norman Shaw's 'Old English' houses (photo: Mosette Broderick).

Island – but to assume that the contribution of English domestic architecture to the world was concerned with *style* is to misunderstand the intentions of the architects and, indeed, to misinterpret Muthesius who was anxious to stress 'that the greatest merit of the English house as it stands completed before us is that it is *English*, that is, it conforms totally to English conditions, embodies totally English ways of life, is totally suited to local climatic and geographical conditions and in its artistic design it must be considered totally a product of a native artistic development. Its exemplary qualities for us are therefore limited. And as we have also to develop the German house to conform to German conditions, the prime purpose of a study like the present one must be to show how closely all the external forms of the English house meet the natural conditions obtaining in

SCHLOSS CECILIENHOF, POTSDAM, perhaps the most unlikely example of architectural Anglophilia. This half-timbered English-style house was designed by Paul Schultze-Naumburg and built for the Crown Prince of Imperial Germany in 1914–15, while German and English troops were fighting each other in France and Belgium. In 1945 this house was the scene of the Potsdam Conference (photo: Gavin Stamp).

England, rather than to pick out fine examples that would be worth copying in our situation.'[8]

Nationalism and Conservatism

The lesson of the English House, today as in 1904, is probably most concerned with the creative development of national and vernacular building traditions, yet art-historians – some of whom could actually read Muthesius – have often concluded that the English domestic revival of the later nineteenth century was somehow *progressive* in that it pointed a way forward to the twentieth century. In fact we know that those domestic practitioners, like Voysey and Baillie Scott, who had the misfortune to live on through the 1930s, did not much care for the New Architecture and the machine aesthetic, which, for them, represented a negation of their ideals of craftsmanship and individualism. Voysey did not like being called a 'pioneer' of what he did not approve, and once wrote that 'I am sure those who express such views have no intention of libelling me. I make no claim to anything new.'[9]

Nor did the English House have anything to do with that international, *fin de siècle* modernism of art nouveau, which Muthesius also disliked. He wrote that, fortunately, in England 'there are no startling exhibition-pieces and there is, thank heaven, no trace of art nouveau. Everything breathes simplicity, homeliness and rural freshness, occasionally, indeed, verging on the vernacular. But a fresh breath of naturalness wafts through the house and a sound down-to-earth quality is combined with a sure feeling for suitability. What we principally find here is a practical, indigenous and pre-eminently friendly house; and instead of a sham modernity expressing itself extravagantly in whimsical artificiality we find a purely functional, unaffected design that many may already regard as more modern than all the fantastic excesses of a so-called modern style.'[10]

At about the same time, W. H. Bidlake – a fine domestic architect – wrote that 'The Arts & Crafts movement has prospered amazingly, it is becoming a mighty force.... So far, so good. But excesses of enthusiasm came, wild and foolish excesses, that proved to be a reversion to pre-historic barbarity. The "New Art" craze came into being, and it is still so recent that we can hardly yet realize that it was

and is a nightmare and not a permanent reality.... To be merely original is easy enough. The New Art having detached itself from the past, sought originality first, an aggressive and self-advertising originality, showing no respect for the virtues of reticence and the sense of fine proportion.

'Still, too much stress may be laid on the New Art movement, for it has not taken any real hold on British domestic architecture, which has quietly and steadily progressed, unaffected by the New Art eccentricities. It is to the work of men like Mr Lutyens, Mr Guy Dawber, Mr Lorimer, Mr Ernest Newton, Mr W. H. Brierley, Mr E. S. Prior, Mr Gerald C. Horsley, Mr E. J. May, Mr Herbert Baker, Mr Arnold Mitchell, Mr R. W. Schultz, that we must turn if we wish to realize the high achievement of the art at the present time. And the one quality which is written upon the work of these masters – written in characters so distinct that he who runs may read – is, reticence. There is no parade of effort, no striving for effect, no desire to advertise the architect at the expense of his building, and, one may add, at his client's cost. For, although the client may not suffer pecuniarily, it must be a daily torture to a sensitive man to be confronted continually by the misdirected efforts of his architect's undisciplined originality.'[11]

Bidlake here might well have had Mackintosh in mind, for Mackintosh's architecture and furniture did not usually manifest the English virtues he so succinctly summarised. Even Voysey could write dismissively of the Glasgow 'spook school', and it was the English concern with sound workmanship and practicality and the suspicion of the contrived manner of the 'New Art' that made Mackintosh less admired in London than in Vienna and caused such men as Norman Shaw and E. S. Prior to protest against the Donaldson bequest of art nouveau furniture to the Victoria and Albert Museum.

Voysey was the most narrow of a very insular school of architects, but the achievements of late-Victorian domestic architecture in Britain were known and admired abroad. Thanks, in particular, to his seductive perspective drawings of his houses in the weekly architectural journals, Norman Shaw's work was known in the United States in the 1870s and had a strong influence on what was to become the indigenous and highly creative development of American domestic architecture: the Shingle style. On the Continent it was principally

A   SCOTNEY CASTLE, Kent, Anthony Salvin, 1837–44

B   ST COLUMB MAJOR OLD RECTORY, Cornwall, William White, 1849–50

C LEYS WOOD, Groombridge, Sussex, Richard Norman Shaw, 1868–9

D **STANDEN**, East Grinstead, Sussex, Philip Webb, 1892–4

E SHIPLAKE COURT, Oxfordshire, Ernest George and Harold Peto, 1889–90

F LYMPNE CASTLE, Kent, Robert Lorimer, 1907–9 and 1911–12

G THE NORMAN CHAPEL, Broad Camden, Gloucestershire, C. R. Ashbee, 1905–7

H   HOME PLACE, Holt, Norfolk, E. S. Prior, 1903–5

the *Studio* magazine which introduced the work of Baillie Scott, Voysey, Ashbee and many others, and the influence of British Arts and Crafts architecture combined with that of the writings of Ruskin and Morris can be seen all over northern Europe at the turn of the century. Nevertheless, it must be stressed that the strength of British domestic architecture was first, that it was *national*, if not regional, and second, that it was not so much progressive as *reactionary*, not forward but backward looking.

National Character

The whole extraordinary flowering of architecture in the early twentieth century was essentially nationalist in origin. Whether in Barcelona or Vienna, Chicago or Helsinki, there was a search for a true national style in reaction to the international consequences of nineteenth-century industrial society or to the supposed rigidities of an imported Classicism. The nationalism, indeed racialism, of the Western world at the turn of the century was well expressed by Voysey in 1911: 'Each country has been given its own characteristics by its Creator and should work out its own salvation.... The best architecture in the past has always been native to its own country and has grown out of a thorough knowledge of local requirements and conditions. Requirements include body, mind and spirit. Conditions include Climate and National Character.'[12] This was an attitude shared by Reginald Blomfield, an architect with Classical tastes very different from Voysey's, who nevertheless believed that 'the individuality of race is stronger than that of genius', and that 'It is nothing to us that the French did this or the Italians that: the point is, what has been loved here, by us and those before us. The best English tradition has always been on the side of refinement and reserve.'[13]

For Muthesius the importance of the English House was that it was the first practical expression of this nationalism, this interest in national traditions and in the vernacular. 'The nineteenth century', he believed – albeit erroneously – 'saw the master-mason who had been trained in his guild replaced by the developer over the whole area of everyday practice. His disappearance marked the beginning of the gradual loss of accumulated tradition as a whole and its replacement by the debased standards that we have observed throughout the

OLD WILSLEY, CRANBROOK, a fine example of an old Kentish yeoman's house, of the fifteenth and seventeenth centuries, which was known to young architects like Shaw in the 1860s (photo: *Country Life*, c.1900).

whole of the lower end of the building trade during the nineteenth century. . . . It was England's achievement – and it cannot be rated highly enough – to have been the first to find an escape from this dilemma and to have done so at a time when nothing of the kind was yet stirring on the continent. The escape consisted in the architects recovering the traditions of the old master-mason, abandoning any suggestion of fine architecture and beginning to build simply and rationally like the old guild masons. . . . The beauty of the old guild-masons' buildings, so long despised by architects, had to be rediscovered. Turning to Germany, we see that a general revival of awareness of the beauty of the small, unpretentious house – such as the farm-house or the small-town house – is of extremely recent date. . . . England had made the same discovery as early as the 1860s and it must be said at once that this formed the foundation of the brilliant development in domestic architecture that has since taken place in England.'[14]

This discovery was of buildings which had hitherto been taken for granted, so that by 1900 illustrated books were being published with such titles as *Old Cottages and Farmhouses in Kent and Sussex*. In this last, Guy Dawber, a talented vernacular revival architect, well expressed the attitude of his generation to these buildings. 'The old country cottages and yeoman's houses still remaining are well worthy of care and regard, if only for the simple lessons they teach us, of the beauty of fitness of purpose. They never pretend to be anything but what they are, and there seems to be no effort in either their construction or ornamentation, but merely a simple handing on from generation to generation of well worn and tried tradition. There is, as a rule, nothing fantastic in their outline, or frivolous in detail, qualities which invariably spoil the character of any building by detracting from its simple dignity.'[15] Such cottages and other rural buildings became the model for the new domestic architecture which Norman Shaw called the 'Old English' style. But, as half-timbering and tall brick chimneys were not really suitable for central London (even though plastered and gabled old houses still survived into the 1870s in Holborn and Southwark), an eclectic urban style was evolved out of the study of unpretentious houses of the seventeenth and even the eighteenth century. Kew Palace, with its Dutch gables, rubbed red-

TEMPERATE HOUSE LODGE, KEW GARDENS, one of Eden Nesfields's early buildings, designed in 1867, in which the 'Queen Anne' style is influenced by Japanese art.

brick detail and (albeit later) sashed windows, was a favourite model for what was confusingly and inaccurately called the 'Queen Anne' style.

Muthesius was prejudiced and regarded this movement chiefly as a reaction against the copyism of the Gothic Revival and, worse, the 'cold grip of classicism' which had dominated English architecture since Inigo Jones. 'The change was effected in the 1860s by three architects who took the bold step of abandoning mere pastiche in architecture. Their method was to look for their forms not only, as hitherto, in great works of architecture, such as castles, palaces and cathedrals, but to design more freely, paying attention to utility, material and other purely practical considerations. At the same time they looked towards the simpler country buildings, in particular houses in villages and small towns built in the tradition of the old masons' guilds [a myth, in which Muthesius, like Morris, believed]. The three men were Philip Webb, Eden Nesfield and Norman Shaw.' However, important as these three were, they, along with the whole vernacular revival, were a part of a much larger movement of immense significance, a movement which accounts for the fact that revivalism is still the most vital force in English culture.

Past and Present: the Rejection of Industrialisation

Britain was the first country in the world to industrialise; Britain was also, therefore, the first to react against the consequences of industrialisation, the first in which men tried to recreate that Golden Age which must have flourished before the railways, before the cities and the factory smoke, before the machines, before the jerry-builder, before the enclosures, before, before . . . Some took it back further. For Pugin, of course, and for several generations of High Anglicans, it was the Reformation that had destroyed the vital, organic, Catholic society of the Middle Ages and Pugin satirised the nineteenth-century industrial city to great effect in his *Contrasts* of 1836. For William Cobbett, stomping around the country raging against the ruination of agriculture and the growth of cities, it was the Norman Conquest which had ended English freedom and put the Englishman under the yoke of the Whig aristocracy, now allied with rapacious capitalists.

Lethaby, in his life of Philip Webb, considered that 'The waking up to a conscious response to Nature and to historical association and survivals seems to have come about at the end of the eighteenth century – it was probably enough a manifestation of a protective instinct mysteriously aware of what was to happen in the coming machine age. Wordsworth seems first to have seen things in the new way', and he quoted Burne-Jones, speaking of Rossetti and 'the perfect hunger for romance that was spread abroad in the world at the time he came into it' (i.e. 1828).[16]

A plate from A. W. N. Pugin's *Details of Antient Timber Houses*, published in 1836, illustrating the fate of many of the pre-Renaissance houses he so admired.

It was in the late eighteenth and early nineteenth century that the questioning of the merits of industrial urban society began, and it was intimately linked with the increasingly popular Romantic view of pre-industrial Britain in contemporary literature. Walter Scott was idealising medieval life for his many readers at the time when Cobbett was reaching the political conclusion that the dissolution of the monasteries had been a catastrophe for England. Pugin, another radical Tory, with his reverence for hierarchy and 'propriety', owed much to Cobbett as well as to other conservative philosophers. After Cobbett came Carlyle, cited by Muthesius for calling industrial products 'cheap and nasty'. His *Past and Present* (1843) excoriated modern liberal and democratic ideas and industrial materialist society; instead, Carlyle argued for the conditions which made medieval society so healthy. The 1830s and 1840s, when Carlyle was writing and when Chartism seemed a serious threat to the established order, were also the decades which saw the revival of interest in medieval chivalry and the attempt to recreate the splendour and authority of the medieval Church. Criticism of the present and a Romantic view of the past were intimately linked.

Ruskin and Morris

But no writer had more influence on English architecture than John Ruskin, who, for Muthesius, was 'the prophet of a new artistic culture.... he was also the first to champion the ideals that later became the guiding principles of the new Arts and Crafts movement: simplicity and naturalness in art, honesty in tectonic design, the conditions for which must be sought in the purpose, material and construction, emphasis on the workmanlike, the characteristic, the indigenous, a synthesis of artistic creation and observation of nature.... Ruskin was the first to reach the point of calling in question machine civilization as a whole. He maintained that it made man himself a machine.... The worker, he believed, must once again become a thinking being, able to enjoy the independent creation of his hand; this, he thought, was the prerequisite for human existence.' If Muthesius may possibly have over-emphasised Ruskin's historical importance, he was right to stress that 'It mattered nothing at first that these aims were to some extent backward-looking and that the

prospect of their being realized could scarcely be close; basically they had been formulated on the mediaeval conditions which Ruskin loved and admired beyond all else. Ruskin preached hatred of railways, factories and the creations of recent civilization, from which he shied away throughout his life. But he achieved one thing: he brought an inner composure into the midst of a period of rising industrialism, which was in many ways reckless and destructive of all ideals, and into the rush for money at any price, which dominated English life as it did life everywhere in the nineteenth century.'[17]

Ruskin's concern with the integrity of the individual craftsman, his hatred of the legacy of the Renaissance and of industrial civilisation profoundly influenced the Gothic Revival and inspired Philip Webb and, of course, William Morris, who turned his theories into practical action and who, by his passion and by his example, was the principal individual force behind the Arts and Crafts movement. This was a movement which was inextricably linked with the revival of English domestic architecture, a movement which cannot really be tied to particular styles or architects but which was all-pervasive from the 1880s until well into this century. It is right and proper that a bust of Morris sits in pride of place in the Hall of the Art Workers' Guild, an influential body which had been founded in 1884 by five young architects who had all worked for Norman Shaw and who were all primarily domestic architects: Horsley, Lethaby, Macartney, Newton and Prior.

Morris's social and architectural vision may best be savoured in his Utopian tract, *News from Nowhere*, of 1890, which was a profoundly reactionary and humane vision of a socialist future in the twenty-first century: a post-revolutionary future in which both the artefacts and the attitudes of Victorian society had been destroyed. There is no money as a means of exchange; places like Manchester have simply been removed and London is a collection of villages again, the railways and suburbs having been effaced; Westminster Abbey survives as does the Palace of Westminster – as a dung market – and the British Museum – as a curiosity – but little else. Trafalgar Square had been transformed from 'a great space surrounded by tall ugly houses, with an ugly church at the corner [i.e. St Martin-in-the-Fields] and a nondescript ugly cupolaed building at my back...' into 'a large open space, sloping somewhat towards the south, the sunny side of which had been taken advantage of for planting an orchard, mainly, as I could see, of apricot trees, in the midst of which was a pretty gay little structure of wood, painted and gilded, that looked like a refreshment stall'.[18]

Anti-urbanism

Morris was typical of his generation in being anti-urban. He agreed with his arch-enemy Gilbert Scott about 'The flatness which is utterly intolerable in Baker-street or Gower-street' and which had 'rendered the greatest city in the world a huge wilderness of ugliness'.[19] The Victorians unthinkingly despised the legacy of the Georgian estate builders and of Nash, and most new building in London was picturesque and anti-Classical – red-brick and terracotta gables protesting against Georgian uniformity and Regency stucco. Most people wished to flee the wicked, dirty centre of London altogether: out to the country or, at best, to the suburb. Morris may have ridiculed Victorian suburbs but his vision was essentially suburban – in the best sense. In Piccadilly are 'elegantly-built much ornamented houses, which I should have called villas if they had been ugly and pretentious, which was very far from being the case. Each house stood in a garden carefully cultivated, and running over with flowers.' When the time-traveller – Morris himself – describes the Guest House which he finds on the site of his own old Georgian house in Hammersmith, he might be conjuring up the ideal English Arts and Crafts building of the 1890s: 'It was a longish building with its gable ends turned away from the road, and long traceried windows coming down rather low down set in the wall that faced us. It was very handsomely built of red brick with a lead roof; and high above the windows there ran a frieze of figure subjects in baked clay, very well executed, and designed with a force and directness which I had never noticed in modern work before.... we were presently within doors, and standing in a hall with a floor of marble mosaic and an open timber roof.' *News from Nowhere* was a manifesto for the garden city, a vision of Letchworth as it might have been.[20]

Economics required that Morris's firm operated from Red Lion Square, but Morris's ideal of architecture was always anti-urban, always suburban or, rather, an anticipation of the garden city ideal. He wrote in 1874 of London that 'surely if people lived five hundred years instead of threescore and ten they would find some better way of living than in such a sordid loathsome place.... but look, suppose people lived in little communities among gardens and green fields, so that you could be in the country in five minutes' walk, and had few wants, almost no furniture for instance, and no servants, and studied the (difficult) arts of enjoying life, and finding out what they really wanted: then I think one might hope civilization had really begun.'[21]

A further illustration of the ideal of the English House shared by so many is given by Lawrence Weaver's description published in *Country Life* in 1912 of the house built in 1900 for himself by Hugh Thackeray Turner, a fine architect and Morris's successor as secretary to the Society for the Protection of Ancient Buildings – that influential pressure-group so utterly in opposition to the Victorian progressive spirit. Westbrook (page 102) 'represents the school of traditional architecture which has grown up quietly and surely in England from the seeds sown by William Morris and Mr Philip Webb. Simple, unaffected, owing nothing, or at least singularly little, to the spirit of the Renaissance, it shows what can be done by using local materials in a straightforward yet thoughtful fashion.'[22]

The SPAB, in fact, played an important part in late-Victorian architecture. Not only was it determinedly and vociferously 'Anti-Scrape', but Webb thought, in 1911, that it was 'by far the best modern school of building we have'. Lethaby later wrote that 'The SPAB was itself a remarkable teaching body. Dealing as it did with the common facts of traditional building in scores and hundreds of examples, it became under the technical guidance of Philip Webb, a real school of practical building.'[23]

The Picturesque

That hand-craft is superior to machine-made products, that the use of local building materials is better than standardised industrial ones, were both canons of the Arts and Crafts movement, but they also stem from another strand in Victorian cultural history which lay behind the development of the English House. This, the taste for the Romantic and the Picturesque, was also a reaction against industrialisation but can be traced back to the late eighteenth century, to landscape gardening and the idealising of Nature; to Humphry Repton, Uvedale Price and Richard Payne Knight, to Horace Walpole and Strawberry Hill. In the first decades of the nineteenth century we find, on the one hand, the cult of the Middle Ages in the novels of Sir Walter Scott which so seized the imagination of a generation that it inspired 'Young England', the Eglinton Tournament and helped provoke the revived medievalism of the Church of England; on the other, there was the building of castellated houses: Beckford creating Fonthill and George IV making Windsor Castle more picturesque and Gothic than it ever was.

In tracing the ancestry of the English House, the new villages in the Picturesque spirit are of more interest, as well as the 'rural residences' and 'cottages ornés' illustrated in so many contemporary books. In the eighteenth century old villages could simply be removed by members of the landed aristocracy who wanted to improve the view; by the early nineteenth century higgledy-piggledy disarray was seen as charming and appropriate and was imitated in new buildings: buildings which were a more convincing evocation of the simplicity of rural life than Marie-Antoinette's Arcadian, neo-Classical dairy. Best of all is Blaise Hamlet (page 46), a group of stone and half-timbered cottages with thatched roofs disposed around a green, supremely Picturesque and designed in 1810 by Nash – but they would not have looked out of place in Port Sunlight a century later (page 224).

Picturesque is especially apt as a descriptive term for, as Andrew Saint has demonstrated,[24] painters performed a pioneering role in the English vernacular revival; where painters led, architects followed. Long before Nesfield and Shaw were designing lodges with tile-hung and half-timbered exteriors, and inglenooks inside massive chimney-breasts, Prout, Mulready and other members of the English school of *genre* scene-painting were depicting authentic old versions of such buildings. Penshurst, Kent, with its medieval mansion, became a centre for this school and at Redleaf near by William Wells entertained such painters as Cooke, Cooper, Frith, Landseer, Nasmyth and Turner. Not far away at Cranbrook, another picturesque old village, was another colony of painters. Here Horsley was to start off Shaw's career in 1864; his son was to become Shaw's pupil and a

Streatley Mill (detail) by George Price Boyce.

notable late Victorian architect. Close by is Scotney Castle (page 48), where, around 1840, Edward Hussey created a perfect fusion of picturesque house and landscape; his architect was Salvin, with whom Shaw trained. Nesfield's father was a landscape gardener and in the early 1860s young Shaw and Nesfield were to be found sketching old cottages, farmhouses and barns in Kent and Sussex.

Such was the origin of their 'Old English' style of architecture (*not* to be confused with the more urban 'Queen Anne'), but a central and yet mysterious figure in the development of the style was George Devey, for whom Voysey later worked. Devey came from the world of painters – he had studied under J. S. Cotman – and already by the 1850s he could create picturesque tile-hung gabled cottages almost

THE BISHOP'S HOUSE, BIRMINGHAM, built in 1840–1 and now demolished, was one of Pugin's most interesting domestic designs, remarkable for its straightforward brick construction and comparative simplicity (photos: National Monuments Record).

indistinguishable from their ancient prototypes. Devey acquired a successful – and, at the time, unpublished – practice; his large country houses for Liberal peers and politicians are ponderous piles but his small estate buildings show a subtle appreciation of the qualities of vernacular architecture.

It is still possible to drive through the counties south of London – the real home of the English House – through enchanting villages and past endless tile-hung cottages and be unsure whether they are genuinely old or all designed by George Devey, Norman Shaw, Ernest George, et al., so successful and so widespread was the Victorian vernacular revival. But the success of this architecture did not only depend upon a picturesque eye for the humble, the quaint and the mellow: it also was indebted to that great architectural movement which was the foundation for a century of creative English architecture – the Gothic Revival. Not the Gothic Revival of Wyatt and Fonthill, but that serious, moral approach to plan and elevation, to materials and craftsmanship, that concern with *honesty* which really began with Pugin.

The Gothic Revival

Pugin was most interested in re-creating the numinous splendour of medieval Catholicism in his churches, but he always argued that his 'True Principles' of Gothic architecture applied to all types of buildings and he designed a number of small houses which are remarkable for their reticent informality and rural charm. His now demolished Bishop's House in Birmingham was a prototype for much Gothic Revival domestic architecture. Pugin's importance, particularly with regard to the revival of the crafts of building, was stressed by John Dando Sedding when speaking to the Art Congress in Liverpool in 1888: 'We should have had no Morris, no Street, no Burges, no Webb, no Bodley, no Rossetti, no Burne-Jones, no Crane, but for Pugin.'[25]

By the 1870s, avant-garde architects had abandoned the literal

FLETE LODGE, HOLBETON, DEVON, a building of 1887 by John Dando Sedding which was illustrated by and particularly admired by Muthesius, who wrote that 'It would be hard to imagine a more delightful house ... which, despite a lingering Gothic feeling in its forms, is yet entirely modern in spirit.'

Gothic style – the pointed arch which had so obsessed Pugin – as they experimented with 'Old English' in the country and 'Queen Anne' in town, but they essentially remained Gothicists in their approach to design. As Goodhart-Rendel observed in his celebrated comment on the urban 'Queen Anne' or 'Free Renaissance' style, it was 'a Gothic game played with neo-Classical counters'.[26] Architects retained their fear of Classical formality and symmetry; they designed with Renaissance or with vernacular motifs but still according to Pugin's True Principles. The great domestic architects of the later nineteenth century were almost all Gothic men by training, many having come from the offices of Scott or Street. Voysey always regarded himself as the last disciple of Pugin; he was a Gothic man until the end.

Gerald Horsley, writing in 1906, well expressed the debt of his generation to the Gothic Revival: '. . . its influence was great upon the building of English houses. . . . probably it was chiefly because of its distinct and insular character that the Gothic Revival in England impressed itself so deeply on British Art, and marked at a critical time in many ways a healthy departure from an outworn creed [i.e. the Classic tradition]. The honesty of the movement was the secret of its success. An ardent attempt was made to return to the older English principles in design and workmanship. . . . It is interesting to trace the effect which this Gothic Revival has had upon our domestic architecture. Foremost among its aims we may place the recognition of the craftsman's position and the study and proper use of building materials.'[27]

The New Vernacular: Old English and Queen Anne

As a brave attempt to re-create the Middle Ages and make Gothic a universal style, the Gothic Revival failed. Scott, Street and Waterhouse made noble efforts to make Gothic town halls, Gothic railway stations, Gothic lawcourts, Gothic hospitals, but by the 1870s such buildings were beginning to be regarded as absurd. Gothic always seemed too churchy – and the biggest failure of all was the Gothic house. What was needed was a truly domestic house architecture, something small in scale, pretty, truly vernacular. The dying of the literal Gothic Revival coincided with the birth of the Domestic Revival, as the best pupils of Scott and Street took to the

24

KEW PALACE, a red-brick house of 1631 with Dutch gables and eighteenth-century sash windows which was a particular influence on the 'Queen Anne' style of the later nineteenth century.

new vernacular and to the 'renaissance of the Renaissance'. Their masters, who believed in Gothic as a great moral crusade, were shocked. Scott's last piece of writing was a criticism of 'Queen Anne' and Burges, once a hero of the young, said of it 'I can't dabble with dirt.'[28]

The old Gothic stalwarts rather missed the point. The new movement was indeed anti-Gothic in that the thirteenth century was no longer going to be the perfect paradigm, but it was also anti-Classical in that the academic formality of the Barry tradition remained as unacceptable to the younger generation as to the old – and 'Queen

Anne' was regarded with equal horror by the old Classicists, like Donaldson. Renaissance motifs were indeed used, but only in a picturesque, provincial, illiterate way – just as the so-called 'post-Modernists' of today will do anything with cornices and keystones except use them according to the rules. Until the 1890s absolute symmetry remained anathema to most architects. The new movement was liberating in that it was tied to no one style but to what was appropriate for the site: red-brick neo-Renaissance for the town, wood, plaster, brick and tile for the country. And those who remained most loyal to the principles of Pugin, like Webb and Voysey, were not so much concerned with *style* at all as with what they called *fitness*.

This Domestic Revival was, as we have seen, profoundly anti-Modern. Pugin had said 'I seek *antiquity* and not *novelty*. I strive *to*

KELHAM HALL, NOTTINGHAMSHIRE, a Gothic Revival house of 1858-61 designed by Sir Gilbert Scott which represented everything that younger architects reacted against. This house near Newark has similarities with Scott's later Midland Hotel at St Pancras Station (photo: National Monuments Record).

revive, not invent', and Scott recalled how, on reading Pugin, 'Old things (in my practice) had passed away, and, behold, all things had become new, or rather modernism had passed away from me and every aspiration of my heart had become mediaeval',[29] but the High Victorian Gothic Revival had, in fact, tried to make medievalism modern. This gave it its heroic quality: Butterfield used modern red brick and sash windows, Scott was happy to use iron and plate glass. Gothic was to be not archaeology, but a modern, rational way of building. And herein lay the failure: to the younger generation the results were so aggressive, so hard, so Victorian, so vulgar! A house like Scott's Kelham Hall represents all his son's generation came to despise: a big pile of modern, un-mellowing materials, dark-red brick and plate glass, looking more like a town hall than a country house.

Conversely, Scott, writing in 1878, found the 'Queen Anne-ites' (amongst whom he numbered the 'Old English-ites') very old fashioned, indeed reactionary, for they 'freely adopted lead lights, iron casements, and all kinds of old fashions which a gothic architect would have hardly dared to employ, so much so, indeed, that a so-called "Queen Anne" house is now more a revival of the past than a modern gothic house. . . . The aim of the Queen Anne architects now

A GROUP OF HOUSES, IN WESTBOURNE PARK, HULL, designed by Sir Gilbert Scott's eldest son, George Gilbert Scott junior, and built in 1876–7 in a conspicuous 'Queen Anne' style. Scott originally proposed having busts of Queen Anne herself in relief on the plaster frieze.

seems to be to show that nothing can be too old-fashioned for their style', even though 'it really brings in very much which is highly picturesque and artistic in character such as no "Gothic man" would fail to appreciate.'[30]

Here we have one of the several paradoxes in late-Victorian domestic architecture. The new movement was fundamentally anti-urban, anti-industrial, anti-modern, yet it depended for its life and success upon the wealth and technology of Victorian Britain. Webb may have enjoyed occasional aristocratic patronage, but most of Shaw's clients were *nouveaux riches*: brewers, solicitors, industrialists – and the money came from *trade*. Furthermore, neither architects nor clients could really have indulged in the taste for rural life and the vernacular if it was not for the invention so hated by Ruskin and Morris: the railway.

A Place in the Country

It is not merely a metropolitan prejudice which emphasises the domestic architecture of the Home Counties, for a very high proportion of the famous English Houses of the later nineteenth century are to be found in the counties south of London, counties where there are few great aristocratic estates, for 'no gentleman hunts south of the Thames'. Surrey, Kent and Sussex were open for house building because much of the area consisted of poor agricultural land – particularly the heathland of Surrey. All that was necessary was rapid transport from London. In the late 1860s the Groombridge area, where Shaw built Glen Andred and Leys Wood (page 70), was being opened up by the London, Brighton & South Coast Railway Company, while most of Lutyens's famous early houses are a few miles from Godalming, from whose station his clients could daily be whisked up to Waterloo by the London & South Western Railway. Thanks to railway companies, a lush zone around London – from Hertfordshire through Buckinghamshire, Berkshire, Hampshire, Surrey and Sussex to Kent – became and remains full of desirable 'Stockbrokers' Tudor'; it is the still wealthy 'Gin and Tonic Belt'.

Doubtless this paradox did not worry Shaw's or Voysey's happy clients in the country at weekends any more than it disturbs those people today who drive out to their quiet cottages in Gloucestershire every Friday over motorways which blight the intervening countryside. The Country Life depends upon money and efficient transport. It was a paradox which poor Morris never resolved: an idealist with a private income reacting against the circumstances which made him privileged, working for socialism with the profits made from selling his products. Morris, with his (Georgian!) house in Hammersmith and old country house by the Thames at Kelmscott, railed against 'the hideous vulgarity of the cockney villas of the well-to-do, stockbrokers and other such, ... which marred the beauty of the bough-hung banks',[31] but he, like so many others, was indulging in the favourite pursuit of the educated: belittling the social class from which they spring.

Definitions of social class are notoriously imprecise and often unhelpful – especially in a country where long-established social fluidity and mobility has given vigour and avoided revolution – but it can be stated unequivocally that the revival of domestic architecture in late-Victorian Britain was based initially upon the patronage of the upper middle classes and the results were then applied gradually down the social scale. The English House expressed bourgeois aspirations; indeed it was perhaps the first truly middle-class expression in British architectural history. Peter Davey goes so far as to argue that 'The Arts and Crafts movement was of and for the Victorian upper middle class. . . . The upper middle classes were the only people who could enjoy individual freedom in Victorian England; they were free of the grinding poverty of the lower orders, the inverted snobbery of the lower middle classes and the increasingly rigid formality of the aristocracy. Because Britain was the richest and most powerful nation in the world, they were probably the most free people in the world.'[32]

The old landed aristocracy no longer led architectural fashion. The 1870s were a great divide in many areas of British life and one of the most significant events was the collapse of British agriculture, owing to a succession of bad harvests and increasing dependance upon imported grain brought cheaply from the Mid-West of America by steam railway and steamship. The agricultural depression, which lasted until the 1940s, largely put an end to country house building by the aristocracy who, by the 1890s, were looking for American heiresses to underpin their prestige. The money which paid for Norman Shaw or Lutyens houses did not come from land but from the city or from abroad.

Social Aspirations

The English House represented a new sophistication in social mobility. Earlier in the nineteenth century the successful industrialist, or his son, who moved away from his mill to establish himself higher in the hierarchy of English society would build a country house similar to those built by the older aristocracy. He would use the same architects and the same styles: Italianate, Elizabethan, Jacobean. Even Gothic, associated as it became with High Church ecclesiology, was patronised by the upper class and was far from being a middle-class style. But by the 1870s some of the new rich (excluding the Rothschilds and the more flashy new money, who went for the French château – what Mark Girouard has characterised as the 'nouveau-riche style'[33]) did not want to build the imperious castellated or porticoed mansions of earlier generations but wanted a truly countrified, old and English style of their own.

This was a product of a social revolution in the 1860s so well analysed by Girouard in his study of the Queen Anne style. There was 'A Class in Search of an Image', a new middle class reacting against their serious, moral, muscularly Christian parents. 'Delicacy and refinement were preferred to toughness and vigour, the small scale to the large. . . . Generally speaking, they looked at modern technology with suspicion; artistically it became progressive to be old-fashioned. Dislike of the present led them to the past, dislike of the town to the country. As an antidote to the present they re-created the past as an ideal world of pre-industrial simplicity, at once homely and Arcadian.'[34] An image was made for this class – designed by Shaw, Nesfield, Webb, Godwin, George and the rest. A new interest in houses not as architecture but as *homes*, considering the furniture, the decorations and wallpapers – which owed much to the growing influence of women – is reflected in a number of books published in the 1870s and 1880s, such as Robert Edis's *Decoration and Furniture of Town Houses* (1881) and the several books by that Artistic clergyman's wife, Mrs Haweis: notably *Beautiful Houses* (1881) and *The Art of Decoration* (1889).

A vernacular architecture, a cottage architecture – which is what 'Old English' really was – was not, of course, new; the novelty lay in the fact that for the first time it was respectable to live in it. Nash had designed sweet cottages at Blaise Hamlet (page 46), but these were to house the aged servants of the banker who lived in the big house. Here is the significance of the Red House at Bexleyheath (page 60), so overrated in historical importance as a piece of architecture. As has been frequently observed, Webb was here merely using the secular, domestic Gothic manner evolved by his master Street and by Butterfield for their schools, parsonages and country buildings. But, whereas Butterfield employed this reduced brick Gothic at Baldersby St James (page 54) for farm labourers – the vicar had half-timbering on his house – Webb was designing in this style for a wealthy, artistic client, namely William Morris.

Muthesius was right to single out the names of Webb, Shaw and Nesfield, for they led the way towards the English House which satisfied the aspirations of the middle class: the private country houses – whether vernacular, Old English, Queen Anne, Free Style, Tudor, and, ultimately, neo-Georgian – which also satisfied the English obsession with Nature and the moral, indeed cosmic, rightness of living in the country. It would seem to be deeply rooted in English – and, for that matter, American – culture that living in or retiring to the country should be the aim of life and that living in the city, or even in the suburb, is a regrettable, unnatural, temporary necessity. It is for the country house or cottage that the businessman, the banker, the shopkeeper, the commuter hopes and saves, despite the painful fact that, after a century and more of social and geographical mobility, the ex-urban or ex-suburban middle-class country dweller has no roots anywhere and glamorises the harsh realities of rural life. The result is the deadness of our city centres, the growth of leafy suburbs and the continuing and sustained desirability of 'Stockbrokers' Tudor' and all the other types of suburban house which derive, ultimately, from the work of Webb, Shaw and Nesfield. The image they gave a class has not lost its appeal over a century later.

BEDFORD PARK (see page 206). The olde-worlde charm of this 'Queen Anne' development is well conveyed by this woodcut, but note the railway in the background, without which the retreat to suburbia would not have been possible (from Moncure Conway, *Travels in South Kensington*, 1881).

Country Life

The great popularity of the ideal of the English House in the country may be assessed by the extraordinary number of books on houses which appeared after the 1890s: books by Lawrence Weaver and W. Shaw Sparrow with titles like *The British Home of Today, Flats, Urban Houses and Cottage Homes, Small Country Houses of Today, Modern Homes, Modern Cottage Architecture, Recent English Domestic Architecture*, which poured from the presses of, in particular, Messrs Batsford and *Country Life*. It was a flood of books for people with moderate incomes which continued through the 1920s and 1930s. But this ideal was conveyed by one publication in particular, a magazine which still seems to both English and foreigners alike to express the essence of England – *Country Life*. The first issue appeared in 1897 (the same year as saw the birth of the *Architectural Review*), in which articles on country pursuits and sports were preceded by a portrait frontispiece of the Earl of Suffolk and Berkshire. In a few years its

inspired founder and editor, Edward Hudson, had arrived at the formula which ensures the magazine's continuing success today, with articles on country houses, old and new, to ameliorate the more bucolic subject matter. Most people who read and still read *Country Life* have little chance of achieving the ideal of style and taste presented in its pages, but Hudson tapped a deep-rooted instinct in the English character. He was also a patron and friend of Lutyens, perhaps the most successful architect of all at creating a Romantic, rural, seemingly timeless architecture for the well-to-do. Country life and *Country Life* both encouraged Lutyens's genius.

The desire to live in, or apparently in, the country in England is, of course, of long standing. Nash catered for this aspiration in Regent's Park, where the lessees of his terraces and villas could overlook lawns and trees and imagine they were in the depth of the country. There followed the mid-Victorian estates of suburban villas set in landscaped parks such as Paxton's Birkenhead Park of the 1840s. Then came the famous fusion of the suburban ideal with the new, smart vernacular style in Bedford Park (pages 206–9) to the west of Hammersmith. This 'first garden suburb' (?) was created after 1875 by E. W. Godwin and then by Shaw and it had an inn (significantly called the Tabard after the old inn in Southwark celebrated by Chaucer), a church and a community centre for its determinedly Artistic inhabitants. Muthesius maintained that 'there was at the time virtually no development that could compare in artistic charm with Bedford Park, least of all had the small house found anything like so satisfactory an artistic and economic solution as here. And herein lies the immense importance of Bedford Park in the history of the English house. It signifies neither more nor less than the starting-point of the smaller modern house, which immediately spread from there over the whole country.'[35]

The Garden Suburb

Thereafter, the development of the English House went hand-in-hand with a larger vision, uniting a popular, domestic architecture for all with the desire to escape from the dark, smoky city back to the land: the garden city and the garden suburb. Ebenezer Howard provided the theory in his book *Garden Cities of Tomorrow* and, soon after the beginning of the new century, Letchworth (page 218) was founded, forty miles from London and full of cottages by famous architects like Baillie Scott, and then there came Hampstead Garden Suburb (page 226), planned by Parker and Unwin but with a centre by Lutyens, just beyond the end of the new electric tube railway.

Here is the humanity of the vision, both social and architectural. Most domestic architects were apolitical – probably Conservative, if anything – after all, they worked for the rich if they could, but some, like Lethaby, Parker and Unwin, shared the socialist ideals of Morris and Webb. They believed that the benefits of a good, homely, well-built domestic architecture should not be enjoyed only by the comparatively wealthy but by *everybody*. The detached countrified English House could be built simpler, smaller and more cheaply without losing its charm or its integrity. At Letchworth, Port Sunlight (page 224) and other garden suburbs, architects showed how cottages could be cottages still, decent houses in which ordinary people could

live. Often they had to be grouped together, but the uniformity of the working-class tenement was always avoided. Each tenant could feel he was living in a house – his castle – and in a villagy atmosphere which was healthy. Architects both famous and obscure addressed themselves to the problem of designing cheap but decent housing and several competitions were held, notably the 1905 'Cheap Cottages' exhibition at Letchworth when cottages were built for £150, if possible.

Garden suburbs, garden cities and well-designed public housing represented an ideal which was very English: a confident assumption that the less-well-off aspired to what the better-off had; it was an ideal of levelling up rather than levelling down, an expression of the social fluidity of British society. If the social experiment of an organic community has failed in places like Hampstead Garden Suburb, it is because the houses intended for the artisan have proved equally attractive to the stockbroker. The humanity of the architectural vision was well expressed in the policy of the Architects' Department of the London County Council, which, after 1893, erected in central London estates of working-class housing blocks whose variety, charm and excellent brickwork, owed much to Philip Webb and to other Arts and Crafts architects (page 228). These estates, built in response to the urgent problems of slum-clearance and inner-city housing, were much admired by Muthesius, who called them 'almost model developments as regards the artistic interpretation of these important problems'. However, Muthesius was sure that Ebenezer Howard's answer was the right one, for 'a real remedy can only come through depopulating the large cities, through the removal of the urban population to the open country. England may be the first to solve the problem because the English of all classes have retained their natural love of country life to a greater extent than any other people.'[36] So, at the same time, the LCC also created large 'cottage estates' away from the centre of London, in Tottenham, Tooting (page 230), and Old Oak Common, which were of an architectural quality and utility equal to any of the privately developed garden suburbs.

In the early work of the robustly named Housing of the Working Classes Branch of the LCC's Architects' Department, whether cottage estates or the high-density urban blocks, we are presented with a contrast between the results of the Fabian Socialism of the reformers of the 1890s and those of the totalitarian Marxist ideals which affected the LCC's architects in the 1950s. The policy of providing middle-class domesticity for all was abandoned in favour of a new industrialised aesthetic: a high-rise uniform domestic architecture in imitation of Le Corbusier, mass-produced for a modern classless, collectivist society. Many members of the unfortunate working class who were housed according to this ideal have been suffering ever since, unless they have managed to escape to the individual suburban house which they would always rather have when given the choice. So often laughed at – sympathetically by Osbert Lancaster but patronisingly by others – the great areas of speculative suburbs, detached and semi-detached, which were built between the wars are far from being an ignoble conclusion to the late-Victorian domestic architecture; the houses may be small and repetitive, with their debased motifs ultimately deriving from Norman Shaw and Voysey, but they represent the popular idea of home – the architecture of freedom and choice.

Muthesius well understood the English character in this respect: 'The great store that the English still set by owning their home is part of [a] powerful sense of the individual personality. The Englishman sees the whole of life embodied in his house. Here, in the heart of his family, self-sufficient and feeling no great urge for sociability, pursuing his own interests in virtual isolation, he finds his happiness and his real spiritual comfort.'[37] The same could be said of America, for, in both countries, this individualism, this concern with privacy and with the family as the essential social unit, was the bedrock of the flowering of domestic architecture in the last decades of the nineteenth century. From about 1870 until the early years of this century, it was the single family house – whether in the country, the suburb or even the town – which most interested architects and which filled the architectural journals in both Britain and the United States. The famous and the less famous architects mentioned by Muthesius – the list is comprehensive, but there were more he could have noted – were all primarily house architects.

After Norman Shaw had designed Albert Hall Mansions in 1880, architects did interest themselves in flat architecture and Edwardian London, very envious of the urbanity of Paris, was much more concerned with city life and city architecture. Nevertheless, the urban flat has never overtaken the private house in general popularity. In 1900, the *Building News* observed that 'The apartment house has disadvantages: among them the gregariousness of the occupants. It is very doubtful, we think, whether the English race will ever abandon their own small castles.'[38] Muthesius regarded the block of flats as an aberration in the English tradition, an attitude shared by another brilliant foreign observer, S. E. Rasmussen, in his *London: The Unique City* of 1937. As in later editions of the book the text was altered, Rasmussen's original gloomy conclusion is worth quoting: 'In England new slums largely develop in houses that have been given up by their middle-class owners. On the continent we construct slums. . . . To build flats in slums will not stem the current, London will continue to be a town of one-family houses . . . [but] new London, the capital of English civilization, has caught the infection of Continental experiments which are at variance with the whole character and tendency of the city! Thus the foolish mistakes of other countries are imported everywhere, and at the end of a few years all cities will be equally ugly and equally devoid of individuality. This is the bitter END.'[39]

Muthesius believed that 'the Anglo-Saxon race has been denied the gift of building cities; and this demonstrates another well-known element in his character: the inability of the individual to subordinate himself and his belongings to the whole. . . . The Englishman hurries up to town for the sole purpose of doing business. In the evening he hastens back to the heart of his family and makes no bones about travelling for up to an hour by railway in order to spend his few hours of leisure as far away as possible from the bustle of the metropolis. In England one does not "live" in the city, one merely stays there.' 'This . . . is the reason for the desolate monotony of English cities that every continental has felt, for the hurried and purely commercial dealings in the city streets, for the absence of inviting places where a drink and a rest may be had and which are so highly evolved on the continent.'[40]

This preference for the dull remote suburb over the attractions of the city centre, this concern with privacy and with the individual, was typical of the English and particularly typical of the Victorian age. The formal regularity of Georgian London – in which urban living and the private house had been reconciled – was despised and destroyed wherever possible. The attitude which valued the private house more highly than a uniform, planned city was expressed, albeit in an extreme form, by Voysey in 1919: 'Town planning is the outcome of a belief in a fundamental principle which is false. The principle is collectivism. The drilling and controlling of the multitude.... One noticeable feature of human nature still persists, and that is the hatred aroused by all forms of heresy. The unconventional is suspected, if not positively resented.... Town planning follows the same instinct – conformity is its very essence. Collectivism is its creed.... It is the moral responsibility of individual action that we need to respect and preserve, and the power without responsibility following collective control which we need to prevent.'[41]

Individuality – not eccentricity – in architecture was what was valued and Voysey's uncompromising individualism was respected by most of his Arts and Crafts colleagues who also agreed with him about the almost sacred importance of the home. As John Brandon-Jones has written, 'To Voysey a house was not a machine for living in, it was a home, and a home to him meant spiritual as well as material shelter, a place in which mind and spirit as well as the body could find rest and comfort.'[42] Muthesius was certain that 'there can be no doubt that to live in a private house is in every way a higher form of life. Its most important qualities are ethical and virtually incalculable. Just as a higher force determines that a man shall found a family, so he certainly has an inborn instinct to create a permanent dwelling place for himself and his family, his own little kingdom in which he may rule, spread himself and blossom.'[43]

The Image of 'Home'

This concern with the house as *home* led to a degree of caricature in much domestic architecture, when tall brick chimneys were made much taller than functionally necessary by Norman Shaw or Lutyens (often the chimney-stack was completely useless except as part of the overall composition) or when Voysey made hipped pitched roofs sweep almost to the ground so as to create a dramatic effect of enclosure. This exaggeration of the individual elements of vernacular

HIGH AND OVER, AMERSHAM, a pioneering and controversial house of 1929 in the Modern movement manner by Amyas Connell which, although it uses the Edwardian 'butterfly' plan, is, in its use of materials, imagery and deliberate lack of adaptation to local climate and conditions, the complete antithesis to 'the English House' (photo: National Monuments Record, c.1930).

architecture was done consciously to make them symbols of a 'home' and is very evident in the work of Baillie Scott and, especially, Voysey whose houses can have a naive, fairy-tale character, as has often been pointed out. The enclosing, protective character of a roof was particularly important and, indeed, the symbolic nature of the roof in house design became very evident in the 1930s – both in Britain and in Germany – in the tiresome controversies about the merits of the flat roof, when the superior efficiency of the pitched roof in a wet climate was scarcely the real issue. 'Hatless houses in England seldom look right in the country', maintained Baillie Scott in 1933, objecting to the International style.[44]

Along with the roof, the fireplace was a vital functional and symbolic feature: the 'hearth' to warm the home at the centre of home life, flame as the soul of the house. Although this view of the fireplace was consciously old-fashioned and essentially Romantic, the hearth assumed an almost mystical importance – as it did in the United States with the early houses of Frank Lloyd Wright – and it was usually a dominant architectural feature. Muthesius wrote of the 'ethical significance of the fire-place' – 'To an Englishman the idea of a room without a fire-place is simply unthinkable. All ideas of domestic comfort, of family happiness, of inward personal life, of spiritual

I MOORCRAG, Lake Windermere, C. F. A. Voysey, 1899

J   HILL HOUSE, Helensburgh, Charles Rennie Mackintosh, 1904

K TIRLEY GARTH, Cheshire, C. E. Mallows, 1906–12

L   EYFORD COURT, Upper Slaughter, Gloucestershire, E. Guy Dawber, 1910

M   THE SALUTATION, Sandwich, Kent, Edwin Lutyens, 1911

N   NO. 39 HARRINGTON GARDENS, Kensington, Ernest George and Peto, 1882–3

o   NO. 8 ADDISON ROAD, Kensington, Halsey Ricardo, 1905–7

P LANESIDE, Letchworth, Barry Parker and Raymond Unwin, 1904–5

wellbeing centre around the fire-place. The fire as the symbol of home is to the Englishman the central idea both of the living-room and of the whole house; the fire-place is the domestic altar before which, daily and hourly, he sacrifices to the household gods.'[45] Only the new god Television, allied to central heating, has allowed the traditional British altar to grow cold.

The Georgian house had a diminutive low-pitched roof behind a parapet and reticent chimneys. In reaction the Gothic Revival concentrated on roof and chimney so as to emphasise home and hearth. After Pugin, architects placed chimney-breasts on the outside walls, a neo-medieval feature which, though an honest expression of interior arrangements, lost heat to the outside air. But generous chimney-breasts suggest warmth and comfort, especially if there is an inglenook inside. The ingle – a recessed fireplace with fixed seats either side, often surmounted by a massive hood – was revived by

INGLENOOK AT FARNHAM PARK, BUCKINGHAMSHIRE, by Eden Nesfield. An early example of 1865 (from C. L. Eastlake, *A History of the Gothic Revival*, 1872).

Nesfield and Shaw in the 1860s and assumed a central place in Parker and Unwin's house designs fifty years later. 'There is perhaps no feature in the interior of even an ordinary dwelling-house which is capable of more artistic treatment than the fireplace of its most frequented sitting-room', wrote Eastlake in 1872, 'and yet how long it was neglected! The Englishman's sacred "hearth", the Scotchman's "ain fireside", the grandsire's "chimney corner", have become mere verbal expressions, of which it is difficult to recall the original significance as we stand before those cold, formal slabs of gray or white marble enclosing the sprucely polished but utterly heartless grate of a modern drawing-room.' Illustrating a Nesfield ingle in his *History of the Gothic Revival*, Eastlake noted that 'To draw round such a cosy hearth as this is rarely given to modern gossips.'[46]

A house in Britain could, can never be a '*machine à habiter*' as that ignores the associational, emotional, symbolic and Romantic necessities of the individual. Baillie Scott would often label his interior spaces on the plans by such twee terms as 'bower' and 'den', while that sound builder and sensible designer, Philip Webb, had at heart a very Romantic attitude to house design. Lethaby recalled that Webb 'felt that roofs, chimneys and walls were sacred. When he designed Morris's coped gravestone he said: "It will be a roof for the old man." Once speaking of a too elegantly designed grate and chimney-piece, he said: "Yes, but it is hardly fit for Holy fire." It was the heart in things made which called to him.'[47]

The Simple Life

With individualism went, all too often, another prejudice which seems very typical of the British character, that is, a certain Puritanism or an exaggerated affection for the simple. This was at its most extreme with Webb and Voysey but a narrow, self-denying austerity can be detected in the character of many Arts and Crafts architects (despite all their enthusiasm for Merrie England, one cannot imagine Lethaby or Voysey being happy in a pub and several Arts and Crafts figures seem to have been prim bachelors who made late, and not always successful, marriages). A dislike of vulgar, ostentatious luxury became characteristic of all those reacting against mid-Victorian materialism and Arts and Crafts designers later found themselves opposed to the extravagant 'Louis who?' interiors favoured by the cosmopolitan *nouveaux riches* of Edward VII's circle. Morris, in 1879, announced that 'I have never been into any rich man's house which would not have looked the better for having a bonfire made outside of it of nine-tenths of all that it held',[48] and sentiments in favour of 'honesty and simplicity of life' may be found in most architects' writings. They looked for what was traditional, rural, whatever seemed more *real* in contrast to the products of Victorian industrial civilisation, and the Simple Life enjoyed a great vogue in the 1890s. Morris once said he would be happy to live in one big room, with a bed in one corner and a table in another – but he was rather a slovenly brute of a man. Voysey invited people to 'Try the effect of a well-proportioned room, with white-washed walls, plain carpet and simple oak furniture, and nothing in it but necessary articles of use, and one pure ornament in the form of a simple vase of flowers' – an austere taste which did not prevent him from being a most successful designer of wallpapers.[49]

What is remarkable is that a degree of simplicity of life was adopted even by some of the very rich and not just by the vegetarians and Fabian socialists who made up most of Voysey's clients. Early *Country Life* photographs of Lutyens's first houses often show nothing but wooden furniture – both antique and new – set against the timber and plaster of the interiors and in Weir Schultz's furnishing of Mochrum Old Place for the 4th Marquess of Bute, not a sofa was to be seen but only good, solid Gimson furniture. It was all very earnest, and not a little uncomfortable.

Despite the possible forward-looking qualities of stylelessness and practicality which certain historians have detected, the fact remains that the English House of the later nineteenth century was usually rather primitive, but it needs foreign observers to see that. In considering 'Voysey's approach to strictly utilitarian problems', David Gebhard has found that 'this is an area of British architecture which an American historian finds difficult to look at in a very sympathetic and objective way. If one posits that a core ingredient of modern twentieth-century architecture is the increased ability fully to control our environment, then Voysey would hardly rate very high (nor as a matter of fact would any architect during these decades). While

DEANERY GARDEN, SONNING (see page 96). The hall of Lutyens' house for Edward Hudson as originally furnished (photo: *Country Life*, 1903).

Voysey did on occasion use central hot-water heating, this was usually the result of the pressure of his client, not a reflection of his own desire. His plumbing – compared with American plumbing of the time – was almost medieval. The layouts of his kitchen (and sculleries) and baths were not well conceived, conveniently planned, or visually pleasant places to be in.'[50]

In terms of technology and environmental control the English House was much less sophisticated than domestic architecture on the Continent or in America, and this was simply because of the generally hospitable climate, as Muthesius realised (he could not bear the damp and fog, however). 'The mildness and evenness of the climate account for the insubstantial structure of the English house, especially the meagre thickness of the walls, the absence of cellars, of double-glazed windows, the negligible care bestowed on ensuring that windows and doors fit snugly, the frequent absence of an entrance porch, the universal habit of using the whole attic floor for living accommodation and the heedless exposure of supply pipes and drain-pipes, for the building regulations prescribe that the latter must be on the exterior of the house.... Open fires are the only means of heating the house.... One presumes that the mild climate is also responsible for the fact that the English have made scarcely any use at all of central heating. And even when it is installed it never replaces the open fire, for to the English a room without a fire is like a body without a soul.... The need for adequate ventilation ... accounts, for example, for the Englishman's fondness for sash-windows.... The large amount of ventilation is the cause of the famous draughtiness of the English houses, which has already provoked many a harsh word from foreigners.... The English are more or less impervious to the draught.... They usually sleep with the window open, open the windows in unheated railway compartments in winter and, in general, have nowhere near the same need of warmth as we on the continent have with our over-heated railway carriages and the tropical temperatures in our rooms.'[51] (Alas, that in recent years more comforts are to be experienced in English houses, for, in these times of expensive energy, old-fashioned English fortitude would be a great economy.)

Planning of Houses

It has been argued by James Kornwolf[52] that Baillie Scott and 'Bungalow' Briggs were sufficiently aware of developments in American domestic architecture to experiment with more open planning, but

CAVENHAM HALL, SUFFOLK, a house designed by A. N. Prentice in an eclectic Classical manner which was admired and illustrated by Muthesius for its clever and typical planning. It was built in 1898–9 and demolished in 1949, although the lodges still survive (see page 154) (photo: National Monuments Record).

Baillie Scott's ingenious plans are more interesting on paper than they are in fact and it is probably true to say that most English domestic architects were not at all interested in new types of spatial arrangements. What was important was the convenient disposition of fully enclosed rooms, for the desire for privacy that encouraged the detached house also encouraged privacy within rooms and Muthesius perceptively noticed that a door was usually positioned near the corner of a room, opening inwards, so that 'the person entering shall not be able to take in the whole room at a glance as he opens the first crack of the door but must walk round it to enter the room, by which time the person seated in the room will have been able to prepare himself suitably for his entry.'[53]

The typical late-Victorian house plan is additive and informal, thus allowing a Picturesque and varied external treatment to the house as well as that separation of functions thought so necessary in domestic architecture. The plans of Shaw's larger country houses, designed for weekend entertaining, are usually rambling and drawn out; Webb's are more compact, though always with long service wings. On a

Comparative house plans

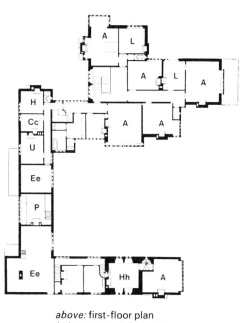

above: first-floor plan
below: ground-floor plan

1. LEYS WOOD, Sussex, 1868, Norman Shaw

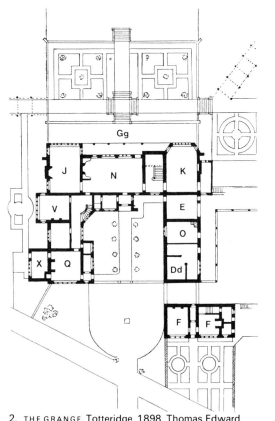

2. THE GRANGE, Totteridge, 1898, Thomas Edward Collcutt

KEY TO PLANS 1–4

A	Bedroom	M	Entrance	Z	Servants
B	Billiard table	N	Hall	Aa	Service area
C	Butler	O	Harness room	Bb	Silver
D	Cleaning room	P	Ironing room	Cc	Spare room
E	Coach house	Q	Kitchen	Dd	Stables
F	Coachmans' quarters	R	Larder	Ee	Storeroom
G	Coal	S	Library	Ff	Study
H	Cook	T	Meat larder	Gg	Terrace
I	Courtyard	U	Maids' room	Hh	Tower room
J	Dining room	V	Morning room	Ii	Upper part of hall
K	Drawing room	W	Pantry	Jj	Veranda
L	Dressing room	X	Scullery	Kk	Workshop
		Y	Seat		

3. REDCOURT, Haslemere, Surrey, 1894–5, Ernest Newton

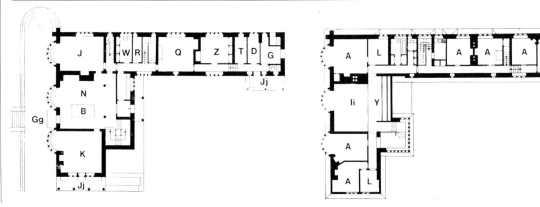

4. BROADLEYS, Westmorland, 1898, C. F. A. Voysey. *left:* ground-floor plan; *right:* first-floor plan

Comparative house plans

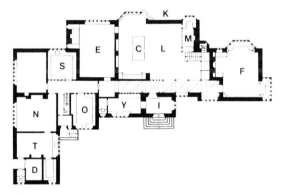

above: first-floor plan
below: ground-floor plan

first-floor plan

SCALE:

5. BLACKWELL, Westmorland, 1898–9, Baillie Scott

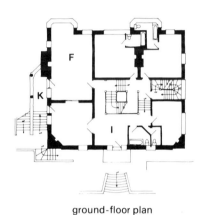

ground-floor plan

8. YEW TREE LODGE, Streatham Park, 1898–9, Leonard Stokes

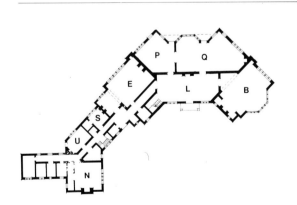

6. HOW GREEN, Hever, Kent, 1904–5, R. Weir Schultz

lower ground-floor plan

7. RED HOUSE, Godalming, Surrey, c. 1899, Edwin Lutyens

smaller scale, the typical Arts and Crafts house has an essentially simple plan of a series of different rooms strung out along corridors, thus securing the vital necessity of privacy; Baillie Scott's type of open, flexible planning was not much imitated as it was both un-English and probably inconvenient. The most sophisticated house planners were Ernest Newton, the master of convenient asymmetry within symmetrical compositions, and Lutyens, who achieved interesting and ambiguous effects by exploiting unorthodox arrangements and the possibilities of suggesting movement along axes.

Compared with contemporary American houses, British houses were no more progressive or 'advanced' in their plans than they were in technical matters, and the large, often double-height, hall which many had was a medieval revival in origin. The only innovation which secured any acceptance was the 'butterfly plan', which became fashionable after Shaw used it at Chesters in 1891. By bending the spine of a house plan, usually at forty-five degrees, more rooms could be made to catch the sun or the view. If three or more such wings were made, the central hall became a more interesting and useful space while, whatever the plan, a change in axis created an unusual and complex external composition.

The Craft Tradition

The affection for simplicity and the primitive was, in part, a reflection of the growing respect for old ways of building, for traditional craftsmanship. The English House was to be built in the old way. Thanks to the Gothic Revival and the Arts and Crafts movement, the standard of building craftsmanship reached a very high pitch by the end of the century and excellent workmanship is to be found even in houses designed by not especially careful or gifted architects. As Horsley noted in 1906, 'So excellent and so thorough has this general craft training become, that good craftsmanship in our homes, in stone, wood, brick, plaster, or metal, is now generally attainable.... It has become an accepted fact in building that no effort should be spared to ensure that all work, in whatever material it is executed, should be carried out in a way which experience shows to be best adapted to the material itself',[54] but it should also be remembered that the high

quality of turn-of-the-century building was assisted by the relative cheapness of both materials and labour. As a result it was possible for architects to specify the special thin, hand-made bricks which add so much to the character of a building.

Quite possibly, the extent to which the old crafts of building had died out during the Industrial Revolution has been much exaggerated – it has been the twentieth century and Modern architecture which has killed them off. That failed architect, Thomas Hardy, recalled in the 1920s how in Dorset cottages 'continued to be built in the old style down to about the middle of the last century, when they were ousted by the now ubiquitous brick-and-slate. By the merest chance I was able, when a child, to see the building of what was probably one of the last of these old fashioned cottages of "mud-wall" and thatch.'[55] In many parts of the country there must have been a very short interval between the dying of an old craft for making a peasant's cottage and its revival by a clever architect for use on a middle-class house. As late as 1909 R. W. Schultz could say that 'There are still some districts where the local wood is comparatively easily procurable in bulk and economically workable, and here the old method of construction still obtains.'[56]

Certainly the old ways of building survived in Surrey which, though close to London, had remained poor and backward. Here enthusiasts for old-fashioned crafts and vernacular buildings like Gertrude Jekyll began to explore the villages and photograph cottages in the 1880s and 1890s. It was in rural Surrey that Lutyens learned how to build by wandering around builders' yards and watching men at work – a sort of training which Arts and Crafts architects like Schultz valued above anything which could be taught in a school. 'My own opinion', Schultz lectured in 1909, 'is that there will be little chance of seeing really good architecture again until architects of the general type that are turned out at the present day cease to exist. Good architecture can only grow out of reasonable building, and reasonable building can only come from a sound constructive basis and a real knowledge of materials, their uses and limitations.... It is not to be wondered at that some of the few best architects of our immediate past have been those who have come from or been through the workshop or builder's yard, and who consequently have brought real practical knowledge to this task of grappling with the problems of design and composition.'[57]

George Jack said much the same about Philip Webb, whose 'influence had always one tendency: it removed "architecture" from the architect's office to the builder's yard and the craftsman's workshop. One remarkable quality was his keen perception of the proper ways in which all kinds of building materials should be used – it was a kind of instinct with him.'[58] Webb's houses were always properly constructed, as were those designed by Lutyens: the half-timbering was real and constructional, properly pegged together. This was an approach which contrasted with that of Norman Shaw, who often used false half-timbering on top of brick to create a purely cosmetic effect. Lutyens, like Webb, was anxious to use local materials in the local manner and at Tigbourne Court he not only used the local stone but managed to make the workmen press little pieces of ironstone into the wet mortar.

This concern with the proper and honest use of traditional materials could reach a somewhat ludicrous pitch. E. S. Prior was so obsessed with the use of local materials – making his houses 'of the soil racy' – that Roderick Gradidge can write with justice about Home Place, Holt (page 122), that 'Particularly rude is the diapering which is quite consciously all over the place, making the house look as though it is covered with a very old Fairisle pullover that had been knitted by an imbecile child. Quaintness can be carried no further',[59] while Gimson, in his Stonywell Cottage near Leicester (page 128), indulged in that contrived barbarism which only great sophistication can permit and built two-foot-thick walls of local stone upon bare rock to create a tiny cottage which, a century before, would have been regarded as a hovel.

Apparent Antiquity

Worse, however – in that it may present a modern observer with moral problems – is the traditional use of materials to suggest a bogus antiquity. One reason for the revival of 'Old English' and the vernacular was to give clients immediate roots in the country and to suggest that a new family had lived on the site for generations: it must never be forgotten that the country house is a social as well as a moral and an aesthetic necessity. Devey often gave his houses a contrived (but unconvincing) antiquity by building rough blocks of stone into the bases of brick walls as if to suggest that his 'Jacobean' house was built on the site of a suppressed monastery, but the master at the art of instant age was Lutyens. There was nothing new in what he attempted: the mid Victorians had often tried by the use of historical styles and by mixing styles to give an impression of age and growth over centuries; Lutyens did the same but with the added ingredient of the superb and convincing traditional use of traditional materials – what Peter Inskip has characterised as 'Archaeology'. For Lutyens, 'the visible result of time is a large factor in realised aesthetic value'[60] and Gertrude Jekyll was therefore delighted that her Munstead Wood (page 94) 'does not stare with newness; it is not new in any way that is disquieting to the eye; it is neither raw nor callow. On the contrary it almost gives the impression of a comfortable maturity of something like a couple of hundred years. And yet there is nothing sham or old about it; it is not trumped up with any specious or fashionable devices of spurious antiquity; there is no pretending to be anything that it is not – no affectation whatever',[61] just the proper and sophisticated use of stone, brick and timber in the old Surrey manner. In some of his houses, as with the isolated pieces of brick amongst the chalk at Marsh Court, Lutyens's use of materials cannot possibly really suggest antiquity; it is an intellectual game with textures and associations: mannerism in materials as well as in style. However, there can be no doubt that many architects were trying to fake antiquity, and this was particularly true with the neo-Tudor which developed into the Stockbrokers' Tudor of the 1920s and 1930s, in which architects employed old timbers from demolished barns to give an old world atmosphere. It was an inevitable and far from unattractive consequence of one strain in the Arts and Crafts movement, and is well exemplified by P. A. Barron's book of 1929 – published at a time when some house architects were faking not antiquity but a machine finish – *The House Desireable: A Handbook for Those Who Wish to Acquire Homes that Charm*, which has a chapter entitled 'New "Old" Houses. The Art of Building with Antique Oak, Bricks, and Mossy Tiles. Modern Homes which look Centuries Old'.[62]

One of the great differences between the recent past and the late nineteenth and early twentieth centuries is in the attitude to age. The late Victorians liked their old buildings to look old and were happy for Nature, with creeper and ivy, to enhance the picturesque and venerable effect made by Time. People today, like the progressive mid Victorians, like everything to be clean and new – even old buildings. The sometimes over-luxuriant growths of ivy have been long stripped off and restorations are not considered complete unless the stonework looks neat and bright. Yet it was against this very type of over-restoration, against the scraping and replacement of old masonry that the Society for the Protection of Ancient Buildings – 'Anti-Scrape' was founded in 1877. Morris, like Ruskin, hated seeing the beautiful and precious effects of time and weather destroyed in favour of a spurious authenticity of design and a good SPAB repair of an old building strengthened the structure and replaced really decayed parts without effacing the appearance of antiquity. This subtle and painstaking approach has been discarded by most of today's restoring architects, who are often just as ruthless as (and sometimes more ignorant than) the over-confident mid-Victorian church restorers like Sir Gilbert Scott.

This changed attitude to antiquity and to materials can now only be appreciated from old photographs. Oxford in 1900 looked wondrously old and venerable, with ivy covering much of the weathered and crumbling stonework; today much of the stone is brand new, the buildings looking nice and smart for the tourists – the best state for the buildings would surely be somewhere in between. Similarly, photographs of Surrey and Sussex cottages taken in the late nineteenth century show the buildings looking convincingly rustic and vernacular; today, if they survive, as likely as not they have been tarted-up as expensive houses with the old brickwork wrongly repointed, the irregular old plaster smoothed out and painted white, the silver-grey old oak timbers painted black and the windows modernised. It is seldom an improvement. The British seem almost to have lost their once highly developed eye for the Picturesque.

House and Garden

In the late nineteenth century together with the concern over the right use of materials went a desire to make a house look right in its

THE STUDIO OF F. D. HARDY, CRANBROOK, KENT (from W. Galsworthy Davie (photographer) and E. Guy Dawber, *Old Cottages and Farmhouses in Kent and Sussex*, 1900).

setting and in its locality. This was achieved by the use of local materials and by siting and shape – Voysey's houses were all of roughcast whether in the Lake District or in west London, but seem to hug their sites in an inevitable and harmonious manner – and also by the design of the gardens. The late-Victorian and Edwardian country house is inseparable from its garden, so intimately connected were the two areas of design. Just as Humphry Repton worked with Nash, so the garden designer Thomas Mawson collaborated with the architect Dan Gibson, while certain architects, like Mallows, Lorimer, Blomfield and Lutyens were celebrated as garden designers. The ability of Lutyens, indeed, to unify house and garden, interior and exterior space, has been compared with that of Frank Lloyd Wright. Unfortunately, gardens are much more fragile and ephemeral creations than buildings and the original setting of many houses can now only be appreciated from old photographs.

The history of the garden in late Victorian Britain cannot receive the attention it deserves here. Muthesius realised the importance of the garden and devoted several pages of *Das Englische Haus* to the subject, writing that 'The modern English view of the garden is that the formal plan should be revived but that at the same time the utmost attention should be paid to the cultivation of flowers and plants, preferably indigenous ones. . . . The garden is seen as a continuation of the rooms of the house, almost as a series of separate outdoor rooms, each of which is self-contained and performs a separate function. Thus the garden extends the house into the midst of nature. At the same time it gives it a framework in nature, without which it would stand like a stranger in its surroundings.'[63]

The story is a complex one, although it is essentially that of the conflict between the formal garden and the Picturesque tradition of the eighteenth century. Hand in hand with the 'Queen Anne' revival in the 1860s went an interest in what Mark Girouard has called the 'old-fashioned garden',[64] that is, the formal gardens of the sixteenth and seventeenth centuries which had so often been swept away by Capability Brown. Such formal gardens, with topiary and old-fashioned flowers, became fashionable amongst the Artistic in the 1870s, and Morris was early in the field in creating one. In the 1890s, the great protagonist of the formal garden in England was Sir Reginald Blomfield – in Scotland it was Lorimer – author of a book on the subject published in 1892. Blomfield was vehemently opposed by the cantankerous advocate of the 'natural' garden, William Robinson. Ultimately more influential than either was Gertrude Jekyll, garden-

BRYANSTON, DORSET, built in 1889–94 for Lord Portman, in which Norman Shaw returned to Classicism and the Grand Manner for the first time (photo: National Monuments Record).

ing correspondent of *Country Life*, who, with her young protégé Edwin Lutyens, did much to end this argument and create some of the most enchanting as well as the most architectural of gardens. Christopher Hussey wrote that their garden at Deanery Garden (page 96), 'at once formal and informal, virtually settled that controversy, of which Sir Reginald Blomfield and William Robinson were for long the protagonists, between formal and naturalistic garden design. Miss Jekyll's naturalistic planting wedded Lutyens's geometry in a balanced union of both principles.'[65] Another designer whose influence and talent must not be underestimated was Thomas Mawson, author of *The Art and Craft of Garden Making* (1900 etc.), while J. D. Sedding anticipated Blomfield's defence of the formal garden with his own book of 1891: *Garden-craft Old and New*.

Return to Classicism

The English House was designed to convey a timeless stability, the stability enjoyed by family life in the confident supremacy of the British Empire. The qualities so often admired by critics in a house – reticence, quietness, sobriety, appropriateness, honesty, solidity – would seem to have been those looked for in the English gentleman.

There would be truth in the cynical suggestion that the English House was the perfect expression of late-Victorian civilisation: the world of the sons of the bourgeoisie moulded by the public schools, insular and of limited imagination, conservative when not Conservative, those who went out to police the Empire and uphold standards of decency and fairness, the generation who later unthinkingly allowed their sons to perish as cannon-fodder in the trenches of the Great War. On the other hand, we can see more positive and timeless qualities in the possibilities of life permitted by the English House than are immediately reflected in that lost – and sometimes over-glamorised – world of late-Victorian and Edwardian England. Would that we could build such houses now.

Circumstances changed early this century. Historians have tended to follow Muthesius and Lethaby in seeing a pure revived Classicism, as opposed to the eclectic and deliberately incorrect picturesque Classicism of 'Queen Anne', as bringing to an end the original phase of what Lethaby called 'the English free architecture'. This 'Grand Manner' began with Norman Shaw's Bryanston (1889) and Chesters (1890) but Voysey thought that it was Lutyens discovering the 'High Game' of Renaissance Classicism which led a whole generation astray. Certainly Edwardian England became more urban and urbane in its architecture, conscious of the city and the Grand Manner and sympathetic to Classical formality. A degree of Classical formality in domestic architecture was also, in part, a reaction to the extreme eccentricity and awkwardness of some Arts and Crafts architecture, that self-conscious originality which could not really be sustained. The realisation that there was more to traditional English domestic architecture than picturesque cottages scarcely undermined standards of building craftsmanship just because it began to be realised that houses of the seventeenth and even the eighteenth centuries were worthy of study. In the 1890s Blomfield, Belcher and Macartney began to look sympathetically at the domestic work of the English Renaissance – it was very important that it was *English* – and in 1906 Gerald Horsley, an impeccably Arts and Crafts designer, was pleased to note that 'other influences have ... broadened the whole outlook; and once again the architecture of the English Renaissance has become a recognised force of the highest importance. We ack-nowledge now, in a manner of which the Gothic Revivalist was incapable, the genius of Sir Christopher Wren, and some of his followers, because it expresses in a perfectly natural manner the change from a mediaeval to a modern England. In looking at a modern and well-designed house, whether in the town or the country, it is interesting to note how the study of the directness and simplicity of the Renaissance ideal has combined with the reverence for craftsmanship and right materials which belongs more properly to the Gothic Revivalists.'[66]

Neo-Georgian was as much the heir to the Arts and Crafts movement as was neo-Tudor and had been used by Webb and Bodley as early as the 1860s. Neo-Georgian houses, well built and gentlemanly in the English tradition, sustained the virtues of the English House for many more decades. In the twentieth century Georgian has become the conventional and favourite style for new country houses. It is very important to distinguish this neo-Georgian from the neo-Classical which was promoted by the architectural schools early this century, for it was these schools which really destroyed the craft basis of architecture by superseding the old system of articled pupillage on which both the Gothic Revival and the Arts and Crafts movement had depended. Modelled on the French *atelier* system which had worked so well in the United States, the old and new established schools in the 1910s replaced practical training with formal academic training on the drawing board alone and encouraged a Beaux-Arts Classical grandeur.

In the 1920s and 1930s this formal approach turned all too easily into acceptance of the new fashion of Continental Modernism and this resulted in an architecture which was utterly inimical to both the building craftsmanship and the sense of tradition which together made the English House. The Modern movement had its contribution to make, but in the sphere of domestic architecture its influence was largely disastrous. It is true that in the 1930s the same sort of wealthy client who had once gone to Voysey or Webb now commissioned Connell, Ward and Lucas or Maxwell Fry to design them avant-garde houses, but while the results may be interesting and striking the new white-walled, flat roofed Modern houses have never secured either the respect or the affection of the British public. It is noticeable that, in Frinton for instance, whereas the ordinary 'Stockbrokers' Tudor' houses of between the wars are well cared for, the once-famous Modern Movement houses of the 1930s by Oliver Hill and other architects look so shabby they seem almost like slums. Architecture is never the creation of architects alone and, as far as the clients are concerned, British insularity and British conservatism lay behind that extraordinary flowering of imaginative, sensible and harmonious domestic architecture which began with the Gothic Revival and which lasted for almost a century after Pugin.

The New Neo-vernacular

Today we can regard the English House with quite as much objective sympathy as Hermann Muthesius. Not only are such houses in good condition and still very desirable but there are significant parallels between the decades which saw its genesis, the 1860s and 1870s, and our own time. The Romantic tradition which was in opposition to industrial society is far from dead: indeed it thrives. The Modern Movement itself has died from popular opposition to the large-scale, to system building, to the worship of technocracy and planning; now we wish again for the small-scale and the crafts, there is enthusiasm for returning to Nature and traditional methods, whether 'real ale' or compost-grown vegetables; ecology and the environment are fashionable. We are all very anti-modern now.

In architecture, the pitched roofs, irregular red-brick walls and small scale of housing schemes built in the last ten years or more all over Britain is evidence – albeit crude and unsophisticated – of a new feeling, or rather an old feeling for the importance of the house, the private dwelling, for family life. No more do public authorities dare impose a concrete, Utopian vision of collectivist, high-rise society upon their tenants, now they have to recognise the ordinary domestic, nay, bourgeois aspirations of ordinary people. An acid test is the condition of council housing: the cottage estates built by the London County Council in the 1900s (page 228) look rather more loved than the vandalised concrete towers of the 1960s. The conclusions Muthesius drew about the importance of living in houses in England are as germane to architecture now as in 1904.

Not that we can expect to see houses of the quality of Deanery Garden or even of those cottages in Letchworth in the near future. Conditions are rather different. Not only are there no longer the many servants for which all domestic architects of the nineteenth and early twentieth centuries planned, but the cost of materials and labour usually makes the attainment of the quality of building craftsmanship of a house of 1900 an impossible dream. But that former high quality should be both a reproach and a goal: the lessons are there to be learned. Muthesius wrote *Das Englische Haus* not for German architects to copy English houses but to teach lessons, to show how fine domestic architecture could arise out of particular national conditions when approached in an inventive, but traditionally-minded way. 'Post-Modern' architects, anxious to build houses and to pick up long-discarded threads, can learn the same lessons. It seems a very modest ambition for British architecture: to return to doing something at which we really used to be rather good.

As far as the general public are concerned, the virtues of this sort of architecture do not usually have to be argued. Such houses are desirable to own and popular to visit, even if many people fail to appreciate that the buildings are nineteenth century and not 'really old'. In 1972 Standen (page 74) was bequeathed to the National Trust, a gift which was almost declined both because the house is 'Victorian' and because it was believed that few would want to see it. In the event the number of visitors has exceeded even the most optimistic estimates. Its architect, Philip Webb, would surely be pleased; I wonder if he would be surprised?

Notes to the Introduction

1. W. R. Lethaby, *Philip Webb and his Work*, 1935, p.128.
2. William Morris, *Address delivered in the Town Hall, Birmingham*, 19.2.1879, p.12.
3. Letter to the author, 11.10.1980.
4. *Architect*, xlv, 1891, p.330: quoted in Donald J. Olsen, *The Growth of Victorian London*, 1976, p.212.
5. Hermann Muthesius, *The English House*, 1979, p.10. This and subsequent quotations are from this first English edition of *Das Englische Haus*, 1904, translated by Janet Seligman.
6. Muthesius, op. cit., p.13.
7. W. R. Lethaby, 'Modern German Architecture and What We May Learn from It', 1915, in *Form in Civilization*, 1922, p.99.
8. Muthesius, op. cit., p.11.
9. C. F. A. Voysey, 'Ultra-Modern Architecture', *Architects' Journal*, lxxxi, 1935, p.404, quoted in R. Gradidge, *Dream Houses*, 1980, p.75.
10. Muthesius, op. cit., p.4.
11. W. H. Bidlake, *The Home from Outside*, in Walter Shaw Sparrow, ed., *The Modern Home*, n.d. (c.1906), pp.22–3.
12. C. F. A. Voysey, *Patriotism in Architecture*, 1911: quoted in John Brandon-Jones and others, *C. F. A. Voysey: Architect and Designer 1857–1941*, 1978, p.12.
13. R. Blomfield, *The Formal Garden in England*, 1892, and *A History of Renaissance Architecture in England, 1500–1800*, 1897: quoted in David Watkin, *The Rise of Architectural History*, 1980, p.97.
14. Muthesius, op. cit., p.15.
15. W. Galsworthy Davie and E. Guy Dawber, *Old Cottages and Farmhouses in Kent and Sussex*, 1900, p.3.
16. *Webb*, op. cit., pp.128 and 30.
17. Muthesius, op. cit., p.13.
18. W. Morris, *News from Nowhere*, (1890) 1912, p.47.
19. G. G. Scott, *Remarks on Secular and Domestic Architecture*, 1857, pp.171 and 167.
20. *News from Nowhere*, op. cit., p.14.
21. Morris to Mrs Alfred Baldwin, 26.3.1874: in Asa Briggs, ed., *William Morris: Selected Writings and Designs*, 1962, p.79.
22. *Country Life*, 20.1.1912, p.93.
23. *Webb*, op. cit., p.138; W. R. Lethaby, *Ernest Gimson: His Life and Work*, 1924, quoted in P. Ferriday, ed., *Victorian Architecture*, 1963, p.265.
24. A. Saint, *Richard Norman Shaw*, 1976, p.24 ff.
25. J. D. Sedding, 'Our Arts and Industries', a paper given to the Liverpool Art Congress, 1888, p.144, quoted by Gillian Naylor, *The Arts and Crafts Movement*, 1971, p.15.
26. H. S. Goodhart-Rendel, *English Architecture since the Regency*, 1953, p.171.
27. G. C. Horsley, *Urban Houses and Cottage Homes*, in W. Shaw Sparrow, ed., *Flats, Urban Houses and Cottage Homes*, 1906, p.106.
28. *Building News*, xxxviii, 1880, quoted in J. Mordaunt Crook, *William Burges*, 1981, p.136.
29. Quoted in P. Stanton, *Pugin*, 1971, p.11; *Personal and Professional Recollections by the late Sir George Gilbert Scott, R.A.*, 1879, p.373.
30. Scott, *Recollections*, op. cit., p.375.
31. *News from Nowhere*, op. cit., p.168.
32. Peter Davey, *Arts and Crafts Architecture*, 1980, p.9.
33. M. Girouard, *The Victorian Country House*, 1971 and 1979.
34. M. Girouard, *Sweetness and Light*, 1977, pp.3 and 5.
35. Muthesius, op. cit., p.31.
36. Muthesius, op. cit., p.60.
37. Muthesius, op. cit., p.7.
38. Quoted by Olsen, op. cit., p.118.
39. S. E. Rasmussen, *London: The Unique City*, 1937, p.404.
40. Muthesius, op. cit., p.7.
41. C. F. A. Voysey, *On Town Planning*, in the *Architectural Review*, 1919: quoted in D. Gebhard, *Charles F. A. Voysey, Architect*, 1975, p.77. An even more extreme and revealing letter by Voysey, written in about 1934, is quoted by Alan Powers in his article on Raymond McGrath in the *Thirties Society Journal*, No. 3, 1983, p.7: 'As a consistent individualist I am violently anti-international, and against Collectivism, mass production of thoughts and sentiments. Regimentation I detest. Also town planning that plays ducks and drakes with private property and vested interest.... All are the outcome of a poisonous socialism and communism.... Going a-whoring with foreign styles has poisoned our Architecture.... Liberty, equality and fraternity are to me poisonous and impossible lies.'
42. J. Brandon-Jones, op. cit., p.12.
43. Muthesius, op. cit., p.9.
44. Quoted in James Kornwolf, *M. H. Baillie Scott and the Arts and Crafts Movement*, 1972, p.457.
45. Muthesius, op. cit., p.181.
46. C. L. Eastlake, *A History of the Gothic Revival*, 1872, p.344.
47. *Webb*, op. cit., p.130.
48. Morris, op. cit., p.21.
49. C. F. A. Voysey, *The English Home*, 1911, quoted in Gebhard, op. cit.
50. Gebhard, op. cit., p.28.
51. Muthesius, op. cit., p.67.
52. Kornwolf, op. cit., pp.47–50.
53. Muthesius, op. cit., p.79.
54. Horsley, op. cit., p.107.
55. Stanley Baldwin, *The Preservation of Ancient Cottages*, n.d., p.13.
56. R. W. Schultz, 'Reason in Building, or the Commonsense Use of Materials', in T. Raffles Davison, ed., *The Arts Connected with Building*, 1909, p.16.
57. Schultz, op. cit., p.12.
58. *Webb*, op. cit., p.125.
59. Victorian Society Notes, *Of the Soil Racy. A Tour of Arts and Crafts Rogues in North Norfolk*, 1971, p.15.
60. Quoted in P. Inskip, *Edwin Lutyens*, 1979, p.27.
61. Gertrude Jekyll, *Home and Garden*, 1900: quoted in R. Gradidge, *Dream Houses*, 1980, p.116.
62. Since this essay was written, in 1980, there has been a growth of interest in the neo-Tudor of the 1920s, with the catalogue of the exhibition of *Ernest George Trobridge, 1884–1942. Architect Extraordinary* held at the Museum of Modern Art in Oxford in 1982 and the publication of an article by Donald Campbell on Blunden Shadbolt (1879–1949) in the *Thirties Society Journal*, No. 3, 1983, pp.17–24.
63. Muthesius, op. cit., p.107.
64. M. Girouard, *Sweetness and Light*, 1977, pp.152–9.
65. C. Hussey, *The Life of Sir Edwin Lutyens*, 1950, p.96.
66. Horsley, op. cit., p.108.

PART ONE / Precursors and Pioneers

Blaise Hamlet / JOHN NASH

It is curious that not only are some of the earliest examples of the revival of the cottage style among the best, but also that their architect was a man principally associated with an urban vision and one considered by later generations to represent the worst aspects of Georgian architecture: John Nash (1752–1835). Nash was the creator of Regent Street, whose stuccoed Classical formality was rejected by the Victorians for both style and for unworthy materials, but he was also the creator of Regent's Park, where Classical palace façades were set against trees and parkland in a quintessentially English vision of the Picturesque. The idea of placing villas in the Park accentuated this vision and was an early expression of the anti-urbanism which produced the English House.

Nash developed his feeling for the Picturesque during his association with the landscape gardener Humphry Repton and he built up a country-house practice. Many of his houses were in the self-consciously Picturesque 'castle style', some were Italian in inspiration, but for smaller buildings Nash often used the cottage style and there is no more charming or successful example of this than Blaise Hamlet, near Bristol. This group of cottages around a green was built for John Scandrett Harford, a Bristol Quaker banker. They were designed in 1810 and, as the column on the green proclaims, completed the following year.

The cottages were built as almshouses and it seems to have been Nash who suggested to Harford that old people would prefer separate cottages rather than the usual formal rows of almshouses. It is, perhaps, surprising to find that Nash, whose London terraces were often so slipshod in detail, should have taken great pains with these little buildings. Summerson quotes Nash writing to his client about some earlier cottages built at Moccas, Herefordshire, in 1804: 'I have the mortification daily to see these minutiae of cottages misunderstood and very much of their good effect depends on the right understanding of their details. They are meant to be essential parts of the construction and growing out of the necessity of the things them-

selves. When this principle is lost sight of they become pretensious [sic] and mere appliqués, than which nothing is more disgusting.'[1] The words might be Pugin's, or Philip Webb's.

The ten cottages are all different and use a variety of materials and roof shapes, but they are unified by the use of the 'continuous penthouse', a projecting pitched roof, of tiles or thatch, above the ground-floor windows, which, especially when combined with a coved plaster cornice, seems to anticipate the cottages of Eden Nesfield of fifty years later. Nash was particularly proud of his tall Elizabethan chimneys, made of special bricks. As a result of this attention to detail, Blaise Hamlet cost £3,800 when Harford originally intended to spend only £2,000. But what divides these cottages from Victorian examples of the genre is that they were built for cottagers, not for gentlemen. Harford himself lived in the plain stone Georgian house designed by William Paty; only much later in the century would gentlemen affect to live in a type of rural house originally built for servants.

Blaise Hamlet / *John Nash*

Scotney Castle / ANTHONY SALVIN

Anthony Salvin (1799–1881) was the most successful country-house builder in early Victorian England. His practice was only emulated in size and scope by that of William Burn in Scotland, who did so much to establish the 'Scottish Baronial' style. Salvin, like Burn, was a highly efficient planner of large aristocratic country houses and was familiar with Picturesque principles. The simple Georgian country-house tradition having broken down, Salvin used a great variety of styles. At Peckforton and for the Duke of Northumberland at Alnwick, he built castles; Harlaxton Manor and Thoresby Hall are great Elizabethan or Jacobean piles, but Salvin made his name with the Tudor style and it was Tudor that he used for the new house at Scotney, near Lamberhurst, Kent, designed in 1835 and built in 1837–44 for Edward Hussey.

The new Scotney Castle (Colour Plate A) is a fine asymmetrical composition of Tudor gables, bays and mullioned windows, all carried out in sharply cut ashlar stone. But Scotney Castle is much more than architecture and its success is not only owing to Anthony Salvin. Old Scotney Castle was a moated castle in the valley with a seventeenth-century house attached. When Hussey decided to build a new house on the hill, he selected a site with the help of William Sawrey Gilpin, nephew of the Revd William Gilpin, the famous writer on the Picturesque. The new house was designed with views of the old in mind, made to look more Picturesque by the pulling down of part of it.

It was at Scotney Castle that Edward Hussey's grandson, Christopher Hussey, wrote his book on *The Picturesque*, published in 1927. 'The picturesque was the artistic tradition in which I was brought up, and I remember clearly the shock with which I suddenly became conscious that it was only one of many aspects of reality. It happened in the library of a country house built, in 1837, by my grandfather. Through the windows of the room you see, in a valley below, a castle, partly ruined, on an island in a lake. A balustrade cresting a cliff forms the foreground, a group of Scots firs and limes the side-screens. Beyond, a meadow melts in the woods, rising to a high sky-line. . . . I had often agreed that it formed a perfect picture. . . . On this particular evening I was pondering on the happy chance, as it appeared to me, of my grandfather's desertion of the old castle, his digging of the new house on this particular spot, and his digging of the stone for building it between the two – in the quarry that makes such a fine foreground to the prospect. It did not occur to me that he was guided by anything more than chance and natural good taste. At that point, however, my eye, ranging the mellow shelves beside me, fell on the book . . . *Sir Uvedale Price on the Picturesque*. . . . And before I had read far I reflected that all those scenes which I instinctively called artistic must be "picturesque", and that I was not being original when I sketched a hovel under a gnarled oak but appallingly traditional – the man wrote in 1794! The very scene before me, so far from being a happy co-incidence, must have been planned on picturesque principles. My grandfather must have evolved it out of that very book. . . . It was humiliating, at the time, to find my aesthetic impulses no more than a product of heredity and environment . . .' – but they are impulses that are deeply rooted in England and explain so much English domestic architecture.

Scotney Castle / *Anthony Salvin*

Betteshanger Manor / GEORGE DEVEY

George Devey (1820–86) is an enigmatic and shadowy figure in the history of Victorian domestic architecture whose importance has only recently been stressed by historians. His comparative obscurity was principally owing to the fact that, to protect the interests of his clients, his work was never published in the architectural weeklies (although this same policy did not affect adversely the reputation of Philip Webb). Devey was, nevertheless, a considerable influence on the younger men, like Nesfield and Shaw, who emerged as domestic architects in the 1860s and 1870s and Voysey was his assistant. Devey was a member of the Theistic Church, founded by Voysey's heretic father who was unfrocked in the Church of England for denying the doctrine of Everlasting Hell.

Devey seems to have been the first Victorian architect to follow the landscape painters in appreciating the rustic charm of Kent and Sussex cottages and villages. He was a good water-colourist in his own right, having taken lessons from John Sell Cotman. In the new cottages and lodges he built all over Kent, Devey was often able to recreate the character of the local vernacular most convincingly: in the group of cottages in Penshurst village, it is difficult to tell which are old, which are constructed out of old materials and which were built by Devey in 1850.

However, in the larger country houses, built for his enviable clientele of aristocrats, Liberal politicians and bankers, Devey's Picturesque style became rather strained and coarse in his attempts to create an impression of great age and piecemeal growth. Clients came to Devey not for vulgar new houses but for houses to suit their aspirations to become landed squirearchical families. Betteshanger Manor in East Kent is a typical example of this.

Betteshanger Manor was built for Sir Walter James, later Lord Northbourne, who was a close friend of W. E. Gladstone and who became Devey's most useful client. The house was begun in 1856

and largely built over the following two decades. It was designed to look as if it had been built over three centuries. The plan is rambling and additive; the styles deliberately mixed. Large pieces of rough stone are built into the bases of brick walls so as to suggest that it is a house built on the site of a medieval building. A tower at the end of a wing looks Tudor; other parts are Jacobean in style while the round, Classical arches of the *porte-cochère* suggest Georgian alterations. Such Romantic conceits and the creation of a bogus antiquity were managed rather more successfully and subtly by later Victorian architects, for in many ways Betteshanger Manor is rather ungainly and crude. Devey's small cottages on the estate now seem to have much greater charm and sensitivity. Betteshanger Manor is now a school for boys.

Betteshanger Manor / *George Devey*

Rampisham Rectory / AUGUSTUS WELBY NORTHMORE PUGIN

Pugin (1812–52), the obsessive Gothicist, the excoriating critic of the Classical – he called it 'Pagan' – tradition in England, was the pioneer in and the initiator of so much in the nineteenth century. He was responsible for the high seriousness of the mid-Victorian Gothic Revival and is the real founder of the Arts and Crafts movement. The Roman Catholic convert, who in his writings linked religion, morality and architecture, attacked contemporary industrial society in his book *Contrasts* (1836) and preached a return to medieval architecture and values, while his *True Principles of Pointed or Christian Architecture* (1841) (the title is most revealing) gave the famous maxims to architects which lay behind so much later fine building: '. . . there should be no features about a building which are not necessary for construction, convenience or propriety', and 'all ornament should consist of enrichment of the essential construction of the building'. These principles, together with Pugin's insistence on 'honest', sound construction, and his defence of traditional methods of building, explain much Arts and Crafts architecture.

Because his idea of architecture was essentially religious, Pugin was principally a church architect, but he was not exclusively one. His books argued that Gothic was suitable for all types of building as it was more than just a style. With Sir Charles Barry, Pugin created the gorgeous interiors of the new Palace of Westminster, the training

of craftsmen for which greatly stimulated the revival of many old building and decorative crafts. He also designed houses. His only large country house was Scarisbrick Hall in Lancashire and other domestic commissions were monastic in purpose, but Pugin also designed a number of small houses and rectories which were full of implications for the development of English architecture. As might be expected from his principles, these are asymmetrical in plan and carefully irregular in massing. Several show a particular sympathy to local materials and building traditions.

Pugin's own house near Salisbury of 1835, St Marie's Grange, was both a medieval fantasy and an early example of a modern, straightforward Gothic house. His second house, the Grange at Ramsgate where he died, was more sober and sensible and he used the plan of it for a number of houses including the Rectory – now Glebe Farm – at Rampisham in Dorset, where he also restored the church and built a school in 1845–6. Built of local stone, Rampisham Rectory is one of the loveliest and simplest of simple vernacular Gothic houses and one in which the elusive character of an anonymous local mason's work was captured. The domestic work of Butterfield, Street and Webb seem to follow on from it and, with its asymmetrically placed gable, bay windows and externally expressed chimney-breast, it seems the model for so many ordinary Victorian houses.

Rampisham Rectory / *Augustus Welby Northmore Pugin*

Baldersby St James / WILLIAM BUTTERFIELD

William Butterfield (1814–1900) was principally a church architect. He was of the generation which was profoundly influenced by the Oxford Movement within the Church of England and followed Pugin in believing in Gothic as the only true Christian style of architecture. Austere and uncompromising, Butterfield was an architect of great, if often idiosyncratic originality. His famous church, All Saints, Margaret Street, London, was really the first in Victoria's reign to take Gothic away from archaeology and open possibilities of making a modern, creative Gothic architecture.

Butterfield's originality expressed itself both in his handling of hard, rather geometrical forms and also in his delight in colour. Partly under the influence of Ruskin, variegated colour effects were achieved by the combination of different building materials – 'structural polychromy' – often arranged in bands or stripes, analogous to the different strata in rock formations. This deliberate suggestion of geology is connected with the Victorian obsession with the weight and quality of building materials, with the massiveness and honesty of the wall.

Butterfield's style can be seen in its most elaborate development in his masterpiece Keble College, Oxford. Not all admired it, however; and many have found his style deliberately coarse and ugly, and his banding at Keble of brick and stone was dismissed as 'streaky bacon'. But there is nothing hard or ugly about Butterfield's smaller domestic buildings, for as a church architect, Butterfield also designed large numbers of schools and vicarages and in such buildings he combined his modern, Victorian Gothic with the Picturesque tradition of Nash. Such buildings had a great influence on the development of English domestic architecture. Philip Webb was one of Butterfield's few intimate friends and Lethaby, Webb's biographer, called him 'more of a builder and experimenter', one of 'the Hards ... thinkers and constructors'.

The charm and subtle simplicity of Butterfield's smaller and secular buildings can best be seen in the village of Baldersby St James in the East Riding of Yorkshire. This whole new village was Butterfield's work and was begun in 1855. It was built by the 7th Viscount Downe, whose father was a clergyman and father-in-law a bishop. From 1846 until 1857 he engaged in extensive building activity on his estates in Yorkshire and Rutland and, at his death, Butterfield described him as 'a most really good man.... It has been one of the pleasures of my life to have been connected so much with his good works and to see how he did them.'[2]

At Baldersby, Butterfield designed church, vicarage, school, agent's house and cottages, all picturesquely arranged. All also demonstrate the practical application of the important principle of 'propriety', for each building visibly demonstrates its importance in an hierarchical scale. The church, built of stone, is most elaborate; the cottages, of simple brick with occasional bands of stone, the least. Some houses have small areas of half-timbering, both to demonstrate their relative importance and to create a rural character. The humblest cottages have no literal Gothic details but simple windows of a traditional vernacular character. Every building, however, is a careful composition of wall planes, hipped roofs and sturdy chimneys and are such truly clever essays in a straightforward cottage style that the cottages would not look out of place in, say, Hampstead Garden Suburb, sixty years on.

Baldersby St James / *William Butterfield*

St Columb Major Old Rectory / WILLIAM WHITE

William White (1825–1900) was, like Butterfield and Street, a Goth-icist associated with the High Church 'Ecclesiological' movement and he, like them, also designed domestic buildings which are of interest in the story of the development of English domestic architecture in Victoria's reign. White is not to be confused with William H. White, Secretary of the RIBA, or William Henry White, who designed build-ings around Cavendish Square. White was a pupil of Gilbert Scott, in whose office he met G. E. Street and G. F. Bodley. He set up practice in Cornwall in 1847. Later he moved to London, where he designed several churches in Battersea and St Saviour's, Aberdeen Park, Is-lington, remarkable for its elaborate polychromy in brick.

William White also built up a significant domestic practice. As well as many rectories, he also designed several country houses. These include the eccentric Quy Hall in Cambridgeshire and the massive granite Humewood Castle in County Wicklow. The Old Rectory (now the Old Rectory Guest House) at St Columb Major (Colour Plate B) belongs to an earlier phase of his career, but although this building is clearly in the Gothic manner of Pugin, the design also exhibits the designer's originality.

There are several buildings by White in the small Cornish hill town; these include Bank House and Penmellyn House. The Rectory was built in 1849–50, and is one of White's first buildings. Compared with Butterfield's rectories, the Gothic detail is rather literal and elaborate, and the dispositions of gables, buttresses and chimneys are picturesquely arranged in the manner of Pugin. Perhaps the most remarkable feature of the building is the staircase, spaciously arranged around a central court with flights and arches supported on chamfered granite piers.

As well as an enthusiastic Gothicist, White was also a mountaineer, an advocate of Swedish gymnastics, an inventor and an opponent of shaving. Mark Girouard, in *The Victorian Country House*, observes how White 'spent much of his life balanced on the boundary between crankiness and brilliance; in the end he fell off on the wrong side, and a large proportion of his last years were wasted in trying to prove

that Shakespeare was Bacon. The crankiness should not be allowed to obscure the brilliance. As an architect he is one of the most interesting and least known of Victorian Gothic Revivalists.'

56

St Columb Major Old Rectory / *William White*   57

Upton Magna Rectory / GEORGE EDMUND STREET

G. E. Street (1824–81) was the greatest architect of the High Victorian Gothic Revival. His finest work exhibits all the muscular characteristics of Victorian 'Vigour and Go', but while he reinterpreted Gothic precedents with much originality, his work does not have the personal idiosyncrasies of Butterfield nor the contrived eccentricity of some of the other Gothicists. In the 1850s, Street was in the vanguard in adopting ideas from Italian Gothic and much of his work is distinguished by structural polychromy and other exotic features. But in his later buildings, such as his masterpiece the Royal Courts of Justice in the Strand, Street returned to more English precedents while never losing his interest in the expressive possibilities of heavy masonry and the wall plane.

The effort involved in designing the Law Courts put Street into a comparatively early grave, but while he was almost as prolific an architect as Sir Gilbert Scott, his work is always carefully thought out and detailed. He could not delegate, and his close interest in the details of buildings led him to be concerned with craftsmanship. Street studied the craft of the blacksmith so that he could design ironwork in sympathy with the medium and the craft. The railings of the Law Courts, or around the church of St James the Less, Pimlico, with their naturalistic, plant-like forms, are of particular beauty. Out of Street's office came the Arts and Crafts movement: Philip Webb was his chief assistant and William Morris was, briefly, his pupil. Another assistant was Norman Shaw. And while Street's pupils and assistants later rejected the muscular Gothic of their master, they learned much which was of lasting value.

Street's larger domestic jobs, such as Cuddesdon College, Oxfordshire, are brilliant compositions of windows, chimneys and angular geometrical forms, all disciplined by the plane of the wall. His smaller schools and vicarages are similar to the contemporary work of Butterfield. Some, such as the buildings attached to the church of All Saints, Boyne Hill, Maidenhead, are rather stridently mannered. The (old) Rectory at Upton Magna, Shropshire, built in 1864, is a later

and quieter work. It does, nevertheless, demonstrate Street's remarkable talent at handling architectural form.

The Rectory is built of brick, but given variety by being laid in a diagonal herring-bone pattern beneath relieving arches above windows. These arches, flush with the wall plane, typically demonstrate that Victorian Gothic delight in expressing constructional truth. Elsewhere there is half-timbering, with brick infill, or 'nogging', to give a rural, vernacular character which is unusual in Street's work. But the overall impression is one of formal discipline, with the carefully composed elevations of windows, gables and hipped roofs. There are also unusual features which emphasise the quality of the wall and which are typical of Street: the strange high plinth, or 'shoulder' of brick which rises to first-floor height – except where broken by windows – and the mannered, stunted buttress at the corner, ending a long run of blank wall. It is details like the handling of wall planes which show Street's consummate mastery as an artist.

Upton Magna Rectory / *George Edmund Street* 59

Red House, Bexleyheath / PHILIP SPEAKMAN WEBB

Philip Webb (1831–1915) was one of the greatest of English domestic architects (see also page 74). Muthesius recognised him as one of the three who, in the 1860s, broke with the revival of formal historical styles and interested themselves in creating a domestic vernacular manner (the other two being Nesfield and Shaw): 'There can be no doubt that he occupies a position of the first importance in English architecture', he wrote. Webb's biographer, the Arts and Crafts architect W. R. Lethaby, believed that 'every piece of building work done in England during the last generation which has any life in it, is either the direct, if bungling attempt of some practical builder, or it derives in some way from the experiments of Webb. Any work that has a soul of good in it must have been thought of, not as architectural style and grandeur, but as sound and expressive building – there is no persistence in anything else.'[3]

Sound building was characteristic of Webb. His assistant, George Jack, wrote of his 'silent influence. This influence had always one tendency: it removed "architecture" from the architect's office to the builder's yard and the craftsman's workshop. One remarkable quality was his keen perception of the proper ways in which all kinds of building materials should be used – it was a kind of instinct with him.'[4]

Possibly Webb's importance has sometimes been over-emphasised at the expense of other architects, but there can be no doubt of his influence. Even though almost none of his work was ever published in the journals, it was known and admired by a younger generation of Arts and Crafts architects – not least by Lutyens, who thought that 'had Webb started his career under the influence of Alfred Stevens rather than of Edmund Street, had he come into touch with those who could have bent his constructive genius to the grand manner of architecture, there would have been produced a man of astounding mark in the authentic line of Western architecture.'[5] Certainly Webb never wanted to shed the stern conscience of a Gothicist and even after he moved beyond the secular Gothic manner of his master, Street, towards an almost astylar eclecticism, his work often retained a rather puritanical awkwardness. Nevertheless, his buildings always compel admiration for the sophisticated and sympathetic use of build-

ing materials, for the delicacy of detail and for common sense.

The celebrated Red House was designed in 1858 soon after Webb left Street's office. It was built in 1859–60 for his lifelong friend, William Morris. Hermann Muthesius thought Red House, 'unique in its time', but it was not, although many historians have regarded the building as of revolutionary importance. In fact, the design owes a great deal to the parsonage style of Butterfield as well as to Street. The hipped dormer roofs raised just proud of the main roof plane are typical of Butterfield, as was the use of conventional sash windows rather than Gothic casements – Morris thought his house was 'in the style of the thirteenth century'[6] – while the tight composition of acute triangular gables on the entrance front, as well as the mannered projecting first-floor bay corbelled out upon a buttress, are reminiscent of Street. Red House is a very brilliant essay in the parsonage manner, but what *was* remarkable was that it was built entirely of red brick for a gentleman of means rather than for a poor clergyman or a farm labourer – Pugin's scale of propriety had been inverted. The furnishings were deliberately simple and the plan of the house really rather crude.

Red House, Bexleyheath / *Philip Speakman Webb*

West House, Glebe Place / PHILIP SPEAKMAN WEBB

In the ten years after he designed Red House for William Morris, Webb's style evolved into something much less Gothic which drew upon wider sources of inspiration. By the end of the 1860s, he was happy to employ Classical elements in his work, such as straightforward Georgian sash windows, so producing a reticent but stylish eclectic architecture. This can be seen in two houses in London designed in 1868. One was the town house in Palace Green, Kensington, built for George Howard, later 9th Earl of Carlisle, the teetotal patron of the Pre-Raphaelites. The other was the house in Chelsea built for the painter, G. P. Boyce.

West House was built on a corner of the garden of Chelsea Rectory in 1868–9. George Price Boyce was a water-colourist who painted the sort of old and picturesque rural architecture which Webb and his contemporaries had learned to admire. His new house, however, was not in a rustic style but in a version of the 'Queen Anne' manner thought appropriate in towns and much more Georgian than the Palace Green house, which still has a Gothic character. All is in red brick, with rubbed-brick cornices. The entrance front, with the projecting first-floor bay above the porch, and its sash windows, would be almost neo-Georgian if not for the hipped roofs and the odd, almost Byzantine details of the front porch; the garden front has a double-height bay window and vestigial pediments in rubbed brick. The whole composition is clever and strange – strange partly because an extra wing was added to the south-west when Boyce married in 1876. This, which bridges a passage from Glebe Place to the hidden garden, has tile-hung gables and the appearance of battlements achieved by playing with the planes of brickwork – a trick Lutyens would use forty years later.

After Boyce's death in 1897, the house was sympathetically extended to the north by an unidentified hand. At the same time, however, Boyce's large first-floor studio, with its wooden gallery, was divided up. The present owner of West House is attempting to restore the interior to its original appearance.

West House, Glebe Place / *Philip Speakman Webb*

Valley End Rectory / Great Malvern Villas / GEORGE FREDERICK BODLEY

G. F. Bodley (1827–1907) was the greatest late-Victorian church architect. He is not generally thought of as a domestic architect and he was not mentioned by Muthesius in his study of *Das Englische Haus*. Nevertheless, in the 1860s, Bodley designed a number of avant-garde houses whose reticent, vernacular manner makes them as interesting as the contemporary work of Philip Webb. Indeed, when Bodley was seriously ill in 1868–9, his friend Webb supervised the construction of some of these houses and it may be wondered whether Bodley's early use of Georgian detailing may have influenced Webb's work rather than vice versa. Later, the two men grew apart, Webb remarking after Bodley's death that 'he was a man of some taste and discrimination, and for a while I had at one time pleasure in his companionship; it died away under the "Restoration" [i.e., the campaigns of the Society for the Protection of Ancient Buildings], separator of friendly familiarity, his respectability increasing and mine going-going-gone!'[7]

A pupil of Gilbert Scott, Bodley as a young man was one of the most original of muscular Gothic architects and he was a very early patron of Morris & Co. in his churches. In 1869 he formed a partnership with Thomas Garner (1839–1906) and their later work, if no less interesting, is more conservative and refined. In 1888, at the first Arts and Crafts Exhibition, Bodley remarked to his pupil, C. R. Ashbee, that, 'I seem to see here the ghosts of all my former friends.' Bodley declined to follow the path taken by Webb. When questioned about his early houses by F. M. Simpson in 1896, Bodley was characteristically diffident: '... I do not think it worth while to mention these things. It would suffice to say that I was early in the field. "Our little systems have their day." But our systems are not worth much, and certainly do not last long, though art is long and buildings are stubborn facts.'[8] Indeed, several of Bodley's early houses do survive as stubborn facts to show just how good a domestic architect he could be. These include All Saints' Vicarage at Scarborough, a house at Cefn Bryntalch, near Welshpool, a vicarage at Valley End (above and page 65) and a collection of villas at Great Malvern (pages 66–7).

The Old Vicarage at Valley End, in remote Surrey heathland near Windlesham, was built to serve a little hamlet where Bodley erected

a church in 1867. The brick church is Gothic; the vicarage is not, and if *1866* was not visible on a gable, it would be very difficult to date. With its simple brickwork and Georgian sashes, freely disposed, the house has a totally convincing anonymous and provincial character; only the three hipped gables towards the garden – a motif later used by Webb – hint at the hand of a very subtle architect.

Four houses in Ranelagh Road, Malvern Link, Worcestershire, were built for the Revd George Herbert, founder and first vicar of the slum church of St Peter's, Vauxhall, as a retreat from London. Philip Webb supervised their construction and they were completed in 1869. These houses are not really 'neo-Georgian' as they are artful and unprecedented compositions of sash windows, weather-boarding, Palladian windows and Classical porches, but they are certainly one of the earliest and most subtle revivals of the elegance of Georgian domestic architecture. Edward Warren wrote of them in 1910 that 'their charm is that of Jane Austen's heroines; it is an affair of character and staid refinement combined with a certain little air of dignified propriety.'[9] In 1879 they were taken over by the (Anglican) nuns of the Community of the Holy Name. In 1893 Ninian Comper added a chapel.

Valley End Rectory / *George Frederick Bodley*

Great Malvern Villas / *George Frederick Bodley*

Great Malvern Villas / *George Frederick Bodley*   67

Stowford Cottages / WILLIAM EDEN NESFIELD

W. E. Nesfield (1835–88) was one of the most brilliant and influential architects of the 1860s who with his friend and sometime partner, Norman Shaw, really invented both the 'Old English' and the 'Queen Anne' styles which were the foundations of English domestic architecture for the next few decades. Hermann Muthesius wrongly assumed that Nesfield, although important, tended to follow Shaw's lead when, in truth, both young architects learned from each other as they explored possibilities and precedents for a new vernacular domestic architecture.

Although in partnership as Nesfield and Shaw from 1866 until 1869, the two architects never collaborated on a design but kept to their own jobs. The son of a successful landscape gardener and the nephew of the architect Salvin, Nesfield had rather less of the Gothic in him than Shaw, whom he met when in the office of Salvin's friend William Burn. Nesfield's eclecticism was brilliant and charming, but he was not able to sustain it much beyond the end of the decade. His Temperate Lodge at Kew Gardens, near Kew Palace, designed in 1867, was one of the first 'Queen Anne' buildings, with its large coved cornice and rubbed-brick pilasters. In his country buildings, Nesfield was early in reviving tile hanging and leaded-light windows in his supremely pretty compositions. Kinmel Park, a large house in Wales, combined Classical elements from Hampton Court with Aesthetic movement motifs, such as 'pies' or Japanese-style roundels.

Moving in advanced artistic circles, Nesfield was one of the first architects to be influenced by Japanese art. The Pre-Raphaelite painter, Simeon Solomon, wrote of Nesfield to the poet Swinburne that he was 'one of our very best architects, a man of great knowledge, invention and consummate amiability. He is a fat, jolly hearty fellow, genuinely good natured, very fond of smoking, and I deeply grieve to say of women.'[10] Nesfield was a gentleman architect who considered himself the social equal of his clients. He did not build much and, eventually, his career was tragic. He allowed his output to decline, gave up practice in 1880, took to drink, married a divorcee and died comparatively young.

The Stowford Cottages near Crewe Hall in Cheshire were built between 1865 and 1867 and this semi-detached pair is one of several examples of estate building designed on the Crewe Hall estate for Lord Crewe. In this characteristically sweet and elaborately detailed design, Nesfield packed in most of the elements of the 'Old English' style which he and Shaw had developed from old vernacular cottages in Southern England: tile-hanging, tall chimneys of rubbed brick, artful gables with only part of the roof hipped, leaded-light windows. The first-floor bays project forward of the ground floor on deep, coved plaster cornices. Sometimes Nesfield would press the ends of his regular supply of bottles into the wet plaster; here they are decorated with 'pies' and other patterns incised into the plaster.

Stowford Cottages / *William Eden Nesfield*

Leys Wood / RICHARD NORMAN SHAW

The name of Norman Shaw is inseparable from the history of English domestic architecture in the nineteenth century (see also pages 174 and 206). Richard Norman Shaw (1831–1912) established himself as the doyen of domestic architects in the 1870s and he almost made the 'Old English' style his own. Shaw dominates the profession in the latter half of Victoria's reign and, although he also designed churches and public buildings like New Scotland Yard, he was primarily a house architect. His work was of immense influence, partly owing to his own beautiful pen drawings of his buildings which were exhibited at the Royal Academy in the 1870s and which, thanks to the invention of photolithography, could easily be reproduced in the weekly architectural journals. It was through his drawings that the 'Old English' style crossed the Atlantic and became, in the hands of H. H. Richardson and McKim, Mead and White, amongst others, transformed into the Shingle style of the East Coast.

Shaw had a large practice and out of his office came many of the best Arts and Crafts architects of the next generation. A superb stylist – albeit often at the expense of the structural honesty so evident in the work of his less prolific contemporary, Philip Webb – and immensely inventive, Shaw managed to keep abreast of architectural fashion until the end of his life. Although he disapproved of Shaw's move to a full-blooded Classicism around 1890 with his two big houses which anticipated Edwardian Baroque – Bryanston and Chesters – Muthesius considered Shaw a giant. 'He always produces something that is his alone, something original and surprising to the spectator. He invariably uses traditional forms, though he is no longer bound by them: he takes liberties with them and uses them only as instruments for his own ideas. Norman Shaw is the first in the history of nineteenth century architecture to show this freedom from the trammels of style . . . he was the first of the modern architects.'

It is particularly sad that the main part of Leys Wood, near Groomsbridge, Sussex, was demolished in the 1950s, for it was Shaw's first and most influential large 'Old English' house. In 1870 Shaw exhibited a spectacular bird's-eye-view drawing of the house at the Royal Academy, showing its dramatic situation on a rocky bluff. The first designs were prepared in 1866 for James Temple, a rich cousin

of Shaw's and a director of the Shaw Savill shipping line. The house was built in 1868–9.

Although Leys Wood represented a departure from the stiff domestic Gothic of Scott and Burges, Shaw's design was illustrated in C. L. Eastlake's *History of the Gothic Revival* of 1872. Eastlake wrote that 'at Leys Wood and mansions of a similar kind there is absolutely nothing in external appearance to distinguish the design and workmanship from those of a building executed when this type of architecture was in ordinary use. The irregularity of plan, the random intersection of roofs, the dormer windows half hidden in odd corners, the fenestration introduced at external angles of the house, the open defiance of those principles of symmetry which were once considered essential to grace in the old and academical sense of the word, all promise a complete and thorough change in the aspect of our rural architecture, at least if such a work as this becomes popular, of which there is every probability. For with all its quaintness there is nothing in the interior of the house at Leys Wood incompatible with modern ideas of comfort or convenience.'

Close by, Shaw's contemporary house, Glen Andred, still stands but only the tile-hung gate-tower and stable wing of Leys Wood (Colour Plate C) survives today on its lush, Romantic site: twentieth-century maisonettes have triumphed over 'Old English'.

Grims Dyke, Harrow Weald / RICHARD NORMAN SHAW

Grims Dyke is today the best-preserved and most accessible example of Norman Shaw's 'Old English' style. Shaw's biographer, Andrew Saint, considers that 'no suaver or more approachable specimen of the smaller English country house of the 1870s can exist than Grims Dyke.... It is like some Victorian fruit cake, full of rich and diverse ingredients: not classic, not by any means right for all types of digestion, yet masterly on its own terms and utterly English, perfect in fact for the afternoon of British bourgeois civilization.' The ingredients are indeed varied: brick, half-timbering with 'brick-nogging' infill, tile-hanging, leaded lights, and the picturesqueness of the composition of gables and tall chimneys is enhanced by a kink in the plan.

Grims Dyke was built in 1870–2 for the painter Frederick Goodall, who specialised in biblical and Egyptian pictures. The house was aligned along the ancient Grime's Dyke in Middlesex, but, as Goodall's studio required north light, part of the house was set on a different axis – giving, for once, functional justification for a picturesque feature. In 1880, Goodall moved to St John's Wood – possibly his paintings were declining in popularity – and he was succeeded by the banker, Robert Heriot, who added a billiard-room in 1883 to designs by Arthur Cawston.

Grims Dyke's most famous owner acquired the house in 1890. This was W. S. Gilbert, who, in 1883 had already built a 'Queen Anne' house in London, designed by Ernest George and Peto (page 176). Gilbert brought in George to make alterations to Grims Dyke, the principal change being the conversion of the studio into a drawing-room, resplendent with a massive alabaster chimney-piece in a florid German Renaissance manner typical of George and Peto – although Gilbert supplied the original sketch.

Gilbert enjoyed himself at Grims Dyke, entertaining young ladies in the room he renamed the 'Flirtorium' and filling house and grounds with a menagerie of exotic animals: parrots, a donkey, lemurs, a fawn and Siberian cranes. He also bathed almost daily in a lake formed in part of the dyke. There, in 1911, two young ladies went for a swim and got into difficulties. The aged dramatist went to their rescue and died of a heart attack. As Andrew Saint notes, even after Gilbert's

death the history of the house has been a little bizarre, as it was used as a most appropriate setting for Hammer horror films such as *Curse of the Crimson Altar* and *Cry of the Banshee*. Today the house is a country club and restaurant.

72   Grims Dyke, Harrow Weald / *Richard Norman Shaw*

Grims Dyke, Harrow Weald / *Richard Norman Shaw*

73

Standen / PHILIP SPEAKMAN WEBB

Standen (Colour Plate D) is one of the loveliest houses south of London: lovely because of its unpretentiousness and the beauty of its construction. It is typical of an architect who took such care over details and materials that he never took on more than one job at a time. Standen, near East Grinstead in Sussex, is one of Webb's last buildings. It was built in 1892–4 for J. S. Beale, a successful solicitor. Webb treated Beale as he treated his aristocratic clients: firmly. He had his own ideas. When Webb's house Clouds burned down his clients, the Wyndhams, had to live in the servants' wing and were agreeably surprised to find it comfortable: Mrs Wyndham observed that this was an advantage of employing an architect who was a socialist.

At Standen, Beale had already cut back rock to build the house. When Webb was approached, he insisted that the site be changed. When Standen was finished, Beale gave his architect a snuff box, engraved with the inscription: 'When clients talk irritating nonsense,

I take a pinch of snuff.' Webb also insisted on preserving the original Hollybush Farm on the site. This was an old tile-hung cottage of the sort Webb liked and he incorporated it into the stable yard. This old building in fact set the tone of the whole design, which is rambling, varied and informal, nestling in the side of a hill rather than sitting on the top of it. Standen is, in fact, almost absurdly informal, for it employs an amazing variety of building materials and tries to give the impression that it has grown over the years. In fact, the only addition made to the original design was a stone bay added to the drawing-room for a piano. All the materials – two sorts of brick, stone, roughcast, tile-hanging, weather-boarding – are superbly employed, but there are odd conceits, such as the projecting bay in the centre of the five-bay gabled weather-boarded and tile-hung garden elevation. This, with its projecting canopy, looks like a blocked door: but it is not.

Webb designed the house for comfort, and the interiors are re-markable for their common-sense detailing as well as the imaginative and unhistoricist character of their vaguely Classical forms. It is a house which is traditional and truly vernacular, and yet not derived from any obvious source – the true aim of a traditionalist architect. There is also evident that puritanical awkwardness which was typical of Webb. Once he wrote to his client about having to 'refrain from a lovely fruit pie and strawberries with cream set out to tempt me from the path of wisdom'. As Mark Girouard remarks, 'One can't help feeling that Webb would have been a happier man and a greater architect if he had helped himself to more strawberries and cream.'[11]

Today Standen is owned by the National Trust and open to the public.

Rousdon / ERNEST GEORGE and THOMAS VAUGHAN

In the 1880s, Ernest George was Norman Shaw's chief competitor in the lucrative and desirable sphere of country-house architecture. Both architects had talented offices adept at producing 'Old English' and otherwise traditional and manorial houses for the new rich. George eventually evolved a distinct style of his own: especially for his town houses (see page 176). In the 1870s, however, he was still strongly under the influence of Norman Shaw, the older man. Ernest George (1839–1922) had been articled to Samuel Hewitt. He first set up in practice in partnership with Thomas Vaughan (1836–74). Vaughan was succeeded by Harold Ainsworth Peto (1854–1933), son of the Samuel Morton Peto and brother of the builders, Peto Brothers – a connection which proved valuable. Peto was succeeded as George's partner by Alfred B. Yates.

George was an accomplished water-colourist and etcher, specialising in mellow and picturesque subjects. Eventually he was able to make his buildings look as good as his sketches, but this cannot be

said of his first big country-house commission, Rousdon, which has a certain hardness of texture. Indeed, the house seems almost as much a product of the Gothic Revival as an essay in the new 'Queen Anne' style; nevertheless, it is a very accomplished and Romantic performance. Rousdon was designed in 1874, the year of Thomas Vaughan's early death. It was built on an exposed cliff-side site on the South Devon coast, and made of materials able to resist the weather: the walls have a 9-inch brick lining, 1 inch of asphalt and 24 inches of locally quarried flints. The house was finished in 1883.

It was built on biscuits: the client was Sir Henry Peek, Bart., MP and the owner of Peek Frean biscuits.

The style of Rousdon owes much to Norman Shaw, especially the tower which is very reminiscent of that over the stables at Leys Wood (page 70). It is, however, a much bigger house than anything Shaw had yet designed, with the principal rooms and a great hall arranged around a courtyard and the service areas given discreet access by a sunken road. Much of the house is late Gothic in style, with pointed arches evident; only in places does the design burst into the domestic manner of half-timbered 'Old English'. All is immensely solid and medieval in character, and, with corner turrets, gables and chimneys, suitably picturesque. Rousdon is now All Hallows School.

The Rousdon Estate was large and is filled with smaller buildings, all designed by George and Vaughan. These include a large stable block and the church of St Pancras, the latter, appropriately, purely Gothic in style.

Rousdon / *Ernest George* and *Thomas Vaughan*

Shiplake Court / ERNEST GEORGE and HAROLD PETO

In Shaw's office there was a joke that a card had been printed advising unsuitable clients to try Mr Ernest George. The joke was rather unfair, for not only was George a competitor, he also produced architecture of, at times, as high a standard as that by Shaw. In the 1880s, the offices of Norman Shaw and Ernest George and Peto were the only ones a bright young architect would wish to enter and it is surely significant that many of the best Arts and Crafts architects of the 1890s had worked for Ernest George. The list includes Guy Dawber, Robert Weir Shultz, Arnold Mitchell, Herbert Baker and, not least, Edwin Lutyens.

On his annual Continental holidays, George was an inveterate sketcher and the material he assembled would be used in the designs for town houses. For the country, he tended to design very convincing re-creations of the mellow country houses of the past, often managing to give them the quality of his own water-colours. This was partly because George's buildings are beautifully made. He took particular care over details like leaded-light windows and was always careful in the choice of building materials.

Ernest George was not, however, by any means an innovator. Houses like Batsford Park are large and convincing re-creations of Elizabethan houses. Muthesius considered that Ernest George 'has done little to further the development of modern ideas. Such was probably not his intention. He took all the richness of accumulated experience from the large English mansion and used it skilfully to build new houses which he intended should equal the old in comfort and romantic character.... His plans are among the best achievements of contemporary architecture. They have a consistent clarity and simplicity which is pleasing.'

Shiplake Court, Oxfordshire, is a good example of a mature Ernest George and Peto house (Colour Plate E). It was designed for Robert Harrison, a stockbroker, and built above the banks of the Thames near Henley in 1889–90. Shiplake Court is a Romantic re-creation of a Tudor house, with walls of mellow red brick with silver-grey diaper patterns. As often with George's houses, the windows are particularly beautifully detailed. The panes of leaded lights are placed in thick oak frames, which have weathered well and increase the ancient charac-

ter of the house. Ironically – and rather typically – modern technology was combined with nostalgic style: the house was lit by electricity from the beginning.

Shiplake Court is now a school.

Shiplake Court / *Ernest George* and *Harold Peto*

Great Bedwyn Vicarage / GEORGE GILBERT SCOTT JUNIOR

George Gilbert Scott Junior (1839–97) was the eldest son of Sir Gilbert Scott and the father of Sir Giles Gilbert Scott, the architect of Liverpool Cathedral. 'Middle' Scott built comparatively little and is even less well known as a domestic architect than as a designer of churches. Scott, like his friend G. F. Bodley (and with whom and Thomas Garner he founded the decorators and church furnishers, Watts & Co.), designed refined late Gothic churches, often with Renaissance details. His most famous building was the church of St Agnes, Kennington, now destroyed. Also like Bodley, Scott designed houses which were not Gothic but almost Georgian in inspiration.

In 1878, Scott was described by E. W. Godwin as 'a master and a leader in the "Queen Anne" revival'.[12] His earliest house, Garboldisham Manor, Norfolk, has unfortunately been demolished. This was Jacobean in style, with prominent Dutch gables, and was very different from the work of Nesfield and Shaw in the late 1860s. Most of Scott's surviving domestic works are small houses, usually vicarages, built of red brick and with a certain idiosyncrasy in the handling of gables, tall chimneys and sash windows. His remarkable enlargement of the vicarage at Pevensey was almost pure neo-Georgian.

G. G. Scott junior's career was strange and tragic. He was briefly a Fellow of Jesus College, Cambridge. In 1880, he shocked his family by becoming a Roman Catholic. Scott became consumed by a violent hatred of Gladstonian Liberalism and his behaviour became increasingly erratic; in 1884 he was found to be of unsound mind. He died in 1897 while staying, inexplicably, in his father's famous building: the Midland Grand Hotel at St Pancras Station.

The vicarage at Great Bedwyn, Wiltshire, is a product of Scott's short creative period as an architect. It was built in 1878–9 at a cost of £2,314. Scott employed the local silver-grey bricks together with red-brick dressings – a combination which became very fashionable after the turn of the century. With its gables, sash windows and undisciplined Classical details, this house succeeds in suggesting the rural anonymity of an altered seventeenth-century rectory. Only some of the details and the bay window, placed centrally, reveal it to be the work of a clever architect. The building is no longer a vicarage and is known as Glebe House.

80

Great Bedwyn Vicarage / *George Gilbert Scott Junior*

The Croft, Totteridge / THOMAS EDWARD COLLCUTT

T. E. Collcutt (1840–1924) was a successful late-Victorian architect not normally known for his domestic work, although he was in G. E. Street's office at the same time as Norman Shaw. He is best known for his Free Renaissance-style urban buildings – christened 'bric-a-brac' by Goodhart-Rendel – which often sported coloured banding in brick and terracotta. Collcutt was the architect of the Palace Theatre in Cambridge Circus, the Savoy Hotel and the now demolished Imperial Institute in South Kensington. He first rose to prominence by winning the competition for Wakefield town hall in 1877 with a 'Queen Anne' design strongly influenced by Shaw.

It is therefore rather surprising to find Collcutt singled out for praise in *Das Englische Haus*, but Muthesius wrote that 'the houses of T. E. Collcutt are distinguished for the energetic yet pleasing design which is so refreshing in his other buildings. Collcutt's means of expression, like George's, are Elizabethan in form, but he is more personal in his use of these forms which he displays in sharply outlined, fairly modern-looking buildings.'

The Croft is one of several houses which Collcutt designed in Totteridge, a Hertfordshire village then well outside London but easily accessible by train. Totteridge became a very desirable location and many expensive Victorian and Edwardian houses were built around the old church and green. Collcutt built the Croft for himself in 1895; its size and opulence suggest how successful the architect's career had been up to this date. The house is in a style very different from that Collcutt was using just a few miles away in central London; here in the country, Collcutt, like other architects, thought a different style appropriate and he employed his own version of 'Old English'. The Croft has an interesting, almost neo-medieval plan arranged around

the entrance court and the house contains a great hall – a feature which Pugin and Shaw took from medieval houses and which Shaw used in rather larger houses than this one.

The Croft was built in a typically varied range of materials: brick, stone, roughcast and timber, and tiles. The timber gallery overlooking the garden is an unusual feature and the design of the gable above the entrance particularly well handled. The Croft admirably conveys the countrified pretensions of its successful builder.

The Croft, Totteridge / *Thomas Edward Collcutt*

Belgrave Cottages, Eaton Hall / Wrexham Road Farm / JOHN DOUGLAS

John Douglas (1829–1911) was the most successful Victorian architect in the north-west. He was a contemporary of Shaw and his career in the Cheshire area, designing 'Old English' houses, mirrored Shaw's on a regional level. Douglas was a pupil of the church architect, E. G. Paley, and, like Shaw, moved away from Gothic in search of a vernacular domestic style. But his solution was different, because of the area where he practised. Whereas Shaw revived the tile-hanging of the south, Douglas revived the black-and-white half-timbering which is actually indigenous to Cheshire (the half-timbering, that is: the strident black-and-white painting may well be a Victorian taste). More than any other architect, Douglas transformed Chester from a Georgian city into one of half-timber, for very few of the traditional black-and-white gabled buildings so admired by tourists were actually standing before the 1850s.

Muthesius wrote that Douglas 'devoted himself most lovingly to the re-introduction of the style, mastered it down to the last detail and produced buildings of great charm. His buildings always reflect consummate mastery of form and are yet simple enough in feeling and natural-looking fitness for purpose to stand comparison with older houses. His most charming creations include a whole series of small buildings (lodges, farm-buildings, workmen's houses, schools, etc.) in the vicinity of Eaton Hall, the Duke of Westminster's seat in Cheshire.' Douglas's firm became Douglas and Fordham in 1885 and Douglas and Minshull in 1898.

The 3rd Marquess and 1st Duke of Westminster carried out a massive amount of building on his Eaton estate after his accession in 1869 and a variety of architects were employed. As Muthesius noted, many of the smaller lodges and cottages were designed by Douglas and their informal, vernacular manner was in marked contrast to Eaton Hall itself, a vast pile in a ponderous Gothic as rebuilt by Waterhouse. Belgrave Cottages (page 85), built in 1871, are typical of Douglas: a picturesque composition of gables employing a variety

of building materials. Douglas does not use half-timbering here but brick and tile-hanging more typical of Norman Shaw. Typically, he could not bear to make this semi-detached pair absolutely symmetrical. One gable is taller and enlivened with a diagonal pattern of brick and plaster rather than the tile-hanging on the other. Belgrave was a tiny hamlet which gave its name to part of the Duke of Westminster's London property.

Wrexham Road Farm (above), near Chester, was a model farm designed by Douglas in about 1875–80. The farm buildings themselves – eminently practical – are of brick and half-timber, while the farmhouse (page 86), of 1880, is of Jacobean inspiration, built of brick and stone. Some of Douglas's larger houses were in a French Renaissance manner rather than Anglo-German half-timber.

Belgrave Cottages, Eaton Hall / *John Douglas*

Wrexham Road Farm / *John Douglas*

PART TWO / The Country House

Bullers Wood / ERNEST NEWTON

Ernest Newton (1856–1922) deserves to be better known than he is. Almost exclusively a country-house architect (see page 158), he was much less interested in conspicuous originality of expression than his contemporaries like W. R. Lethaby or E. S. Prior. As a result, Newton has enjoyed rather less attention from historians than other late-Victorian architects, but his quiet and painstaking attention to convenience, detail and the siting of houses ensured him great respect among his contemporaries and he had a large and very successful practice. Quite undoctrinaire about style, Newton realised from the beginning of his career that Georgian was the natural and gentlemanly manner of building in the south of England, but his own Georgian manner was never formal and rigid; rather it was adapted to his sensible, convenient plans with generous bay windows.

Muthesius wrote that Newton was 'one of the busiest architects in England and therefore represents the good principles of current thinking about the house in perhaps its most accessible form.... Our interest is immediately engaged by the masterly way in which the qualities of the material are handled and shown to advantage, the excellent work in every material, the subtle juxtaposing of colour in the different materials. Although they are far removed from any elegance, they reflect a high level of refinement.'

Newton entered Norman Shaw's office as a pupil in 1873; later he became chief assistant. With his colleagues in Shaw's office – Lethaby, Prior, Macartney and Horsley – he founded the Art Workers' Guild in 1884, a body dedicated to the encouragement of co-operation between architects, artists and other artist-craftsmen. In 1903 Newton published *A Book of Country Houses* about his own work and, after his death, his son W. G. Newton produced *The Work of Ernest Newton* (1925).

After leaving Shaw in 1879, Newton's practice did not take off for

some time. His first important commission came in 1888 when he was asked by a Bromley merchant called Sanderson to enlarge a mid-Victorian stuccoed villa. The result, Bullers Wood at Chislehurst, built in 1889–90, is a house of red brick with stone dressings whose long elevations are unassertive and subtle compositions of deep projecting bays and chimney-breasts, all in a style which is a fusion of Georgian and leaded-light Tudor. The elegant interiors are largely Classical in style, with much white-painted woodwork at the outset, and with Jacobean touches. As Roderick Gradidge writes, 'it seems that Newton never gave his clients anything that they did not entirely want and need – for this reason his houses are difficult to write about, but they are clearly easy to live in.'[13]

Bullers Wood / *Ernest Newton*

Avon Tyrell / WILLIAM RICHARD LETHABY

The considerable reputation of W. R. Lethaby (1857–1931) rests more upon his writings than upon his executed works. This seems paradoxical as the essence of his philosophy was that practical work was the best foundation for a good modern architecture. Lethaby despised drawing-board architecture using historical styles, and admired architects who made something new out of sound building: architects like Butterfield and, above all, Philip Webb, whose biography he wrote. But it was with Norman Shaw that Lethaby acquired his architectural education, succeeding Ernest Newton as chief assistant in 1879 and setting up on his own ten years later. Lethaby, complex and intense, was very different from Shaw, who had a great regard for Lethaby as a fine draughtsman and a talented designer: 'No, on the contrary, it is I who am Lethaby's pupil'[14] – and allowed him considerable independence in the office work.

On his own, Lethaby built comparatively little – a handful of houses, an insurance building and a church – and it was the worry and strain of getting All Saints', Brockhampton, built which made Lethaby give up architecture for writing and teaching. A founder of the Art Workers' Guild in 1884, Lethaby was a disciple of Ruskin and Morris. He also had a weakness for arcane exoticism, which he explained in his book *Architecture, Mysticism and Myth* of 1892. This book about architectural symbolism was responsible for much Byzantinesque mannerism in Arts and Crafts architecture.

Muthesius warmed to Lethaby's moral high-mindedness and Lethaby seems to have been Muthesius's guide in the selection of buildings discussed in *Das Englische Haus*. In the book, he was described as 'one of the architects who today uphold and continue the best traditions of English house-building. He brings a delicate, distinctive atmosphere to the sombre grandeur of the English house. Modern in the best sense in thought and sensibility and certainly hostile to any hint of romanticism, he cannot help imbuing his buildings with an exalted aesthetic and spiritualised atmosphere which immediately charms the spectator.'

Avon Tyrell, near Christchurch, Hampshire, was Lethaby's first independent work. Shaw, with characteristic generosity, used to set up his assistants with a job when they left his office and when Lord

Manners asked Shaw to recommend an architect, Shaw suggested that Macartney, Newton and Lethaby submit drawings and photographs to him. Lethaby was chosen and found himself, like his hero Webb, a socialist designing a large country house for a peer. Building began in 1891. The basic ingredients of the design owe much to Shaw – red brick, tile-hung gables, etc. – but they are put together in a manner which is typical of Lethaby: a certain awkwardness of proportion and austerity in contrast to Shaw's exuberance and with flattened, rounded mouldings.

On paper the design looks splendid, but in the execution a certain hardness crept in. The rooms are grouped under a long, high unbroken roof-line, such as a Goth like Butterfield might admire: none of Shaw's usual nightmare of valley gutters here. The composition of the long garden elevation reflects Ruskin's *Lamp of Life*: the rhythm of the projecting bays differs from that of the flattened gables above, and the whole elevation is not quite symmetrical. At one end the massive blank chimney-breast has the interesting detail of a pattern of stone blocks. Is this an intellectual stylisation of Devey's sham antique? The house is now a school.

90

Avon Tyrell / *William Richard Lethaby*

Pleasaunce Cottage, Dormans Park / ROBERT ALEXANDER BRIGGS

Although his work was not of any particular originality or sophistication, R. A. Briggs (1858–1916) became well known as he was a successful self-publicist. *Bungalows and Country Residences*, first published in 1891, was one of several books produced by Briggs in which he illustrated his own work. As a result, he became best known as 'Bungalow' Briggs.

James Kornwolf, the biographer of Baillie Scott, suggests that Briggs's work is of interest because it shows the influence of the American Shingle style on England around 1890. In the 1870s, the publication of Shaw's drawings transmitted the 'Old English' style across the Atlantic, where it was transformed into a picturesque Shavian style with wooden shingles replacing the tile-hanging. In the 1890s, the interconnecting spaces, low spreading roofs and extravagant verandahs of American country houses were, in turn, occasionally imitated in Britain. Certainly Briggs's work has an American character.

Bungalow Briggs designed several houses in Dormans Park, a curious development north of East Grinstead built after the railway was opened in 1884. It was a private, gated estate of week-end cottages for bachelors – whether intended for any nefarious activities is not recorded – which was originally named Bellagio. An attempt was made to justify this name by damming a stream to create a rather smaller version of Lake Como.

The houses built on the Bellagio estate were often described as bungalows, even though the buildings were of several storeys. Briggs explained that by the Indian term 'bungalow' he had in mind a relatively primitive small house, such as might be found in the Colonies. 'What we mean by a bungalow is an artistic little dwelling, cheaply but soundly built with a proper regard to sanitation, and

popped down in some pretty little spot with just sufficient accommodation for our particular needs. It is not necessary that an English bungalow, like its Eastern original, should be a one-storied building.'

Pleasaunce Cottage was built in 1889 for C. Quentin. Apart from the substitution of tiles for the original thatch and the glazing in of the verandahs, the house is unaltered today. The construction was largely of wood above dwarf stone walls, and the American character of the structure is evident. Inside there is a double-height hall with a gallery – also rather American, even if the American idea may originally have come from Pugin and Shaw. The woodwork was 'stained very dark brown, and coated with boiled linseed oil'.

Pleasaunce Cottage, Dormans Park / *Robert Alexander Briggs*

Munstead Wood / EDWIN LANDSEER LUTYENS

Out of the Gothic Revival, out of the Arts and Crafts movement with its concern with honesty of construction and truth to materials, and building on the work of Philip Webb and Norman Shaw in creating modern but traditional houses for the country, came Edwin Lutyens to create the most stylish and clever English houses of them all (see also page 168). Sir Edwin Lutyens (1869–1944) went on to become an Imperial architect, the designer of New Delhi, the Cenotaph and grand Classical buildings, but had he died in 1900 he would be remembered as a masterly and inventive domestic architect.

Muthesius was impressed: 'He is a young man who of recent years has come increasingly to the forefront of domestic architects and who may soon become the accepted leader among English builders of houses, like Norman Shaw in the past. Lutyens is one of those architects who would refuse to have anything whatever to do with any new movement. His buildings reflect his attachment to the styles of the past, the charms of which he finds inexhaustible. . . . But just as a really important artist cannot ignore the demands of his time, so Lutyens's new buildings do not really look ancient at all. On the contrary, they have a character that, if not modern, is entirely personal and extremely interesting.'

These remarks certainly apply to Lutyens's first masterpiece, Munstead Wood, near Godalming, Surrey, a house built for the formidable gardener, Gertrude Jekyll, who had such a profound influence on the development of Lutyens's career. Lutyens had first met her in 1890 and had already designed a cottage for her, the 'Hut', at Munstead. Munstead Wood was as much the result of his client's influence as of his own ideas. It was built in 1896–7 by Thomas Underwood, a local builder from Dunsfold, and the stonemason was William Herbert of Witley.

Munstead Wood was planned around three sides of an open court, facing north, with the first-floor gallery cantilevered out over the middle side. As with most Lutyens houses, Munstead Wood is entered by a complex and subtle route. The front door is hidden behind an arch – reminiscent of the work of the American, H. H. Richardson – cut through the end of the solid stone wall of the entrance front and leading straight into the garden. The appeal of the house comes from

Lutyens's use of the local Burgate stone combined with red brick, timber and great sweeps of tiled roof.

Miss Jekyll wrote that 'from the way it is built it does not stare with newness; it is not new in any way that is disquieting to the eye; it is neither raw nor callow. On the contrary, it almost gives the impression of a comfortable maturity of something like a couple of hundred

94

years. And yet there is nothing sham-old about it; it is not trumped up with any specious or fashionable devices of spurious antiquity; there is no pretending to be anything that it is not – no affectation whatever. But it is designed and built in the thorough and honest spirit of the good work of old days.'[15] Unfortunately, in the 1930s, the bushes and trees of Miss Jekyll's garden were cut back to much further away from the house, and alternate timber mullions in the windows have been removed.

One explanation for the quality of Munstead Wood is Lutyens's architectural education: wandering around his native Surrey watching builders at work and learning about composition by drawing the outlines of buildings in soap on a piece of glass held up to the subject. He had a most remarkable three-dimensional sense of form. Lutyens spent less than a year in Ernest George's office before setting up on his own.

Munstead Wood / *Edwin Landseer Lutyens*

Deanery Garden / EDWIN LANDSEER LUTYENS

Muthesius remarked of Lutyens's houses that 'as regards the ground plan, he seeks unusual solutions by introducing, or rather re-introducing, the idea of the enclosed courtyard; in siting a house he seeks to relate it as closely as possible to the surrounding terrain by developing the architectonic idea in the form of terraces, flower-beds, pools, box hedges and pergolas. In this connection he is the most zealous champion of the new movement in gardening.'

These remarks certainly apply to Deanery Garden, one of Lutyens's finest Romantic vernacular houses, described by Christopher Hussey as 'without overstatement, a perfect architectural sonnet', and built at the very turn of the century for a client who did more than anyone to promote the Edwardian 'dream house': Edward Hudson, founder and managing director of *Country Life* and one of Lutyens's greatest and most influential patrons. Deanery Garden at Sonning was designed in 1899 as a bachelor retreat near the Thames and was completed in 1901.

Taking a cue from the old wall which surrounded the enclosed site and which was incorporated into the design, Lutyens built the new house of special thin pinky-red bricks, white clunch (or chalk) and oak. The house surrounds three sides of a courtyard – the fourth being the old entrance wall – and is linked to the gardens by a series of vistas along dominant axes. One axis leads from the understated outside door in the wall, along a cloister by the courtyard, through the house past the double-height, half-timber hall and out into the garden. The other axis leads from the courtyard through the cloister and out into the side garden at a right-angle to the principal axis.

The garden elevation is one of Lutyens's finest, with the great timber oriel window of leaded lights balanced by a tall and cleverly modelled chimney-breast on the other side of the garden door. This elevation was lengthened in 1912, presumably by Lutyens, for a new owner, C. W. Christie-Miller. At the same time a new wing was added in the same brick but in a more suave and streamlined Tudor style, with parapets and 'battlements' created by planes of brickwork – an idea which may derive from Philip Webb. Here also are more of the large brick chimneys, usually placed on the diagonal, which are such a conspicuous feature of Deanery Garden. The style of the house may be traditional, but it is full of unusual ideas, typical of the architect, like the use of clunch, combined with brick in the cloister and infilling the properly pegged and jointed timberwork of the hall.

The house cannot be separated from its garden: as in the work of Frank Lloyd Wright, the two are bound together architecturally. The garden, designed with Gertrude Jekyll, is really a series of gardens, each enclosed and interesting but related to the other parts and to the house by vistas and by walls. It is a composition of levels and textures, of grass and water and stone, which, as Hussey observed, 'at once formal and informal, virtually settled that controversy, of which Sir Reginald Blomfield and William Robinson were for long the protagonists, between formal and naturalistic garden design. Miss Jekyll's naturalistic planting wedded Lutyens's geometry in a balanced union of both principles.'[16]

In 1903, *Country Life* – and, therefore, Hudson himself – felt that 'Mr Lutyens never designed a more perfect house or charming garden.... So naturally has the house been planned that it seems to have grown out of the landscape rather than to have been fitted into it.'

Deanery Garden / *Edwin Landseer Lutyens*

Deanery Garden / *Edwin Landseer Lutyens*

Deanery Garden / *Edwin Landseer Lutyens*

99

Red House, Godalming / EDWIN LANDSEER LUTYENS

Lutyens became very successful very quickly because of the seemingly effortless beauty and mellowness of his traditional-looking houses. There was also, however, always a vein of wilful originality, if not eccentricity in his work, which usually expressed itself in the highly mannered Classical forms of his chimney-pieces. Sometimes this eccentricity was on a larger scale, as with the curious duality in the design of Overstrand Hall, Norfolk, and the almost art nouveau quality of Les Bois des Moutiers at Varangeville-sur-Mer, near Dieppe, one of Lutyens's best and best-preserved early houses. Such houses usually received less attention from the architect's admirers.

The Red House in Frith Hill Road, Godalming, is one of Lutyens's most remarkable and least-known houses. It was omitted from Lawrence Weaver's and A. S. G. Butler's surveys of Lutyens's work doubtless because it was too eccentric for their tastes and did not relate to the mainstream of his practice. The house was built for the Revd W. H. Evans, a master at Charterhouse school which is just across a deep valley from the (now demolished) boarding houses next door. The precise date of the house is not recorded: it may be as early as 1897–9.

On its difficult, steeply sloping site, Red House is most cleverly planned. The front door, in the centre of the quiet, low and rather Georgian street front of the house, meets the square central staircase about half way up its full height, for there is a floor above and a floor below. In fact, they are not really floors, for all the rooms are arranged in a sort of spiral around this staircase which manages to climb gently through the whole height of the house. This means that the floor levels on one side of the house are different from on the other, but this can only be seen in elevation: from far below on the garden side, the projecting bays manage to conceal the difference.

This garden front, at the top of a steep slope where once there was a Jekyll garden, is reminiscent of the front of Norman Shaw's own house in Hampstead – where the floor levels are also irregular. But the Red House elevation, with its bays rising from the ground through four storeys to a straight parapet, has a castle-like quality which is enhanced by the recessed planes of brickwork making 'battlements' – a Philip Webb trick – and makes this Surrey house seem to antici-

pate Castle Drogo. All is in red brick, with bands of wood and leaded-light windows wrapping around the corners in a 'Modern' way. At the side of the house is a strange, double-height bay, which gives garden access to rooms on two floors. Inside, there are some of Lutyens's most peculiar and mannered chimney-pieces.

Having become an hotel, Red House was recently threatened with demolition and is in poor condition. The present owner is hoping to restore it as a house.

Red House, Godalming / *Edwin Landseer Lutyens*

Westbrook / HUGH THACKERAY TURNER

Thackeray Turner (1853–1937) was one of the best Arts and Crafts architects of his generation and, apart from two notable London churches, designed nothing but houses, yet he is not mentioned in *Das Englische Haus*. Though a pupil of Sir Gilbert Scott and chief assistant to poor, mad, G. G. Scott junior, Turner's buildings show more of the influence of William Morris and Philip Webb. He became the second secretary of Morris's Society for the Protection of Ancient Buildings, serving from 1885 until 1911, and his practicality and tact did much to further Anti-Scrape – the principles of anti-restoration. In London, Turner was in partnership with Colonel Eustace Balfour, surveyor to the Grosvenor Estate and the brother of the future prime minister. Balfour and Turner's London town houses and flats are suave and original developments of 'Queen Anne' Tudor. These included Lygon Place, Ebury Street, near Victoria Station, and the now demolished town house for Alfred Beit in Park Lane: Aldford House. In the country, Turner's independent work was more rugged and earthy.

Turner built Westbrook, on a hill above Godalming, for himself in 1899–1900. The builder was Walter Holt, of Croydon, and the plasterwork was carried out by Turner's craftsman brother, Laurence. The house is made of local Burgate stone and is sober, appropriate and undemonstrative: there are none of the tricks found in Lutyens's contemporary houses nearby. Westbrook manifests a quiet but sensuous joy in the quality of materials – stone, wood, plaster, tile, marble – all of which are superb and soundly combined. Marble is used in thin slabs for a chimney-piece and the floor-boards are impressively wide. It is a well-made, comfortable house, right in the landscape and not trying too hard to exhibit originality: the only feature which is at all wilful is the entrance porch, with stubby Byzantinesque columns carrying a generous timber lintel, above which rises a low stone gable. Elsewhere, tiles are used in the Roman manner to make the piers of a pergola.

Writing in 1912, Lawrence Weaver considered that Westbrook 'represents the school of traditional architecture which has grown up quietly and surely in England from the seeds sown by William Morris and Mr Philip Webb. Simple, unaffected, owing nothing, or at least singularly little, to the spirit of the Renaissance, it shows what can be done by using local materials in a straightforward yet thoughtful fashion.'[17]

Turner also designed the gardens at Westbrook, with the sunken octagonal pool enclosed by a tall and very architectural hedge.

Westbrook / *Hugh Thackeray Turner*

Westbrook / *Hugh Thackeray Turner*

Westbrook / *Hugh Thackeray Turner*

Lympne Castle / ROBERT STODART LORIMER

No one architect in England was as important as Sir Robert Lorimer (1864–1929) in Scotland in the revival of old building crafts and of traditional vernacular architecture. He is represented here by one of his two houses in England. A Romantic, a Scottish nationalist, and a disciple of William Morris, Lorimer believed that the last healthy, indigenous architecture in Scotland had been in the seventeenth century, before being supplanted by a Classicism imported from England. Sometimes called the 'Lutyens of Scotland', Lorimer's work was both similar to and yet different from that of his great English contemporary. Being inspired by the vital craftsmanship, especially plaster-work and woodwork, in Scottish castles and tower houses, he remained almost more interested in the crafts themselves than in an overall harmonious design. He was reluctant to follow Lutyens along the path towards an intellectual Classicism.

Born in Edinburgh, Lorimer was first a pupil with Sir Robert Rowand Anderson before coming south to work with Bodley and Garner, in whose office he learned about Gothic and encountered the English Arts and Crafts movement in London. Lorimer's first job was the restoration of Earlshall, Fife, begun in 1891. Here, as elsewhere, he repaired the old work in the old way and made new additions, in a traditional manner, subservient to the old work – an approach which contrasted with earlier reconstructions of Scottish tower houses. Also interested in seventeenth-century Scottish formal gardens, Lorimer's work in garden design is analogous to that of Lutyens and Jekyll in England.

Muthesius appreciated Lorimer's importance in Scotland where 'he was the first to recognize the charm of unpretentious old Scottish buildings, with their honest plainness and simple, almost rugged massiveness. He saw no necessity for imitations of early Scottish styles, with pinnacles and towers and projecting barbizans; he had steeped himself in early art sufficiently to recognize and re-assess its more intimate charms. In short, Lorimer has begun to do in Scotland what Norman Shaw's group did in London thirty-five years ago. Lorimer's achievements in house-building in Scotland today are by

far the most interesting of any that can bear comparison with the Mackintosh group.'

Lympne Castle (Colour Plate F) on the Kent coast was restored and enlarged for F. J. Tennant in 1907–9 and 1911–12. The job might have gone to Lutyens as Edward Hudson was hoping to buy the castle until outbid, so he transferred his attention to Lindisfarne. In 1906 the fifteenth-century castle overlooking Romney Marsh was derelict. Lorimer restored it sympathetically and added a large extension containing dining-room and kitchens, and another wing of servants' quarters by the road at the other end of a walled garden. Although built in rubble stone to harmonise with the castle, the new buildings do not imitate the castle but are domestic in scale. As Christopher Hussey, Lorimer's first biographer, wrote, 'In contrast to Sir Edwin Lutyens, whose first care is to produce a united and homogeneous whole and who is inclined in the process to alter the values of the original part, Lorimer started out with the conviction that additions must be definitely subordinate in importance to the ancient nucleus and, while harmonizing, form a contrast.'[18] Such, of course, are the principles Morris enshrined in the Manifesto of the SPAB.

Lympne Castle / *Robert Stodart Lorimer*

The Norman Chapel, Broad Campden / CHARLES ROBERT ASHBEE

C.R. Ashbee (1863–1942), architect, artist, craftsman, writer and social reformer, took his Arts and Crafts ideals further than most. Goodhart-Rendel recalled that 'if you had taken him up, you really were in with the revolutionaries'.[19] Lutyens described him as 'that most – to me – distasteful Ashbee, artist and furniture freakist',[20] but this comment may have been a reaction to Ashbee's Uranian ideal of friendship. Ashbee was the son of the celebrated pornographic bibliographer who disinherited him after he sided with his mother when she left her husband. After being educated at King's College, Cambridge, he trained as an architect with Bodley and Garner. His Christian Socialist conscience took him to Toynbee Hall in the East End of London, where he lectured on Ruskin to working men. Out of this commitment grew the Guild and School of Handicraft, founded in 1888 and occupying Essex House in the Mile End Road. The Guild executed Baillie Scott's designs for the interiors of the new palace at Darmstadt in 1897. The following year Ashbee set up the Essex House Press with the presses from Morris's Kelmscott Press. Also in the 1890s, Ashbee was active in the campaign to save ancient London buildings from demolition and he founded the Survey of London.

In 1902, further to fulfil the ideas of Morris, Ashbee took his guild away from the East End to Chipping Camden, so that his craftsmen could enjoy idyllic, rural surroundings. However, this Cockney invasion of rural Gloucestershire was not an unqualified success and, with commercial firms able to undercut the price of products made by Ashbee's craftsmen, the Guild went bankrupt in 1908. Ashbee had a small architectural practice, much of it consisting of building houses in Cheyne Walk, Chelsea (see page 194), where he lived. All of Ashbee's executed work was domestic, including the careful restoration of Cotswold cottages. He was a friend of Frank Lloyd Wright, with whom he corresponded.

The Norman Chapel at Broad Campden in Gloucestershire (Colour Plate G) is almost the perfect English House, for much of the structure is genuinely old. In 1903, when Ashbee surveyed the building, it consisted of the derelict nave of a Norman church, complete with chancel arch, which had been made into a house in the fourteenth or fifteenth century by the insertion of a floor. There were also two-storeyed domestic wings which had been added at about the same time to the west and south. Ashbee wished to restore the Norman Chapel as a house for himself, but could not afford to do so. In the event, he carried out the work in 1905–7 for his friend Ananda Coomaraswamy, the Singhalese scholar and a very sympathetic client. The nave was planned as a music-room, the room above that a library, and the later additions thrown together as a dining-room. The old buildings were treated according to SPAB Anti-Scrape principles. Where unstable, the nave walls were carefully taken down and rebuilt, supported by stout new buttresses. Ashbee's new service wing to the north-east was made of roughcast brick so as 'to harmonise and yet not compete with the stonework of the two earlier periods'. The newer stone-faced wing to the west is a later refacing and extension of Ashbee's work.

The room intended as a music-room was first used to house the remnants of Ashbee's Essex House Press, which he ran jointly with Coomaraswamy from 1907 until 1910. After 1911 Coomaraswamy let the Norman Chapel to the Ashbees, who lived there until 1919.

The Norman Chapel, Broad Campden / *Charles Robert Ashbee*

Vann / WILLIAM DOUGLAS CAROË

As the inspiration for the 'Old English' country house was both a love of old vernacular buildings and a desire for modern houses to look convincingly old, it is not surprising to find that some architects converted genuine old buildings into houses. Old timbers were better than new ones, old buildings had an unaffected picturesqueness which some had qualms about faking. This desire for the 'olde' reached an extreme pitch in the 1920s when neo-Tudor architects like Blunden Shadbolt faked old cottages with absurdly wobbly roof-ridges and made them out of old timbers taken from demolished houses and barns.

Edwardian architects were rather more reasonable and converted barns into houses in an honest manner, even if the structures were sometimes taken from other sites and re-erected. Lutyens did this at Great Dixter and Caroë did the same at Vann, near Godalming.

William Douglas Caroë (1857–1938) was the son of the Danish consul in Liverpool. He was articled to J. L. Pearson, architect of Truro Cathedral, and was primarily a church architect, becoming architect to the Church Commissioners. Caroë was the architect with whom Eric Gill trained and whom he criticised, albeit un-named, in his *Autobiography* (1940). Gill's dismissal of Caroë as conservative and unoriginal was very unfair, for his churches are elegant developments of Gothic precedents carried out with a beauty in the handling of materials which shows an allegiance to the ideals of the Arts and Crafts movement.

Caroë built Vann for himself and his descendants still live in the house. Vann is a clever and confusing mixture of old and new. The core is a medieval farmhouse with later additions, and there is an old timber barn by the road. Caroë joined all these together with a new connecting wing and made the whole into a convincingly rustic house. The work took some time: one rainwater head is dated 1908,

another 1929. Caroë was a good and sensitive restorer of churches and his skill in dealing with old buildings is evident at Vann. He delighted in the quality of materials, old and new, and unified the house with tile-hanging, wooden shingles and weather-boarding. The leadwork is of particularly high quality – Caroë was past Master of the Plumbers' Company. Of the interiors, the most impressive is the barn, converted into a large games-room, open to the roof timbers and with an upper timber gallery above the fireplace. All the new woodwork, furnishings and fittings were introduced with sensitive respect for the rugged character of the original buildings.

Vann / *William Douglas Caroë*

The Barn, Hartley Wintney / ROBERT WEIR SCHULTZ

Another architect who chose to live in a converted barn was Robert Weir Schultz (1860–1951). Notwithstanding his name, Schultz was a Scot, born in Port Glasgow. The name has caused confusion for, in 1915, he was persuaded to change it by his wife in order to sound less German. Henceforth he was R. W. S. Weir. Schultz trained in the office of Rowand Anderson in Edinburgh and then in London with both Norman Shaw and Ernest George, but the principal influences acting on him were the work of Philip Webb and his lifelong friend Lethaby. From them he acquired his deep respect for building crafts and a contempt for architecture merely created on paper in offices. He did not, however, adopt their socialism and Schultz enjoyed a most successful career, working for a range of rich clients, from hereditary peers to South African diamond millionaires. Also, unlike some of his equally uncompromising brothers in the Art Workers' Guild, Schultz's career did not decline after the turn of the century, even though he had no patience with Edwardian Classicism.

Schultz was firmly in the Arts and Crafts tradition, but there was another aspect to his career evident in some of his work. He was an expert on Byzantine architecture and from 1887 until 1890 he travelled in Greece, partly with Sidney Barnsley. Schultz put his Byzantine studies to good effect in his work for his best and most interesting patron, the 3rd Marquess of Bute, who earlier had commissioned Burges to design Cardiff Castle. For Bute Schultz designed, amongst other things, a subterranean Byzantine chapel in Regent's Park.

In 1899, Schultz bought twenty-six acres of land at Phoenix Green, Hartley Wintney, Hampshire, in an area where he designed several houses. On this land were two old barns, one of which he converted into a house for his own use. When he married in 1911, Schultz added a wing to the Barn which, characteristically, is subordinate to

the old building. All is immensely reticent and rustic, most of the exterior being weather-boarded. Inside there are white walls and fine timberwork to make an appropriate – and authentic – Arts and Crafts setting for Schultz's collection of both old furniture and modern pieces by his friends Lethaby, Ernest Gimson and others.

Schultz was also adept at garden design and, at the Barn, created a series of gardens divided up by pergolas and hedges. The topiary, the planting and the convincing rusticity of the overgrown surroundings and exterior of the house shows Schultz to have been a disciple of Gertrude Jekyll.

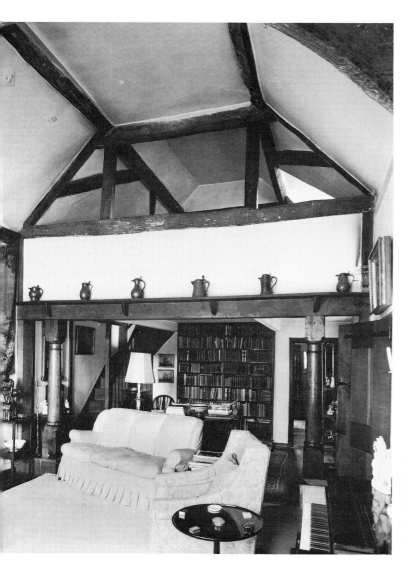

The Barn, Hartley Wintney / *Robert Weir Schultz*

How Green House / ROBERT WEIR SCHULTZ

Most English houses were not particularly inventive in their planning, for very good reasons. One innovation which was adopted by several architects, however, was the 'butterfly' plan. Another name for it, the 'double suntrap plan', suggests a practical reason for its adoption. Radiating wings broke up the rectilinear mass of the house and made its outline more interesting, but the junction of wings with a central core could produce an awkward internal plan. A butterfly plan was adopted by Norman Shaw at Chesters in 1891 and several examples were built after the turn of the century.

How Green House near Hever, Kent, was Robert Weir Schultz's only executed attempt at a butterfly plan and David Ottewill considers the result to be 'probably his finest house designed when he was at the height of his powers'.[21] The house was built in 1904–5 for Mobray V. Charrington. Although the butterfly is not placed sym-metrically facing south, the intention was to catch as much sun as possible and to give several rooms views over the River Eden. Wings radiating at forty-five degrees enclose the entrance court, one wing being extended into servants' quarters. These gabled elevations are entirely tile-hung, while the garden elevation is of brick and plaster. The gap between the smaller radiating wings is filled by first-floor balconies and a double-height central bay window.

Butterfly plans can produce awkward roof junctions, but Schultz managed to handle the complex shapes of gables and wings with skill and without creating awkward valleys and changes in height. There is a certain contrived awkwardness about the house but, as always with this architect, it is well built. Always sensitive to locality, Schultz here used the Surrey manner of style of Shaw and Lutyens.

How Green House / *Robert Weir Schultz*

Happisburgh Manor / DETMAR JELLINGS BLOW

The strange and sad career of Detmar Blow (1867–1939) is a parable of the ideals and temptations of late-Victorian and Edwardian society. It was a career which moved from the innocence of the Arts and Crafts towards something grander and more worldly, as did the career of his contemporary Lutyens. Lutyens survived this loss of innocence, Blow did not.

Blow was brought up in the very bosom of the Arts and Crafts movement. He was discovered by Ruskin sketching in Abbeville Cathedral in 1888 and taken up, introduced to his architect and craftsmen friends and persuaded to give up his training in an office and learn about the realities of sound architecture by apprenticing himself to a builder. When Ernest Gimson asked Blow to supervise the construction of his Leicestershire cottages (page 128) he had already built some cottages in Yorkshire and had acted as clerk of works for Philip Webb on the restoration of a church. Absolute and confident familiarity with the nature of building materials is evident in all of Blow's country work and his cottages and houses are among the most mellow and Romantic of Arts and Crafts buildings.

But Blow was also cannily aware that fashions were changing and architecture moving in new directions. He adapted himself to the new Imperial mood and Edwardian Baroque manner by teaming up with a Frenchman, Fernand Billerey. Blow and Billerey were thus able to compete with Mewès and Davis, the Anglo-French architects of the smart new Ritz Hotel. Billerey became a partner in 1905 and probably was solely responsible for the town houses of the Edwardian rich, like the interior of 10 Carlton House Terrace done in a chic French manner for Lord Ridley, while Blow continued to build traditional, earthy country houses like Wilsford Manor of 1904, which is often mistaken for a real Elizabethan manor house.

Blow, like Lutyens, made a good marriage, wedding a daughter of Lord Tollemache in 1910. In 1914 he set up as a country gentleman by building Hilles for himself, a fine traditional stone house in the Cotswolds. He increasingly moved in the world of the rich and important, of men like Kitchener, but his undoing was getting involved with Bendor, the very unpleasant 2nd Duke of Westminster. After enjoying his confidence for some years, Blow was obliged to resign from his position with the Grosvenor Estate in Mayfair in 1933 and died a broken man, never receiving the honours that Lutyens enjoyed.

Happisburgh Manor was designed at a happier stage of Blow's career. It was built in 1900 as a holiday home on the north Norfolk coast for the Cator family. Blow adopted the 'butterfly' plan for the house; the idea was not his but Ernest Gimson's, 'who sent the little butterfly device on a postcard'. At the centre of the butterfly is a single-storey entrance-hall cum dining-room, from which four wings radiate at sixty degrees. Blow contrived to fill the awkward triangular spaces left over with staircases and bathrooms. There were eighteen bedrooms in all. Happisburgh Manor is very earthy and 'of the soil racy' in its building materials. It is faced in local flint with red-brick dressings and decoration. The house was, and is, thatched and cost as little as £4,000. The Cators were Catholic and 'AVE' and 'MARIA' appear on the gables. Today the house is St Mary's country club.

Further along the Norfolk coast are other eccentric Arts and Crafts holiday homes: Lutyens's Pleasaunce and Overstrand Hall, and Prior's Home Place (page 122).

Happisburgh Manor / *Detmar Jellings Blow*

The Barn, Exmouth / EDWARD SCHROEDER PRIOR

E. S. Prior (1852–1932) was a characteristic product of late-Victorian England: confident, hearty and independent. He best represents the individualist, eccentric strain in the Arts and Crafts world, although his unusual designs managed to attract sufficient clients to sustain his comparatively small practice. Blomfield noted that Prior 'never went with the crowd, indeed his instinct was to turn his back on it and go the other way, and I think he really enjoyed being in a minority of one'.[22] He was helped by being an athletic Old Harrovian and a Cambridge graduate. In 1912 Prior became Slade Professor at Cambridge.

Prior was a pupil of Norman Shaw – 'perhaps the most gifted pupil of them all'[23] – and a co-founder of the Art Workers' Guild. He was also a fine writer and historian, although his view of medieval art was somewhat limited by his rigid adherence to the doctrines of Ruskin and Morris about the dominant role of the craftsman in architecture. He published *The Cathedral Builders of England* in 1905 and *A History of Gothic Art in England* in 1900. He designed more buildings for schools and universities – in a variety of styles – than houses, and his church at Roker in Sunderland is one of the very best Arts and Crafts buildings: a strange and thoughtful combination of contrived primitivism and sensible modernity. All Prior's work can be described as either original or eccentric, but his perversity was always tempered by common sense.

The Barn at Exmouth exhibits Prior's originality. Built in 1895–7 for Major H. B. Weatherall, it cost over £7,000 which was not cheap for a small house. The Barn combines the fashionable 'butterfly' plan with Prior's obsession with the use of local building materials. Two roughly symmetrical short wings are placed at forty-five degrees to a small, tall central block, but Prior made the whole composition much more complex by contriving to have three separate roof-ridges which produce deliberate collisions of gables. The plan also generated some very odd internal spaces.

Prior strongly believed that, 'There are Nature's own textures for

us to use . . . we may borrow from her and show the grain and figure of her works, the ordered roughness of her crystallisations in granite or sandstones, or the veining of her marbles . . . our work in each must take a character from the material. . . . As evidence of our delight in texture, we may leave our wood or stone as it comes from the chisel or saw, to show the fracture the tool has made,'[24] – sentiments which echo Ruskin. The walls of the Barn are blocks of local sandstone – he was anxious to obtain the biggest possible – with rubble and local pebbles randomly mixed in as arbitrary and 'natural' a manner as possible. Two columns on the verandah are of Dartmoor granite, as are the 5-foot-wide caps which rest on stone balls on top of the monstrous round chimneys.

The local council objected to the original thatched roof; Prior said he would cover it with 'an incombustible solution' but, in 1905, the thatch caught fire and the house was burned out. When it was rebuilt the following year, slates were put on the roof.

The Barn, Exmouth / *Edward Schroeder Prior*

Home Place / EDWARD SCHROEDER PRIOR

If E. S. Prior's ideas produced a rather awkward architectural expression at the Barn at Exmouth, a larger and much more successful design was realised in the following decade on the north Norfolk coast – the home of eccentric Edwardian houses. The 'butterfly' plan was again employed and Prior's obsession with the rightness of using a rugged combination of local building materials was, if anything, even stronger. The resulting house, Home Place (Colour Plate H) is, perhaps, the most compellingly strange and wonderful of all English houses of the period.

Home Place was built outside Holt for the Revd Percy R. Lloyd in 1903–5 at a cost of £8,000. Prior here placed the wings at sixty degrees to the larger central range, which created more useful internal spaces. The central hall – double-height – is large and of a sensible shape, if with odd wood detailing, unlike that at the Barn. Externally, Prior contrived a series of elevations which are picturesquely composed and wildly varied in texture, shape and the disposition of architectural features.

Writing in *Country Life* in 1909, 'W' (Lawrence Weaver?) wrote that, 'Mr Prior is a staunch protagonist in the demand that a building shall be racy of the soil it stands on. While his attitude does not stand

in the way of importing such small quantities of material from outside districts as are needful to give a touch of variety, it stands firmly for a main construction which shall be purely vernacular. Flint and gravel were the local materials and they postulated the use of concrete.' Indeed, Home Place shows a sensible and sophisticated early use of concrete (a material used by several Arts and Crafts architects) and inside the house the unaffected use of mass concrete for vaulting can be seen with the wooden shuttering marks left visible. In the local tradition, pantiles were used for the roof and the walls were further enlivened by tiles and a brown stone from near Sandringham. The walls were basically of concrete construction but faced in these natural materials in a contrived arbitrary pattern, affecting the randomness of geology – as did High Victorian polychromy years before – so that, as Roderick Gradidge once observed, Home Place looks 'as though it is covered with a very old Fairisle pullover that had been knitted by an imbecile child. Quaintness can be carried no further.'[25]

Country Life continued that, 'Mr Prior's work is governed by the strong conviction that a house should not be a *design* but a *building*, conditioned not only by the needs of the man who will live in it, but by the local experiences of construction. From this follows the disregard of conscious styles and manners.' Yet the overwhelming impression given by Home Place is of the personality of its architect – not the case with a house by his friend Ernest Newton.

Home Place has been a convalescent home since the 1930s and the garden front has been altered by the erection of a sun lounge between the arms of the butterfly. Near by there still stands a very odd cottage by Prior of 1907: a wooden first floor with pantiled roof stands on an absurdly solid arched masonry base, as if the ruins of an ancient building has been adapted as a house. Lutyens's Methodist Chapel at nearby Overstrand is not dissimilar in form. Perhaps there is something in the Norfolk air which accounts for all this strange architecture.

Home Place / *Edward Schroeder Prior*

Kelling Hall / EDWARD BRANTWOOD MAUFE

Prior's Home Place engendered another butterfly-plan house just a few miles away, but while Kelling Hall was clearly inspired by its Holt neighbour, the eccentricities in Prior's design have been ironed out. Kelling Hall was the first country house built by Sir Edward Maufe (1883–1974). Maufe, whose original name was Muff, built little before the Great War. Although he designed a number of suave, vaguely Spanish Colonial style houses between the wars, he was principally a church architect and is best known as the winner of the competition for Guildford Cathedral, held in 1932.

Kelling Hall was built in 1912–13 for H. W. A. Deterding, director general of the Royal Dutch Petroleum Company. Although Maufe designed the house almost a decade after Muthesius wrote *Das Englische Haus*, the vitality of the English vernacular tradition is in no way diminished. However, while Maufe employed the butterfly plan

used at Home Place and also faced the house in local flint, he did not have Prior's obsession about the use of materials. The brick used for dressings was not local but imported from Holland. Nor does Kelling Hall exhibit the contrived oddness of Home Place; the style is a more straightforward Tudor – really the Tudor of Lutyens's Overstrand Hall not far away. The fenestration is more disciplined, the eaves and the brick banding in the flint walls – the flint being knapped and not left whole, as at Home Place – keep firmly horizontal and the projecting Tudor bays rise to a straight parapet. The house is an elegant fusion of rusticity and sophistication.

Maufe did not forget the butterfly plan. Seventeen years later he used it for Yaffle Hill, a house near Broadstone in Dorset designed in a very different style to flint and brick Tudor.

Kelling Hall / *Edward Brantwood Maufe*

Stonywell Cottage / ERNEST WILLIAM GIMSON

Ernest Gimson (1864–1919) took the ideas of William Morris to one logical but extreme conclusion: he eventually gave up architecture and retreated to the country to make furniture. He represents an extreme, if typical, reaction to nineteenth-century industrial civilisation for, helped by private means, he utterly rejected the sophisticated technologies provided in his time and employed only traditional methods and crafts. On this level, Gimson exemplifies the escapism of the Arts and Crafts movement, yet much of the furniture he designed (*not* made with his own hands) is elegant and highly sophisticated.

Gimson was the son of a Leicester engineer who took him to hear Morris lecture in 1884. The young man was impressed. Morris advised him to go to the office of J. D. Sedding to learn about architecture. While articled to Sedding in 1885–7, Gimson met Ernest Barnsley (1863–1926) in the office and his brother Sidney (1865–1926) who was then working for Shaw. Gimson and the Barnsleys were involved in the furniture-making venture of Kenton and Co. in 1890–2. In 1893 they all moved to the Cotswolds and in the following year set up a workshop in Pinbury. In 1902 a new workshop was established at Daneway. Gimson designed furniture, metalwork, plasterwork, needlework and bookbinding. Most of his architecture consisted of small cottages built by the traditional methods he was so anxious to revive. An exception is the fine timber assembly hall at Bedales School, of 1910.

It is curious that, while Gimson's furniture is so very sophisticated, in his architecture he took the primitivism implicit in the Arts and Crafts movement to an absurd extreme. This can be seen in Stonywell Cottage, one of three cottages he designed in Charnwood Forest near Leicester for members of his family. Stonywell Cottage was built in 1898 for his brother Sidney. It must surely be the most reactionary building of the nineteenth century: there is none of Nash's wit in making a picturesque cottage out of the ingredients of a hovel. Nor was there intended to be, for Stonywell Cottage is a simple building built in the traditional way. It is the product not of the revival of an old style but of old skills.

Lawrence Weaver recorded the greatest compliment paid to its architect: 'an old inhabitant of the district, who had been absent

some years, greeted Stonywell on his return with the puzzled observation, "odd that I should have forgotten this old cottage".'[26] The cottage was not, in fact, completely traditional in that old cottages were erected according to customary practice and this one had to be drawn out on paper as a design, but its convincing ruggedness comes from there being a clerk of works on site who directed the workmen. This was the young architect Detmar Blow.

The 'Z' plan of the cottage, nestling against an outcrop of rock, is simple indeed, but such contrived simplicity is a product of extreme Romanticism and therefore not so very far removed in spirit from the rustic timbers of Stockbrokers' Tudor. One bedroom can only be approached by a step-ladder. The lintel over the fireplace is a $1\frac{1}{2}$-ton slab of slate discovered near by by Blow in an old quarry. The walls are 2 feet thick. Originally Stonywell Cottage was thatched but, after a fire in 1939, stone slates were put on the roof. Gimson's cottages provided little help towards giving Arts and Crafts ideas a practical application, let alone suggesting how the working classes might be housed in a more humane manner.

Stonywell Cottage / *Ernest William Gimson*

Perrycroft / CHARLES FRANCIS ANNESLEY VOYSEY

C. F. A. Voysey (1857–1941) remains rather an enigma, not easily to be categorised. He was not always true to the ideals of the Arts and Crafts movement, certainly not a 'pioneer' of the Modern movement; what is most conspicuous in both Voysey's writings and his work is his intense individualism. Although his style was imitated, there was nobody quite like him and yet, in his independence of convention, his insularity and his puritanism, he was typical of a strand in English life which flourished in the 1890s. Voysey's achievement was to give a compelling image to the ideal of domesticity, an unequivocal expression of the English love of home and belief in the virtues of the simple, outdoor life. Huge, enclosing, sweeping roofs coming almost to the ground, exaggerated chimneys, white walls pierced by small bands of leaded-light windows framed in stone, an outside water-butt, downpipes painted a vivid green and a heart-shaped cut-out on every piece of metalwork – the Voysey style is unmistakable.

Once Voysey had invented the style, he never developed it but employed it everywhere – whether in the Lake District or in Hammersmith – thus ignoring the Arts and Crafts belief in the value of local building traditions. Yet his houses are always well sited, hugging the ground they lie on. They are also beautifully and sensibly made, even though often poky and crudely planned, with distressingly low door lintels. Voysey was a puritan and he imposed his beliefs on his clients. He was fortunate in finding enough vegetarians and Fabian socialists to keep him in business.

Voysey was peculiar. His father had founded the Theistic Church after being expelled from the Church of England for heresy. Voysey deeply mistrusted Abroad and, much later, was irritated when parallels were drawn between the homely simplicity of his houses and the mechanistic white aesthetic of the International style. 'I make no claim to anything new.'[27] He regarded himself as a disciple of Pugin and his approach as Gothic. He was articled to the Gothic Revivalist J. P. Seddon, friend of the Pre-Raphaelites, and then worked for George Devey before setting up on his own. In 1911, in *The English Home*, in opposition to the revival of the English Renaissance, he wrote that 'The Gothic process is the exact opposite; outside appearances are evolved from internal fundamental conditions; staircases

and windows come where most convenient for use. All openings are proportioned to the various parts to which they apply, and the creation of a beautiful Gothic building instead of being a conception based on a temple made with hands, is based on the temple of the human soul.... Do we not all desire peace, repose, protection, warmth, cheerfulness and sincerity, open, frank expression and freedom from chafing convention in our homes? Surely, then, the Gothic principle can help us to attain all these qualities.'

Perrycroft, Colwall, Herefordshire, was built in 1893–4 for J. W. Wilson on a dramatic sloping site in the Malvern Hills. It was Voysey's first big house, and all the elements are present which he would continue to employ for the rest of his career: roughcast, buttressed walls, massive wide chimneys, horizontal bands of leaded-light windows, huge, unbroken sweeps of roof, and, overall, rather horizontal proportions. The only relic of Voysey's earlier, more Tudor designs is the outbreak of half-timber on the top of the tower which draws attention to the servants' entrance at the expense of the main porch. The house is now used by a youth organisation.

Perrycroft / *Charles Francis Annesley Voysey*

Voysey had definite views on what made a home. 'There are certain qualities that may be regarded as essential to all classes of homes, but there are certain other qualities, like grandeur, splendour, pomp, majesty and exuberance which are suitable only to comparatively few. In the category of qualities of general need, we should put repose, cheerfulness, simplicity, breadth, warmth, quietness in storm, economy of up-keep, evidence of protection, harmony with surroundings, absence of dark passages or places, evenness of temperature, making the home a frame to its inmates, for rich and poor alike will appreciate these qualities.'[28]

Muthesius recognised both Voysey's originality and his puritanism. 'In both interiors and exteriors he strives for a personal style that shall differ from the styles of the past. His means of expression are of the simplest so that there is always an air of primitivism about his houses. This lends them their charm, for deliberate originality in architecture can lead those who are less brilliant into absurdities. Yet

Voysey's total abandonment of historical tradition does rob his houses too of that firmly established conviction that we admire so much in the houses of the Norman Shaw group.'

That Voysey did not really abandon tradition can be seen in two of his finest houses which are near neighbours in the Lake District. Broadleys (above) was built overlooking Lake Windermere in 1898 for A. Currer Briggs, the son of a colliery owner. Voysey here adopted an L-shaped plan, with a narrower kitchen and servants' wing, as at Perrycroft but here handled more successfully. The most impressive feature at Broadleys is the sequence of bow-fronted bays overlooking the lake. These rise above the eaves of the huge roof to finish with a

stone cornice and a flat lead roof. The central of the three bays, almost all of stone mullions and transoms, lights a double-height hall with a gallery – an unusually grand and spacious feature for Voysey. Broadleys now serves as a club.

Moorcrag (above and Colour Plate I) was built near Broadleys in 1899, first designed in 1898 for J. W. Buckley. Here the L-plan has been abandoned for a compact long block, dominated by gables at either end and by a huge expanse of roof. The drama of the house on its sloping site results from Voysey sweeping the roof down almost to the ground at the lower end of the site, whereas other architects might have emphasised the greater height allowed by the falling ground. The gardens were originally laid out by Thomas Mawson. Moorcrag is in a good state of preservation but has been divided into two houses.

Dixcote, Streatham Park / WALTER FREDERICK CAVE

Dixcote in North Drive, Streatham Park, a suburban rather than a country house, looks like a Voysey house. Voysey, indeed, prepared the first designs for it in 1897 for R. L. Essex. This contained a few Classical details which Voysey soon abandoned. He then prepared a revised and simpler design, which Mrs Essex disliked, so he resigned as architect. The design by Walter Cave, carried out in about 1899–1901, was apparently similar to Voysey's first project.

Muthesius commented how Voysey was good at 'displaying his own personal art to good advantage'. He was certainly successful at getting his designs published, particularly in the *Studio*, and as a result, his style and his mannerisms were much imitated, both at home and abroad. One follower of the Voysey style was Walter Cave (1863–1939). Muthesius wrote that Cave, 'another member of the inner circle of the Art Workers' Guild, uses forms of expression that are close to those of Voysey. Like Voysey, he favours certain characteristics of the "new Art", such as tapering uprights and elongated mouldings, closely-set supports for banisters, rough plaster and slate roofs for exteriors. The external appearance of his houses is almost more successful than Voysey's, his surfaces have a broader sweep and the whole is more expressive.' Cave later went down the Classical path which Voysey would not follow. His block of flats in Earl's Court, Coleherne Court, is eclectic Free Renaissance in style while the stone front of Burberry's in the Haymarket of 1912 is sober and Classical – and rather good. Later, Cave was the consulting architect to Whiteley Village in Surrey, the community of almshouses established by the murdered founder of the department store.

Dixcote, Streatham Park / *Walter Frederick Cave*

Blackwell / MACKAY HUGH BAILLIE SCOTT

Considering the work of the celebrated Baillie Scott (1865–1945), Muthesius thought that, 'all the coolness and naked rationality which distinguishes the Anglo-Saxon south seems already to have vanished. We seem already to have stepped into the world of fantasy and romance of the ancient bardic poetry that was once supposed to have been the legacy of the misty figure of Ossian and gave the world a new thrill of emotion from the heart of Scotland. With Baillie Scott we are among the purely northern poets among British architects.' In fact, Baillie Scott was born in Ramsgate and trained as an architect in Bath. He was very successful in promoting himself, so that his reputation is now difficult to separate from his actual achievement.

Despite his usual eye for sound work, Muthesius was captivated by the sheer artiness of Baillie Scott and, considering him 'one of those architects who have discovered entirely personal means of expression', put him with C. R. Mackintosh, who was also more appreciated on the Continent than in London. And as with Mackintosh, Baillie Scott's work was known abroad through the charming water-colours of his interiors. The fact is that Baillie Scott's reputation rests more upon his designs than upon his executed work. During his long period on the Isle of Man, 1899 until 1901, he was tireless in sending drawings and water-colours to the *Studio*. As a result, an invitation came in 1897 to decorate a dining-room and drawing-room for the Grand Duke of Hesse in Darmstadt. In the same year Baillie Scott designed an absurd tree hut with an elaborately decorated interior for Queen Marie of Romania.

Baillie Scott's interiors were certainly remarkable. In their open planning he may have been influenced by American houses, while his careful colour schemes and designs for furniture and decoration were strongly tinged by art nouveau. However, Scott's reputation as a 'pioneer' is debatable. On the Isle of Man his work moved from the Tudor manner of Ernest George to the simple white style of Voysey. This simplicity is often misleading, as it is less evident in the buildings than in the water-colours which conjure up an almost child-like world of domesticity and fairy-tale Romance. As Scott himself wrote, 'The natural reaction from the dry mechanical routine of modern life leads to a demand for Romance in every form. In the form of fiction

it supplies a retreat, an escape for the mind to an enchanted realm where thrilling deeds may be done without danger, and beautiful habitations enjoyed without expense. In the treatment of a house a more real and permanent haven may be secured. Here at least we may say there shall be no ugliness. On crossing this threshold we pass into charmed territory.'[29]

Blackwell, at Bowness-on-Windermere, is one of Baillie Scott's best-known houses and is largely unaltered. It was built in 1898–9 for Sir Edward Holt. The gabled roughcast exterior is well massed but scarcely very interesting or subtle in detail. It is the interior which is remarkable. There is a dark panelled dining-room with a peacock frieze, a white-painted drawing-room with an art nouveau chimney-piece and, in the centre of the house, a double-height hall. This is an impressive and complex space for, in places, the ceiling is lower. Under one low area was the billiard table – so often confined to a remote 'masculine' part of the house – and above the inglenook fireplace is a little enclosed gallery, looking down on to the hall. This was not a new trick, however, but one used by Shaw in his own house and by George for W. S. Gilbert. Although abstracted to a geometrical pattern of black and white, the Tudor sources of this hall are clear. Muthesius thought Blackwell 'one of the most attractive creations that the new movement in house-building has produced'.

Blackwell / *Mackay Hugh Baillie Scott*

Hill House, Helensburgh / CHARLES RENNIE MACKINTOSH

C. R. Mackintosh (1868–1928) was, of course, a Scot and, until he left Glasgow for London in 1913, designed no houses in England. So important a figure was he, however, and so interesting are his Scottish houses, that he cannot possibly be omitted from this study of the English house, even though his work was much more admired in Vienna than in London. Voysey referred to Mackintosh and his circle of Glasgow designers as the 'Spook School' and Mackintosh's designs for furniture at the Arts and Crafts Exhibition of 1896 in London were criticised for their decadent artiness and bad construction. He was not invited back.

But for Muthesius, Mackintosh was 'one of Britain's, if not one of *the*, most outstanding younger architects of the day', a judgement which posterity has endorsed. '... the essence of the art of the Glasgow group in fact rests in an underlying emotional and poetical quality. It seeks a highly charged atmosphere or more specifically an atmosphere of a mystical, symbolic kind. One cannot imagine a greater contrast in this respect than between the London architects working in the new forms, the most sedulous of whom is Voysey, and the Scottish architects around Mackintosh. The former seek extreme plainness in which imagination is suppressed, the latter are virtually governed and led by imagination.'

Mackintosh designed no complete houses in England – his work for Bassett-Lowke in 1916 consisted of remodelling a terraced house in Northampton – but he designed five in or around Glasgow. Hill House, Helensburgh, was the largest of these (Colour Plate J). It was designed in 1902 for W. W. Blackie, the publisher, and completed in 1904. The exterior is harled – the Scottish version of roughcast – and is splendidly rugged in its massing. Mackintosh here was making a modern interpretation of a traditional manner just as his English contemporaries were, but to English (or German) eyes, unfamiliar with the shapes and detailing of old Scottish tower houses, Hill House may seem more original than it actually is.

Every detail, inside and out, was designed by the architect, including elegant and idiosyncratic electric light fittings and built-in wardrobes in characteristic style. The detailing is flat, flimsy and somewhat impractical. Mackintosh demanded absolute control over his client's lives – something most other architects would not have expected nor their clients tolerated. It is said that even the trees were clipped to look like those in his stylish, clever drawings. Even Muthesius saw the drawbacks of this approach: 'once the interior attains the status of a work of art, that is, when it is intended to embody aesthetic values, the artistic effect must be heightened to the utmost.... Whether such enhancement is appropriate to our everyday rooms is another question. Mackintosh's rooms are refined to such a degree which the lives of even the artistically educated are still a long way from matching. The delicacy and austerity of their artistic atmosphere would tolerate no admixture of the ordinariness which fills our lives. Even a book in an unsuitable binding would disturb the atmosphere simply by lying on the table.' In this, Mackintosh certainly was a pioneer of the Modern movement.

In 1972 Hill House was sold to the Royal Incorporation of Architects in Scotland and in 1982 it was transferred to the care of the National Trust for Scotland. Much careful restoration work has had to be undertaken, for Mackintosh's exterior treatment, despite its apparent ruggedness, was impractically detailed and proved vulnerable to the Scottish climate. Not for nothing were English Arts and Crafts architects suspicious of this Scottish artist.

Hill House, Helensburgh / *Charles Rennie Mackintosh*

The Leys, Elstree / GEORGE WALTON

George Walton (1867–1933) was born in Glasgow and much of his work has definite affinities with the Glasgow school of Mackintosh. He gave up training as a bank clerk to become an interior decorator and designer; it was as a designer of interiors that he was most accomplished, and much influenced by his friend Voysey. After designing one of Miss Cranston's famous tea rooms in Glasgow, Walton moved to London in 1898, and most of his limited number of jobs were carried out after that date. His White House at Shiplake of 1908 has been mutilated, so that The Leys at Elstree, Hertfordshire, remains his only complete house. Much of Walton's work was carried out for the Central Liquor Traffic Control Board after the public houses of the Carlisle district were nationalised in 1916. Muthesius admired Walton: 'Almost from the beginning his work had a delicate, mature, solid and pleasing quality. He is more down-to-earth, that is, the demands of pure utility are more to the fore in his work than in that of the Mackintosh group, but he is nonetheless a poet from whose creations a subtle spiritual atmosphere always radiates.'

The Leys was built in 1901 for the photographer J. B. B. Wellington, who was the first manager of the Kodak works at Harrow. Walton had already designed some London shops for the Kodak company. Wellington was a keen billiards player and the plan of the house is therefore arranged around a large, central triple-height billiards-hall, into which galleries on both first and second floor look down. The first-floor gallery is reached by a screen of narrow upright timbers, very much in the manner of Voysey. The influence of Voysey is strong in the principal entrance front of the house. There is a massive roof whose eaves are broken by the rise of one bow-fronted bay – just as at Voysey's Broadleys (page 132). But the combination of red brick, roughcast, and half-timber is very unlike Voysey, who would never have designed a symmetrical façade. The rear elevation is much less Voyseyesque, for there is a large Palladian window lighting the hall which is placed between two projecting wings, each of whose mannered gables are bisected by tall chimney-breasts. There is an odd,

Glasgow-school quality about the house which is also evident in the brick coach-house of 1901. An extra wing was added to The Leys in 1923 by Walton.

Since 1947 The Leys has been in community use and it is now owned by the London Borough of Brent who carefully restored the house in 1980.

The Leys, Elstree / *George Walton*

Banney Royd, Huddersfield / EDGAR WOOD

and is in a simplified Tudor style, which occasionally breaks out into art nouveau detailing, as with the entrance porch, whose attenuated mouldings are strongly reminiscent of Mackintosh. The influence of Mackintosh is also evident in the interior of the house, where there are several elaborate chimney-pieces in an art nouveau style. 'Inside', wrote Muthesius, the house 'reveals in both the arrangement of rooms – all of which are extremely comfortable and attractive in shape – and in their colour-schemes and decoration, a great creative power in which a certain poetic gift is dominant and actually lends the room their essential quality.'

Edgar Wood (1860–1935) was the most important Arts and Crafts architect in the north of England and he was described by Muthesius as 'one of the best representatives of those who go their own way and refuse to reproduce earlier styles'. Wood was born in Manchester where he trained as an architect. He designed churches, schools and a few houses. His work in the 1890s was largely in a mannered vernacular style with decided overtones of art nouveau. One of his most remarkable buildings is the eccentric Christian Science church in Manchester. In about 1904 Wood entered into an informal partnership with the Manchester architect J. H. Sellars, and together they designed buildings of a modern-looking rectangularity, often with flat concrete roofs. A house, Upmeads at Stafford, of 1908 is in this manner. Wood himself followed the teachings of Ruskin and Morris, drew from nature, worked as a craftsman and wore tweeds, knickerbockers and a cloak.

Banney Royd, in Halifax Road, Edgerton, on the outskirts of Huddersfield, was Wood's largest house and was built in 1900–1 for W. H. Armitage. The house is built of rough-hewn local sandstone

Banney Royd, Huddersfield / *Edgar Wood*

143

Tirley Garth / CHARLES EDWARD MALLOWS

C. E. Mallows (1864–1915) was one of the finest architectural draughtsmen of his generation, a master of what Goodhart-Rendel called 'dazzle' technique. His delicate drawings of houses and gardens, executed in soft pencil, conjure up all the domestic and rural charm of the English house. In view of his talent, it is sad that Mallows had comparatively few opportunities to convert his drawings into reality: Tirley Garth suggests that he was able successfully to interpret the mellow softness of his drawings into bricks, stone, wood and mortar. Mallows was born in Bedford, where he was articled to F. T. Mercer. Several architects employed his talents, notably William Flockhart, before Mallows set up in practice with F. W. Lacey in 1886. He was in partnership for a time with G. Grocock, also of Bedford.

Tirley Garth, Willington, Cheshire (Colour Plate K) is Mallows's largest and best house. Its building history was complex and Mallows prepared several designs before work went ahead. Building began in 1906 for Bryan Leesmith, a director of Brunner, Mond & Co., the chemical firm which later became ICI. Leesmith, however, ran into financial difficulties and in 1911 the incomplete house was sold to the firm which, in 1912, leased it to R. H. Prestwich, a Manchester textile manufacturer who became chairman of Burberry's. Prestwich finished the house to Mallows's design.

Tirley Garth was planned round a courtyard, or cloister garth, which has arches reminiscent of Lutyens. On one side is a double-height great hall, panelled in oak, which has an open timber roof and a huge mullioned bay window overlooking the gardens. The external style of the house is a sort of smooth Tudor, with roughcast walls and dressings of sandstone quarried on the site. The details are magnificent, but the elevations are somewhat confused and the symmetrical garden front, with its tall chimneys, decidedly strange. However, the house is designed to be seen as part of a series of vistas from the gardens. These were laid out in a series of terraces and enclosed spaces, separated by rustic stone walls, designed by the garden designer Thomas H. Mawson in collaboration with Mallows. These gardens, even more than the house, show the influence of Lutyens

but the overall character of Tirley Garth is very special and unusual.

Prestwich died in 1940 and his daughter then bought the house from ICI and gave it to Moral Re-Armament.

Tirley Garth / *Charles Edward Mallows*

Bishopsbarns, York / WALTER HENRY BRIERLEY

Walter Brierley (1862–1926) dominated Edwardian domestic architecture in Yorkshire and has been called 'The Lutyens of the North'. Brierley was based in York and was trained as an architect by his father, from whom he eventually inherited a practice begun by John Carr in the eighteenth century. Most of Brierley's work was domestic and his houses, whether in an Arts and Crafts Tudor style or neo-Georgian, are unassertive and fit well into the landscape. He also restored sympathetically the interiors of several Georgian country houses, such as Sledmere, which had been destroyed by fire caused by electric wiring systems – a hazard in Edwardian England.

Bishopsbarns was built by Brierley for himself in 1905 on a small suburban site in St George's Place, York. The house was placed close to the street, concealing a large garden behind. Bishopsbarns was built of special 2-inch handmade bricks, relieved by bands of the same handmade tiles as were used on the roof. The windows are of leaded-lights in English oak frames. Inside, there is fine Arts and Crafts plasterwork in a Classical style. The exterior, however, is in a loose Tudor style, long and low in proportion, with details which owe much to the work of Ernest Newton. Newton's influence is particularly obvious in the flattened top of the Venetian window in one of the projecting bays on the street elevation. So as to avoid

strict symmetry, the balancing bay is almost devoid of fenestration.

Brierley's garden was laid out with the advice of Gertrude Jekyll.

Bishopsbarns, York / *Walter Henry Brierley*

Thistlegate, Charmouth / FRANCIS WILLIAM TROUP

That F. W. Troup (1859–1941) is not as well known today as he ought to be is typical of the Webb–Lethaby strain within the Arts and Crafts movement. He was a good, responsible and careful architect concerned with sound workmanship and satisfying clients, not with self-advertisement. Troup was a Scot, born in Aberdeenshire. Having been articled to Campbell Douglas and James Sellars in Glasgow, he then worked for J. J. Stevenson in London. Troup was a disciple of Lethaby and a friend of Robert Weir Schultz, with whom he shared an office. But whereas Schultz's practice remained small in scale and traditional in manner, Troup attempted to come to terms with modern conditions and, in 1913, designed Blackfriars House in New Bridge Street in the City of London, a white faience-covered steel-framed office building of commendably rational and sensible expression. Troup was also the designer of the new hall of the Art Workers' Guild, built at the back of a genuine Queen Anne house in Queen Square in 1914. Busts of the heroes of the Arts and Crafts movement, like Morris, Crane and Lethaby, sit in Classical niches of typically Arts and Crafts incorrectness.

Thistlegate, now called the Dower House, on Axminster Road near Charmouth, Dorset, was built in 1911 for Mrs Capper Pass, for whom he had already designed a village hall in Wootton Fitzpaine. Mrs Capper Pass's house is carefully nondescript, sensibly planned, well detailed but in no way assertive or self-conscious. Built of thin red bricks, the house is traditional and domestic in character, but cannot be labelled 'Tudor' or 'Old English'. The entrance front is symmetrical yet not symmetrical, with its entrance off-centre under a segmental brick arch. The garden front has quiet idiosyncrasies: a polygonal projecting bay with no facet parallel with the main wall plane, and a sort of free-standing balcony on simple brick columns. The garden itself is formal in the Scottish manner, similar to the seventeenth-century gardens revived by Schultz and by Lorimer.

Like many of the best Arts and Crafts buildings, this house by Troup only reveals its qualities by careful inspection with an eye for reticent but sensible detail. Its apparent ordinariness is the product of careful thought and, characteristically, it has lasted well.

Thistlegate, Charmouth / *Francis William Troup*

The Fives Court, Pinner / ARNOLD DUNBAR SMITH and CECIL CLAUDE BREWER

Smith and Brewer were admired by Muthesius as 'their works show extreme tastefulness together with a primitive simplicity that borders upon the vernacular'. Cecil Brewer (1871–1918) was R. W. Schultz's assistant when in 1895 he and Smith (1866–1933) won the competition for the Passmore Edwards Settlement in Tavistock Place, which was assessed by Norman Shaw. This building, in a free style, with an upper storey of white plaster above red brick, was very influential, particularly on some of the housing of the London County Council. Most of Smith and Brewer's early work was domestic, until the partnership won the competition for the National Museum of Wales in Cardiff in 1909 with a design in a large-scale American Beaux Arts manner. Later they designed the new building in the Tottenham Court Road for Heal's department store.

Ambrose Heal junior had already commissioned Smith and Brewer to design The Fives Court at Pinner. Heal, a furniture designer who created the progressive reputation of his family's firm in the early twentieth century, was sympathetic to the Arts and Crafts movement. The Fives Court, a small house, was built in 1900 and was illustrated in *Das Englische Haus*. In 1908 the house was carefully extended. Built of white roughcast brick, the influence of Voysey is particularly evident in the shape of the wide stocky chimneys. It is a house of great simplicity and charm. Its name came from the fact that a game

of fives could be played against the garden wall between two symmetrical sloping extensions – one for coal, the other for bicycles. The house is sometimes attributed to Brewer alone.

The Fives Court, Pinner / *Arnold Dunbar Smith* and *Cecil Claude Brewer*

Littleshaw, Woldingham / LEONARD ALOYSIUS STOKES

Leonard Stokes (1858–1925) was one of the most resourceful and impressive of Edwardian architects and he had a large and distinguished practice. Most of his practice consisted of designing church, school and monastery buildings for the Roman Catholic Church but he was also responsible for a series of telephone exchanges. He also designed houses, including one large country house, Minterne Magna, of 1903–7, for Lord Digby (see also page 202). Stokes developed a characteristic style which was a mannered and horizontally proportioned development of Tudor and late Gothic and often embellished with good architectural sculpture. Stokes had worked in the offices of Street, Collcutt and Bodley before setting up on his own in 1883.

Muthesius noticed his houses and considered that 'Leonard Stokes is certainly one of the most interesting and talented architects in England today.' He thought that Stokes's buildings 'are always arresting because of the reposefulness of their broad surfaces and the spacious, robust placing of their masses. This is well illustrated in his own house at Woldingham, Surrey. In his non-classicising houses at least, he also treats the few details entirely as he pleases, in a free and witty manner that is attractive in its mixture of forcefulness and charm. His ground plans are no less lucid and definite than his architecture; the same bold steely thread runs through them.'

In fact, although he did design it for his own use, Littleshaw, the house Muthesius noticed in Woldingham, is not wholly typical of Stokes. It was built in 1902–4 and is faced in roughcast rather than

being built straightforwardly of brick, like so many of the architect's best buildings. It is an unpretentious, practical essay in a simple vernacular style but it is strongly reminiscent in its shape and details of The Fives Court at Pinner (page 150), designed by Smith and Brewer a few years before. A particularly happy feature is the long run of glazed verandah which overlooks the sloping, terraced garden.

Littleshaw, Woldingham / *Leonard Aloysius Stokes*

Cavenham Park Lodges / ANDREW NOBLE PRENTICE

A. N. Prentice (1866–1941) is by no means a well-known Edwardian country-house architect, yet Muthesius devoted a considerable amount of space to illustrating his work. Prentice was a Scot who trained as an architect in Glasgow before coming to London and working for Collcutt. He made his name by the publication of his book on *Renaissance Architecture and Ornament in Spain* in 1893. He built up a successful country-house practice – not with designs in a Spanish style, which only became fashionable in England after the Great War – and designed Witham Hall, Lincolnshire, Chapelwood Manor, Sussex and Notgrove Manor, Gloucestershire, as well as many houses in Broadway, Worcestershire. He also designed the interiors of steamships on the Australia and South America runs.

It is odd to find Muthesius paying so much attention to Prentice as he did not sympathise with his Classical tastes. 'An artist who has moved steadily closer to this latest classicising trend is A. N. Prentice, who first made his name with his fine drawings of Spain. One must regret this change of heart all the more since in his first projects Prentice raised great hopes of a more independent attitude and at the beginning was in every way one of the more promising talents. His taut, forceful style of drawing, of which he is an undisputed master, has had a great influence on the youngest generation. His groundplans are always extremely lucid and precise.'

The house by Prentice which Muthesius illustrated was Cavenham Hall, otherwise Cavenham Park, Suffolk. It was originally built in 1898–9 for H. E. M. Davies, a South African gold tycoon, but shortly afterwards the shooting estate was bought by Adolph B. H. Goldschmidt, JP, the grandfather of the chairman of Cavenham Foods, Ltd. Cavenham Park was a large house of dark-red narrow brick with grey stone facings built in an eclectic Georgian manner. The design was of no particular distinction but as well as reproducing photographs of both house and stables, Muthesius illustrated the ground plan of the house to make a point about planning and the Englishman's desire for privacy.

'The greatest care is also taken to see that those seated in a room are disturbed as little as possible by the opening of a door. The most important point is that people should not be disturbed and this is reflected mainly in the direction in which the door opens. The rule known to every Englishman says that the door must open towards the main sitting area in the room, which usually means towards the fireplace; in a study it opens towards the desk, in a bedroom towards the bed.' On the plan of Cavenham Hall, every door was placed towards the corner of a room, opening inwards and hinged on the side furthest from the corner.

Cavenham Hall (see page 35) was unfortunately demolished in 1949 but the lodges survive, combining half-timber with Classical details.

Cavenham Park Lodges / *Andrew Noble Prentice*

Greystanes, Mill Hill / GILES and ADRIAN GILBERT SCOTT

In the Edwardian years, enjoying the flowering of the revival of English domestic architecture and with the wealthy taking an interest in the subject, there were few architects who did not try their hand at designing a house. With the generally high standards of design and construction prevailing and with many good models available – published in the many books and journals – the results were seldom unsuccessful. The single Edwardian house designed by the architect of Liverpool Cathedral and Battersea Power Station and built in a plush outer London suburb is as unusual as it is unexpected.

Sir Giles Gilbert Scott (1880–1960) won the competition for the Anglican Cathedral in Liverpool in 1903 at the age of twenty-two. Apart from completing this last great Gothic Revival masterpiece, most of Scott's career was devoted to designing churches and public buildings. He designed very few houses: one was his own, Chester House, Clarendon Place, Bayswater, of 1924–5, a much admired essay in a Georgian manner. From the early years of his practice, Scott's younger brother Adrian (1882–1963) acted as assistant until he had established his own name as a designer of Roman Catholic churches. In the years before 1914, Giles Scott had comparatively little work but he still often passed on small jobs to his younger brother to carry out; these included the cottages in Melbourne Road, Bushey, built in 1906–7 for Sir Hubert von Herkomer.

Greystanes, a house in Marsh Lane, Mill Hill, was built in 1907 for A. E. Colebrook. Scott first corresponded with this client in 1906 but the actual construction was supervised by his brother and the drawings were labelled 'G. & A. Gilbert Scott'. The style of the house is strange: a mixture of gabled vernacular with segmental Classical pediments reminiscent of the contemporary eclectic work of Beresford Pite. The materials of which the house is built are also unusual: the

wooden-framed leaded-light windows are flanked by bands of thin grey bricks proud of the wall plane, while the walls themselves are plastered white. Giles Scott wrote to Colebrook that the house was to be of 'plastered brickwork (not pebbledash, roughcast, to which I share your objection)'. The prominent tall chimneys also attract attention to themselves by bands of brick. The front door is protected by a deliberately massive canopy, supported on corbels, which acts as a balcony. The drawing-room cum billiard-room has not one but two chimney-pieces.

Greystanes, Mill Hill / *Giles* and *Adrian Gilbert Scott*

Redcourt / ERNEST NEWTON

By 1900, domestic architects were no longer afraid to look to the Classical tradition for inspiration. The moral objection of Gothic Revivalists to Renaissance formality had been slowly overcome by architects who realised that the English Georgian manner was not only commonplace but a natural way of building in many parts of the country. A pioneer in the use of Classicism in house design was Norman Shaw, as we have seen, but also very influential in this was his pupil Ernest Newton (1856–1922).

Redcourt, Haslemere, Surrey, was built in 1894–5 for Louis Wigram. It is the quintessential Newton house. By 1894 he had formed his style (see also page 88): a sort of vernacular Georgian with segment-headed windows which derives from Shaw but which also has Lethaby's manner of flattening gables and mouldings. The style is by no means correct or academic Georgian, for the style was always loosely adapted to convenient plans. As Newton himself wrote, 'the planning is without doubt the most important thing in the designing of a house. "To be happy at home is the ultimate result of all ambition." No one can be quite happy in an ill-planned house any more than in ill-fitting clothes, and although the "cut" and "style" are much, they count for nothing in a garment which pinches and annoys the wearer in a hundred ways.... Although house building is very much a practical art, the practical requirements may be met gracefully and pleasantly; there is scope for dignity, humour and even romance.... A natural architecture is a rational healthy builder's art expressing itself soberly through the medium of masonry and carpentry.'[30]

At Redcourt, the two principal elevations – east and south – are as formal as any Arts and Crafts architect could tolerate. Axial symmetry is broken by irregular fenestration, reflecting internal arrangements, and on the garden front the splendid lead-covered curved bay is placed decidedly off-centre. The gardens themselves were laid out by Thomas H. Mawson (1861–1933), author of *The Art and Craft of Garden Making* (1900, etc.), the apologist for the formal garden and a very successful garden designer and town planner.

Redcourt / *Ernest Newton*

Kennet Orley / MERVYN EDMUND MACARTNEY

Sir Mervyn Macartney (1853–1932) does not deserve his comparative obscurity today for he was, in many respects, a most representative Edwardian architect. His writings and his architecture manifest that admiration for the Classicism of Sir Christopher Wren which was widely held. Like Sir Reginald Blomfield, Macartney was a well-connected Oxford graduate, an author and an authority on English architectural history who specialised in producing gentlemanly houses in a quiet, undemonstrative manner for comfortable Edwardians. Also like Blomfield, he had connections with the Arts and Crafts world. He was a co-founder of the Art Workers' Guild, he collaborated with Blomfield, Lethaby and Gimson in the short-lived firm of Kenton & Co. which produced handmade furniture. Macartney was an Ulsterman. From Oxford he went to Shaw's office as a pupil. Later he became editor of the *Architectural Review* and he was the author of *English Houses and Gardens of the 16th and 17th Centuries* (1908), *Recent English Domestic Architecture* (1909) and, with John Belcher, the two large and influential volumes on *Later Renaissance Architecture in England* (1901). A great admirer of Wren, Macartney was appointed surveyor to St Paul's Cathedral in 1906.

Macartney built Kennet Orley, near Woolhampton, Berkshire, for himself in about 1907–9. It is curious, perhaps, that the scholarly surveyor to St Paul's did not produce a more correct essay in the late seventeenth-century manner of Wren. Kennet Orley is in a style which combines Classicism with the practical features of the vernacular tradition. Of red brick, with quoins at the corners, the entrance front is symmetrical, but on the garden elevation there is less of Wren and more of Ernest Newton, for there are odd asymmetries in the placing of the three double-height bay windows and maddening ones with the placing of the chimneys. Even Macartney retained his Arts and Crafts conscience in the Edwardian decade, but the house does have the virtue of quiet dignity and unpretentiousness.

Kennet Orley / *Mervyn Edmund Macartney*

Wittington / REGINALD THEODORE BLOMFIELD

Sir Reginald Blomfield (1856–1942) should not only be remembered as the Blimpish (if pertinent) critic of modern architecture in his book *Modernismus* of 1934, for he was a scholar and an architect whose career perfectly exemplifies the conflicts within the Arts and Crafts movement. Muthesius mentioned Blomfield as one of 'certain other outstanding domestic architects working in London' who was 'entirely on the side of classicising historicism'. Indeed, Blomfield became more and more identified with tendencies which Muthesius and many Arts and Crafts architects condemned and he was an important influence on the development of Edwardian Baroque architecture. This was principally through his books, which provided both architects and clients with seventeenth- and eighteenth-century precedents to emulate. These were *A History of Renaissance Architecture in England* (1897) and *A Shorter History of Renaissance Architecture in England* (1900) as well as books on French Renaissance architecture. Blomfield also had an influence on garden design and he published *The Formal Garden in England* in 1892.

Blomfield was articled to his uncle, Sir Arthur Blomfield, but his early work was most influenced by Norman Shaw, whose biography he eventually wrote. Although an early member of the Art Workers' Guild and involved in Kenton and Co., Blomfield's interests moved away from those of his Arts and Crafts friends as he became an apologist for the Grand Manner. In the 1920s Blomfield and Lethaby came together again in the campaign to save Waterloo Bridge but Blomfield

soon lost any credibility as a conservative when he prepared designs for the rebuilding of Carlton House Terrace. Educated at Haileybury and Oxford, Blomfield developed a lucrative country-house practice with clients with whom he was at ease socially. Blomfield was a sometimes tiresome and cantankerous controversialist whose buildings do not quite live up to the promise of his writings and drawings.

Wittington, near Medmenham in the Thames Valley, is a typical Blomfield house: a grand essay in the William and Mary manner, with pilasters, swags and quoins, which somehow does not manage to have the quiet dignity he admired in the old houses he wrote about.

Wittington is slightly vulgar. It was built for Hudson Kearley, MP for Devonport and founder of the firm Kearley and Tonge, which became International Stores. He became Viscount Devonport in 1917. The history of Wittington is slightly obscure as Blomfield prepared one design for Kearley in 1897 and a larger, grander design in 1908. It is not clear whether the earlier design was built and then altered. Wittington is well built in brick and with stone dressings. That Blomfield had not lost contact with his Arts and Crafts roots is shown by the flint and stone chequerboard patterning on the chimney-breasts on the rather striking and un-Wren-like side elevation.

Eyford Court / E. GUY DAWBER

Sir Guy Dawber (1861–1938) was one of the most accomplished and successful of Edwardian country-house builders. He was renowned for his sympathy for local building traditions and materials, which is particularly evident in his work in the Cotswolds. This knowledge was acquired owing to fortuitous circumstances. Born in King's Lynn, Dawber first worked for Sir Thomas Deane in Dublin until the Land League disturbances stopped building work in Ireland. He then joined the office of Ernest George and Peto in London. In 1887 his eyesight became impaired and he was obliged to leave London, but George arranged for him to act as clerk of works on the building of Batsford Park, the large Elizabethan-style house designed for A. B. Mitford, later Lord Redesdale. Dawber then spent four years studying the local Cotswold vernacular, which few at that date had done.

Dawber first set up his own practice in Bourton-on-the-Water and Lord Redesdale's connections led to many local commissions for building or altering houses. He later designed Swinbrook House for the second Lord Redesdale and both Batsford and Swinbrook loom large in the over-documented lives of the Mitford sisters. Dawber eventually set up an office in London but the bulk of his work was in the West Country. His early designs were the fruits of his studies of vernacular architecture, which were published as *Old Cottages and Farmhouses in Kent and Sussex* in 1900 and *Old Cottages and Farmhouses, and Other Stone Buildings in the Cotswold District* (1905). After about 1905 Dawber followed Lutyens in moving to a formal 'Wrenaissance' manner, but whatever style he used, Dawber's quiet and appropriate houses were always in the local manner of building and were superbly constructed and detailed.

Eyford Court, Upper Slaughter, Gloucestershire (Colour Plate L),

was built in 1910. The design was sufficiently formal to have a full Ionic order on the garden front, although there are other details which no Georgian builder would have used. As originally built on the site of an earlier house, two wings came forward to form an entrance court but these, together with a service wing, were taken down in 1962 when the house was made more compact by G. Forsyth Lawson. Dawber's stonework and details were carefully reused. Dawber's house had replaced one of 1870 – so firmly had taste turned against the mid Victorians by Edward VII's reign. That, in turn, had replaced a seventeenth-century house. Dawber laid out the gardens.

Eyford Court / *E. Guy Dawber*

Barnett Hill / ARNOLD BIDLAKE MITCHELL

Arnold Mitchell (1863–1944) was not one of the élite Arts and Crafts architects but he produced very good work and deserves to be better known today. He had a large and successful practice. Many of his houses are in the Harrow area; his own, The Orchard, in London Road, Harrow, of 1900, is slate-hung and gabled, but many of his buildings are in a Free Renaissance manner. Mitchell was a pupil in Ernest George's office – again, the best architectural stable – and set up in practice in 1886. Somehow, he became known abroad. He designed buildings in Ostend for King Leopold of the Belgians, and also worked in Germany, Austria and Argentina where he was re-

sponsible for three railway termini including the Plaza Constitucion station in Buenos Aires. One of Mitchell's finest buildings is University College School in Frognal, Hampstead, of 1905–6, a Renaissance-style design executed in particularly fine brick. Mitchell also invented the toy, Lott's Bricks.

In 1912 the *Builder* reported that Mitchell believed 'the architect's function is to obtain for the client what he wants and see that he gets it' – not a commonly held view among architects – and Muthesius praised his 'laying great stress on the economic aspect. His ground plans are always practical and interesting, especially in their skilful arrangement and balanced proportions. His vocabulary of forms is less personal and usually tends towards Neo-Classicism.'

Barnett Hill, near Wonersh, in Surrey, is a good example of a 'Wrenaissance' house built on a considerable scale. It was erected in 1905–6 for Frank Cook of Thomas Cook and Sons, the highly successful travel agents. Like the exactly contemporary University College School, Barnett Hill is built of fine orange-red and purplish bricks, with dressings of brown stone. The quality of detail throughout is particularly high. Mitchell designed a main block, with two symmetrical façades, and a long servants' wing. In the H-plan of the main part of the house, Mitchell was determined to secure privacy for the family: he had criticised Lutyens's double-height hall at Little Thakeham for its lack of privacy and at Barnett Hill there is a single-height hall, separated from the longitudinal entrance corridor by doors. The corridor itself is nicely terminated by apsidal ends. Internally, the plasterwork, probably by George Bankart, is particularly exuberant and rich; the oval lantern above the staircase was inspired by that in the seventeenth-century Ashburnham House in Westminster.

Barnett Hill is now used as a conference centre by the British Red Cross Society.

Barnett Hill / *Arnold Bidlake Mitchell*

The Salutation / EDWIN LANDSEER LUTYENS

Of all the architects who followed Shaw in moving towards the Classical tradition, Lutyens was undoubtedly the most brilliant (see also pages 94–101). While others produced over-elaborate Edwardian Baroque or followed the fashion for Beaux-Arts Classicism, Lutyens so well understood the Classical tradition that he was able to develop it and produce such truly inventive buildings as Viceroy's House, New Delhi – an English country house, indeed, on an Imperial scale. Lutyens soon saw the expressive possibilities of what he called the 'high game' of Classicism. In a famous letter of 1903 written to his friend Herbert Baker in South Africa, he wrote how 'In architecture Palladio is the game!! It is so big – few appreciate it now, and it requires training to value and realise it. The way Wren handled it was marvellous. Shaw has the gift. To the average man it is dry bones, but under the hand of a Wren it glows and the stiff materials become as plastic clay.'[31]

Lutyens was delighted by the Mannerist tricks he could play with the orders, and strange Classical details appear in his work almost from the beginning. But his only full-blooded essay in the 'high game' was Heathcote, Ilkley, of 1906. Most of his later houses were in the Wren manner, although idiosyncrasies still creep into the gentlemanly formality of that fashionable style. Voysey considered that Lutyens was the most able of the younger generation of Arts and Crafts architects and he maintained that it was Lutyens's conversion to Classicism which destroyed the development of the traditional English vernacular into something rational and modern, something which he and architects like Lethaby sought. But Lutyens did not betray his origins, for his sense of form and sure touch with materials remained unchanged. Even after the Great War Lutyens could produce a charming vernacular cottage as well as huge banks and war memorials.

The Salutation (Colour Plate M), tucked away behind a wall in Sandwich, Kent, is Lutyens's loveliest and most brilliant essay in the Wren manner. It was built in 1911 for two bachelor brothers, Gaspard and Henry Farrer. At first it seems staid and conventional, but it is not. Although the three main elevations are symmetrical, there are idiosyncrasies in the rhythm of the windows. The geometrical formality of the design is emphasised by the thick glazing bars. All is precise and supremely elegant: Lutyens indeed made what seems in the hands of other architects the 'dry bones' of neo-Georgian or, more correctly here, 'Wrenaissance', into something which glows because of his complete mastery of the style. Inside, the house is far from conventional, as there is an ingenious plan around an impressive staircase and the entrance hall has twisted black marble columns.

The formal axiality of the house extends into the garden, which is divided up into a series of separate gardens by tall hedges. But the Romantic side of Lutyens is still evident, particularly in the extraordinary gate lodge, placed in a narrow street. Two cottages flank the gates, which are surmounted by a deep plaster cornice which is contained by strange Georgian-style dormer windows. As ever, Classical and vernacular are subtly integrated.

The Salutation / *Edwin Landseer Lutyens*

PART THREE / The Town House

No. 8 Palace Gate, Kensington / JOHN JAMES STEVENSON

From the beginning of the movement to revitalise English domestic architecture, most architects realised that a different style was required in the town from that used in the country. The country style was 'Old English' but in London, Shaw and his contemporaries evolved the eclectic 'Queen Anne' style, of sash windows, Dutch gables and Classical detail in rubbed brick. A leading 'Queen Anne' architect was J. J. Stevenson (1831–1908). He was not an innovator like Shaw but he was one of the most vocal apologists for the new styles of domestic architecture. In 1880 Stevenson published *House Architecture* in two volumes.

Stevenson was a Scot who took up architecture having decided not to be a Presbyterian minister. He was a pupil of David Bryce in Edinburgh and then worked for Sir Gilbert Scott in London. First practising in Scotland, he moved to London in 1870 and was in partnership with E. R. Robson from 1871 to 1876, principally engaged in designing a number of the new Board Schools in the 'Queen Anne' style. Stevenson was responsible for several town houses in 'Pont Street Dutch' (to use Osbert Lancaster's term) in Pont Street and Cadogan Square and also for Kensington Court. Stevenson took 'Queen Anne' to the country at Munstead House of 1878 and Ken

Hill, Norfolk, of 1879–81. He also designed a number of houses for dons in both Oxford and Cambridge. Oddly, Stevenson was not mentioned by Muthesius in *Das Englische Haus*.

Stevenson's most influential London house was his own. Called Red House, it was built in Bayswater in 1871–3. The house was not, in fact, red but made largely of London stocks with red bricks used for dressings and the Classical details. These included a niche in the centre of the façade, designed for a blue and white Nankin vase which was considered suitably Artistic. Although not a particularly original design, Red House was imitated as a suitable treatment for a London terraced house, with 'Queen Anne' detail, gabled dormers and projecting bay windows to break up what was felt to be the monotony of the standard London house. Red House was badly damaged by a bomb and later demolished, but No. 8 Palace Gate, Kensington, is very similar to it in style, although entirely of red brick. It was built in 1873–5 for Henry Francis Makins. The house has particularly fine detail in rubbed red brick – the special finely jointed brick used for cornices, swags and other details of the 'Queen Anne' style – and good ironwork.

No. 8 Palace Gate, Kensington / *John James Stevenson*

173

No. 6 Ellerdale Road, Hampstead / RICHARD NORMAN SHAW

The house which Norman Shaw (1831–1912) built for himself on the slopes of Hampstead shows a clever development of the 'Queen Anne' style which Shaw had invented (see also page 206). No. 6 Ellerdale Road was built in 1875–6 and extended in 1885–6. Rather typically with an artist's own house, Shaw's house has an eccentric plan which is ambiguously expressed on the principal street elevation. Shaw played with levels and the positions of windows. The façade, on a sloping site, is basically symmetrical but the two projecting bays are different. That on the right sports three tiers of Shaw's favourite 'Ipswich oriel', a window type found on the seventeenth-century Sparrowe's House in Ipswich that Shaw used on many 'Queen Anne' designs, such as the Swan House in Cheyne Walk. Other windows are scattered about the façade in an artfully random way. The most notable aspect of the interior was the dining-room, where, over a large inglenook fireplace, Shaw had his 'den' or studio, accessible by a private stair and looking down both into the dining-room and onto the garden.

No. 6 Ellerdale Road is now a convent.

174

No. 6 Ellerdale Road, Hampstead / *Richard Norman Shaw*

Harrington and Collingham Gardens, Kensington / ERNEST GEORGE and HAROLD PETO

The terraced houses designed by Ernest George (1839–1922) and Peto in Harrington and Collingham Gardens represent an extreme manifestation of Victorian architectural individualism. Although all the houses are part of an organised development, each house is made to look as different as possible from its neighbour. This reaction against Georgian formality and the dull repetitiveness of Victorian stuccoed Kensington and Bayswater was already evident on the Cadogan Estate in Chelsea, but George made his town houses even more Picturesque, and varied red brick with stone and terracotta. His façades were inspired by the early Renaissance merchants' houses of Holland and Germany and he put his holiday sketchbooks, filled with details of Amsterdam, Ghent, Bruges and Lübeck to good use. George's houses are distinguished by their fine detailing and his leaded-light windows are always of very high quality.

This development was the work of the builders Peto Brothers – brothers, indeed, of George's partner from 1875 until 1892, Harold Ainsworth Peto. Four houses were built first on the north side of Harrington Gardens (Nos. 20–6 even), begun in 1880. In 1881 the south side of the street (Nos. 35–45) was planned to be developed with large houses for individual clients. The most famous of these was W. S. Gilbert, who had No. 39 (page 176 and Colour Plate N) built in 1882–3 out of the profits of the Gilbert and Sullivan operetta *Patience*. Gilbert's house has a particularly flamboyant façade, suiting the man; and is surmounted by a nineteen-stage stepped gable. Inside, the seventeenth-century style was consistently maintained, with an oak-panelled hall, alabaster chimney-pieces and strapwork ceilings.

Collingham Gardens (page 177) was built by Peto Brothers as a speculation in 1883–8. Two terraces of houses were arranged along two sides of a communal garden but, again, the architects succeeded in giving the different houses immensely varied and picturesque façades, both towards the street and towards the garden. Ironically,

the plan of the houses, as with 'Queen Anne' terraced houses in Chelsea, is essentially that of the standard Georgian terraced house.

Muthesius praised Ernest George's success in 'never copying slavishly what he had seen, and the residential quarters that he built are among the finest examples of domestic architecture to be seen in London'. Not everybody agreed. A critic in the *Builder*, commenting on George's highly picturesque drawing of the terrace in Harrington Gardens which was being exhibited at the Royal Academy, wrote scathingly that 'old streets do occasionally assume this kind of appearance of pieces of buildings in ever so many different manners all muddled together ... but to go about to make this kind of thing deliberately is child's play.'[32]

Collingham Gardens, Kensington / *Ernest George* and *Harold Peto* 177

River House, Chelsea Embankment / GEORGE FREDERICK BODLEY and THOMAS GARNER

George Frederick Bodley (1827–1907), who had already designed some advanced 'Queen Anne' houses in the 1860s, entered into partnership with Thomas Garner (1839–1906) in 1869. Bodley and Garner completed one more house before concentrating on church architecture, although, much later, in 1884, Garner alone designed Hewell Grange, a large neo-Elizabethan country house for Lord Windsor. This house was River House, No. 3 Chelsea Embankment, begun in 1876 for the Hon. J. C. Dundas and completed in 1879. With its white cupola surmounting the roof and with the use of London stock bricks with red dressings, River House looks rather different from the nearby red-brick houses built by Norman Shaw on the Metropolitan Board of Works' new Embankment and is more similar in character to the contemporary Board schools designed by E. R. Robson and J. J. Stevenson. However, F. M. Simpson, a former pupil of Bodley and Garner, observed in 1908 that the 'design is based on Kew Palace, the front of which they had measured purposely, and the curious can trace the resemblance between the two buildings, although one is very far from being a copy of the other'.[33]

River House, Chelsea Embankment / *George Frederick Bodley* and *Thomas Garner*

All Saints' Vicarage, Plymouth / JOHN DANDO SEDDING

J. D. Sedding (1838–91) was principally a church architect but Muthesius thought that 'the houses that he did build are as brilliant as his churches'. However, it is arguable that his churches are not that brilliant and that their most notable features were the work of Sedding's assistant and successor, Henry Wilson, who had to finish several of them after his death. Sedding's buildings often do not live up to the promise of his drawings and his considerable reputation may have resulted from his association with the Arts and Crafts movement as well as from the romantic tragedy of his comparatively early death.

Sedding was certainly an important influence within the world of the Arts and Crafts, and good architects who were not in the offices of Shaw or George were in his: these included Ernest Barnsley, Gimson, Alfred Powell and Henry Wilson. He was friendly with younger architects and fulfilled the ideas of Morris and Ruskin by commissioning artists and craftsmen to embellish his buildings. It was Ruskin who, as Lethaby recorded, 'told him that "an architect should always have a chisel or pencil in hand"'. Sedding had been a pupil of G. E. Street, but in his desire to get away from historical styles and to revitalise the crafts in architecture, Sedding moved from Gothic to an often uncertain eclecticism.

Of Sedding's domestic buildings, perhaps the best are the Lodge at Fleet (a big house by Shaw), which was illustrated and admired by Muthesius, and the vicarage in Harwell Street, Plymouth. All Saints' Church itself is hard and dull Gothic and not by Sedding; the vicarage, of 1887, which occupies an adjacent corner site, is an eclectic and picturesque composition which develops the style of Norman Shaw. A fine bird's-eye pen drawing of the vicarage, published in the *Architectural Review* in 1897, shows that Sedding intended the gable and wing to be tile-hung; as executed, these areas are roughcast. This drawing also suggests a source of inspiration for the design, for the feature of the gable above a small pitched roof straddling two projecting bays is strongly reminiscent of American Shingle-style architecture. Sedding's interest in building materials is shown in the care-

ful random design of the courses of stone of which the ground floor is built. Although now neglected, the charm of this house, with its tall chimneys and leaded-light windows, is still evident.

All Saints' Vicarage, Plymouth / *John Dando Sedding*

Sunnydene, Sydenham / JOHN FRANCIS BENTLEY

J. F. Bentley (1839–1902) was another church architect who also designed houses which deserve notice in any survey of late-Victorian domestic architecture. Few, in fact, were private houses, but as well as a number of Roman Catholic churches, Bentley designed several monastic buildings in a delightful and sophisticated Tudor style in brick, beautifully detailed and very unmonastic in character. His skill as a decorator and interior designer is shown in the interiors at Carlton Towers, Yorkshire, which he designed following the death of E. W. Pugin, the architect of the house. Bentley's principal creation was Westminster Cathedral, a building greatly admired by Philip Webb for its constructional integrity and its intelligent development of historical precedents – and the compliment was returned, for Bentley wanted Webb to carry on the building after his death. 'Beyond all doubt the finest church that has been built for centuries. Superb in scale and character, and full of the most devouring interest,' was Norman Shaw's verdict on it.

Sunnydene, a suburban house in Sydenham, is an early work by Bentley and is much more Gothic in style than his later work, but it is full of mannerism and sophistication which distinguish it from the average South London mid-Victorian villa. This house, now No. 108 Westwood Hill, was built in 1868–70 on the top of Sydenham Hill facing the end of the Crystal Palace. It was built for W. R. Sutton, the millionaire carrier entrepreneur. The design has several happy peculiarities, such as the two-storey projecting bay with a gable supported on a single buttress and the herringbone brick pattern in the gable and under the eaves. C. L. Eastlake in his *History of the Gothic Revival* (1872) noticed this house and described it as 'Tudor and Jacobean, a well appointed residence, designed with great care, the garden, etc., being laid out in a style corresponding with the date of the house'. There is no trace now, unfortunately, of the original garden and Sunnydene itself is cut up into flats. The house next door, also by Bentley, is even more mutilated.

Sunnydene, Sydenham / *John Francis Bentley*

Lime Tree Walk, Sevenoaks / THOMAS GRAHAM JACKSON

Until the 1890s, 'Queen Anne' was a middle-class style, but there is one earlier occasion when this progressive style was used for working-class housing. This was for a street in Sevenoaks where the philanthropic client was the father of the architect, who was Sir Thomas Graham Jackson (1835–1924).

T. G. Jackson was articled to Sir Gilbert Scott. Like many of his contemporaries, he reacted against the orthodoxy of Gothic but in Jackson's case the move to a freer eclectic style was in the sphere of university building. In 1876 he won the competition for new Examination Schools in Oxford with an Elizabethan design. This success was followed by a large number of Oxford commissions for collegiate buildings which he designed in his characteristic 'Anglo-Jackson' style, a Free Renaissance Jacobean. Lime Tree Walk in Sevenoaks is a less typical but much more attractive work by Jackson.

Jackson's father, Hugh Jackson, a solicitor, had moved to Sevenoaks. He was interested in the problem of building cheap housing for working men and was distressed by the way the poor were forced out of the town when old cottages were replaced by middle-class villas. 'It was to remedy this state of things,' Jackson later wrote, 'and to do something to counteract the mischievous sorting out of classes into distinct districts for rich and poor, which always has the effect of creating as it were two hostile camps, that we now set ourselves to work. When at last we heard of a field right in the middle of town on which no restrictions would be put we bought it for £4,500 and built, at first, twenty-four cottages. The result was that a great number of families were eventually well and cheaply housed on a beautiful site commanding lovely views equal to any enjoyed by their well-to-do neighbours, and that the workmen were close by their work instead of having to walk miles from home and back again twice a day.'[34]

The cottages were built in 1878–9 in a simple 'Queen Anne' manner, stepping sensibly down a gentle slope. They are very similar

in style to the 'cottage estates' built by the London County Council two decades later. Jackson wrote that he had 'tried to make them beautiful within the proper limits of cottage building; *not the cottage orné*, which is detestable, but with that kind of simple grace which comes from plain sensible construction. I know nothing more difficult of attainment in architecture than that, for the result ought to look as if it had come of itself, not as if it had been designed.' In this worthy aim, Jackson seems to have been quite as successful as Norman Shaw in middle-class Bedford Park (page 206) – which was clearly an influence on Jackson. Curiously, although he may have despised the *cottage orné*, Jackson's words precisely echo the sentiments expressed by Nash about his Blaise Hamlet cottages seventy years before (page 46).

Lime Tree Walk, Sevenoaks / *Thomas Graham Jackson*

No. 44 Tite Street, Chelsea / EDWARD WILLIAM GODWIN

In his remarkable career on the crest of the avant-garde which took him from Bristol to Bohemia, E. W. Godwin (1833–86) designed a handful of town houses which were some of the most interesting of their day. Most of Godwin's domestic work was carried out in the 1870s. Earlier, he had designed in muscular Gothic and was an apostle of Burges. He was responsible for the town halls in Northampton and Congleton. Godwin's furniture designs showed the new mood before his architecture. He was an early collector of Japanese art and designed thin and mannered ebonised Aesthetic furniture. Godwin acquired impeccable credentials in the avant-garde by running off with young Mrs G. F. Watts (the future actress Ellen Terry) and living in sin in Hertfordshire. He increasingly moved in the world of artists and writers, like J. M. Whistler and Oscar Wilde. In the late 1870s, Godwin's house designs provoked hostility and opposition (see page 207). Sadly, between 1881 and his early death, he designed no more buildings and concentrated on interior decoration and stage design – a talent inherited by his son Edward Gordon Craig.

Godwin's battles with the conservative architectural establishment occurred in Chelsea where, in the mid-1870s, the Metropolitan Board of Works had built the Chelsea Embankment and laid out Tite Street. In 1877, Godwin designed the now destroyed White House in Tite Street for Whistler. The following year he designed another house on the west side of Tite Street for Frank Miles, a sad crony of Oscar Wilde's; Tite Street was full of artists. This first design was very rectilinear in elevation and Japanese in style. 'When the first elevation was sent to the Board of Works', Godwin later recounted, 'our respected friend, Mr Vulliamy, said, "Why, this is worse than Whistler's", that it would be useless to lay it before the Board, and that it would not do, and yet I consider it the best thing I ever did. I grant you there was no cornice, no parapet and no string course. But is architecture a matter of string courses and parapets?... The Board refused to let my design be carried out. Well, I made a second design, in which I introduced a number of reminiscences of Holland, and the thing was pronounced charming. This is very sad.' (George Vulliamy was architect to the Metropolitan Board of Works.)

Although less original than the first design, No. 44 Tite Street as built contains many fewer reminiscences of Holland than, say, the houses of Ernest George and is still a clever design relying largely on the handling of wall planes and with little 'Queen Anne' detail. It was approved by the MBW in 1878 and built the following year. Today it is marred by the removal of some of the very necessary glazing bars.

No. 44 Tite Street, Chelsea / *Edward William Godwin* 187

No. 2 Palace Court, Bayswater / WILLIAM FLOCKHART

William Flockhart (1854–1913) is one of those late-Victorian architects who deserves to be more than a vaguely familiar name, for his practice was large and his work good. Flockhart was born in Glasgow and, although he had a London office, he built several large houses in Scotland. His sometime assistant, S. D. Adshead, recalled that 'he was a man with a highly strung and very artistic temperament.... He was well acquainted with all the details of every style, particularly the decadent and baroque styles [sic]. Few architects possessed his knowledge of Louis Quinze and Quatorze and succeeding styles, and he had great appreciation of Tudor, William and Mary and other semi-decadent English styles [Adshead had become a strict Classicist]. These gave him an opportunity for originality of composition, and did not tie him down to the severity of pure style.'[35] A later pupil was Oliver Hill, the domestic architect of between the wars. Goodhart-Rendel considered Flockhart 'an extremely sensitive draughtsman, potentially the best of the lot'.[36]

No. 2 Palace Court, Bayswater, shows the skilled and eclectic use to which Flockhart put his knowledge of styles. The house was built in 1891 for Patrick Ness, 'a rich carriage builder in Long Acre'. The red-brick house is in a sort of vaguely French early Renaissance style, with its depressed segmental arches, but the windows are placed with the contrived randomness of an Arts and Crafts architect and the corner from Palace Court to the Bayswater Road is handsomely and sensibly taken by an oriel turret. Historical styles, in the hands of an eclectic master of composition, could be turned into something refreshingly new and charming.

No. 2 Palace Court, Bayswater / *William Flockhart*

Nos. 8–10 Palace Court, Bayswater / JAMES MARJORIBANKS MACLAREN

The neighbour to Flockhart's Palace Court building was also a Scot but one who has a reputation, and one based on comparatively few executed buildings. The career of James MacLaren (1843–90) was cut short by an early death, but in the 1880s his buildings showed a conspicuous originality which was not lost upon a younger generation of Arts and Crafts architects whose own careers blossomed in the following decade. MacLaren came south to London in the 1870s and may have worked in the office of J. J. Stevenson, but the architect he admired most was E. W. Godwin. The other influence on Mac-Laren's development was American architecture and, in particular, the rugged, massive Romanesque-style work of H. H. Richardson. It is surprising that Muthesius did not notice the work of MacLaren in *Das Englische Haus* for, although he built little, his Bayswater house was an influential design.

In fact, MacLaren's building is a pair of houses built in 1889–90 for Sir Donald Currie. The two houses, with very different and separate entrances, were combined in one asymmetrical elevation. There is much of Norman Shaw in the design: not only his style of sash window but also one of the strange thin oriel windows used on the Swan House in Chelsea. There is also an American influence as well as considerable invention. The Byzantinesque detail and flattened mouldings must have been noticed by Lethaby, a colleague in the Art Workers' Guild. The fine lead gutter and the low-relief naturalistic frieze also fulfil the Guild's idea of architecture as something sculptural and dependent upon fine craftsmanship. Goodhart-Rendel was so impressed by MacLaren's originality that he included him as one of his 'rogue' architects. Of this pair of houses – traditional and yet so inventive – he wrote, 'That this remarkable work should be so little known is a sad proof that novelty, when it is rational rather than sensational, obtains scanty recognition.'[37]

Nos. 8–10 Palace Court, Bayswater / *James Marjoribanks MacLaren*

No. 25 Cadogan Gardens, Chelsea / ARTHUR HEYGATE MACKMURDO

The reputation of A. H. Mackmurdo (1851–1942) as an avant-garde innovator is somewhat problematical. An architect, designer and utopian socio-economic theorist, his proto art nouveau title-pages for his book on *Wren's City Churches* (1883) and for the Arts and Crafts journal *The Hobby Horse* (1884) were certainly strikingly original and his Century Guild played an important role in the Arts and Crafts movement. But the fact has to be faced that the houses he designed himself are muddled, awkward and pretentious – especially his later work in Essex. It may be that those, like Nikolaus Pevsner, who met Mackmurdo late in life and wished to see him as a 'pioneer' of the Modern movement took him too much at his own word.

Mackmurdo's early work was heavily dependent upon that of Norman Shaw. The house in Private Road, Enfield, of 1883 is very strange indeed, in a peculiarly illiterate and contrived neo-Classical manner. But this design may well reflect the influence of Mackmurdo's partner from 1882 until 1890, Herbert P. Horne, who later went off to Italy to write about Botticelli.

No. 25 Cadogan Gardens seems to be Mackmurdo's best and most accomplished building, but even this may not be the result of his own unaided efforts. Margaret Richardson has discovered that the drawings for the building, dated 1892, are signed by Mackmurdo, Hornblower and Walters, for in the 1890s Mackmurdo was in partnership with George Hornblower (1858–1940), a Liverpool Arts and Crafts architect who specialised in houses, and E. S. Walters. The same partnership was also responsible for the other Mackmurdo building near by, in Hans Road.

No. 25 Cadogan Gardens is certainly a clever development of the local 'Queen Anne' style. It is more rectilinear and formal, with a pitched roof above one of Shaw's coved cornices, and an element of ambiguity is achieved by having three double-height oriel windows projecting on one façade and three similarly shaped but flush tall windows on the other – the building being on a corner. The house was built in 1893–5 for Mortimer Menpes, an Australian artist who was a follower of Whistler and a good etcher and water-colourist. Tipped-in colour plates of his paintings illustrate several Edwardian travel books. Menpes was much influenced by Japanese art and the

original interior of his house was exotic and oriental in style. These interiors have since been destroyed, for 25 Cadogan Gardens has since been annexed by the Peter Jones department store behind.

No. 25 Cadogan Gardens, Chelsea / *Arthur Heygate Mackmurdo*

193

Nos. 38 and 39 Cheyne Walk, Chelsea / CHARLES ROBERT ASHBEE

C. R. Ashbee (see page 108) lived in Chelsea and it was along Cheyne Walk that most of his executed designs were built. These were a series of houses with deliberately varied and irregular façades which, Muthesius thought, 'have a certain distinctive quality though they are not always free of affectation'. Sadly, today only two of these houses are left; some were bombed but the house Ashbee built for himself and his mother in 1893–4 and which he called 'the Magpie and Stump' was shamefully demolished in recent years. This house, on the site of an old inn, was No. 37 Cheyne Walk. The two surviving houses were its neighbours, although built a little later.

No. 39 Cheyne Walk was built by Ashbee as a speculation, No. 38 was designed for Miss C. L. Christian, an artist. Both were built at the same time, in 1898–9, but, naturally, the two houses were made to look very different. On Miss Christian's house, the very tall gable houses a large studio. This gable was plastered, to distinguish it from the brick below, and so to evoke the character of old gabled London houses. These were being swept away for street improvements like the building of the Aldwych and Kingsway, but the London County Council's Committee for the Survey of the Memorials of Greater London, under Ashbee's chairmanship, was doing its best to record them.

194

Nos. 38 and 39 Cheyne Walk, Chelsea / *Charles Robert Ashbee*

No. 54 Mount Street, Mayfair / FAIRFAX BLOMFIELD WADE

Fairfax B. Wade (1851–1919) is not a well-known architect and, as No. 54 Mount Street is a house in a Classical style, it is perhaps surprising to find that Muthesius illustrated his work, but Wade had somehow come to the attention of the Germans and he was represented in 'a collection of English houseplans in the private property of HM the Kaiser, published under the highest auspices to further the building of German single-family-owner-occupied houses'. Wade designed a number of interesting town houses in the 1890s, notably Nos. 63 and 64 Sloane Street, Chelsea, of 1894–6. According to Goodhart-Rendel, Wade 'was a fine gentleman of private means and employed gentlemen to do his architecture'.[38] Andrew Saint believes that this comment is unfair and that Wade's architecture suddenly improved after a riding accident made him lead a less social and more sedentary life.

No. 54 Mount Street was built in 1896–9 on the corner of Park Street and is characteristic in scale and opulence of the turn-of-the-century redevelopment of the Grosvenor Estate in Mayfair. The client was Lord Windsor, later 1st Earl of Plymouth, who had earlier commissioned Thomas Garner to build Hewell Grange, a colossal neo-Elizabethan house in Worcestershire. In Mount Street, Wade employed the fashionable 'Wrenaissance' style in brick and stone but with a typical English, or Arts and Crafts, determination to flout the rules of Classical architecture. The fenestration is too crowded, the Classicism itself too exuberant and arbitrary, making the building friendly and jolly. Muthesius selected this house as a 'characteristic example' of a 'palatial type of town house' and illustrated the plans of all five floors. He observed that 'the servants' quarters of the house will be seen to occupy an area as large as, or even a little larger than, the family's quarters' and concluded that 'both for its plan and for the admirable way it has been realised, this house can be regarded as one of the best examples of this type of grand house.' Compared with the simple, spacious plan of a first-rate Georgian town house, Wade's plan is really rather complicated and contrived. This house is now the residence of the Brazilian ambassador.

No. 54 Mount Street, Mayfair / *Fairfax Blomfield Wade*

No. 8 Addison Road, Kensington / HALSEY RALPH RICARDO

Halsey Ricardo (1854–1928) is chiefly remembered for his obsession with strongly coloured and washable building materials. The son of a Jewish banker, Ricardo was educated at Rugby where he admired the polychromatic buildings designed by Butterfield, for whose architecture he became a rare apologist at the turn of the century. Ricardo worked for the 'Queen Anne' architect, Basil Champneys, came under the influence of Philip Webb and moved in Arts and Crafts circles. Ricardo's architectural practice was comparatively small and his work unusual. In the country, as at Woodside, Graffham, of 1905, he adopted a quiet vernacular manner, but in London he demonstrated his belief in the virtue of facing buildings in bright, washable materials in dirty smoky cities. Possibly inspired by Butterfield at a time when glazed tiles and terracotta was available for architecture (although mass-produced details were anathema to those who followed Ruskin and Morris), Ricardo lectured on the need for 'Colour in the Architecture of Cities'. For a number of years Ricardo was in partnership with the potter William de Morgan.

At No. 8 Addison Road, a large town house built in 1905–7 for Sir Ernest Debenham, of the department store Debenham & Freebody, Ricardo was enabled to carry out his ideas on an extensive scale. The whole of the Classical-style exterior of the house is coloured white, blue and green. It is faced with Doulton's tiles and Burmanstoft's Staffordshire glazed bricks, all made to order in the shapes required for cornices, columns, lintels and other details. Inside, there are deep-turquoise tiles, many intended originally for the Tsar of Russia's yacht, *Livadia*, and left over when William de Morgan's firm went bankrupt. The lavish and colourful interior (Colour Plate O) justifies the intentions of the Art Workers' Guild, of which Ricardo was a member, as it displays the skills of several different artists and craftsmen. There is inlaid woodwork by William Aumonier and plasterwork by Ernest Gimson. Ricardo left the dome over the central galleried hall white, but in 1913 it was covered in Byzantine-style mosaics designed by Gaetano Meo and applied by Debenham's own mosaic workers.

No. 8 Addison Road, Kensington / *Halsey Ralph Ricardo*

PART FOUR / The Suburb and the Garden Suburb

Yew Tree Lodge, Streatham Park / LEONARD ALOYSIUS STOKES

By the reign of Edward VII, architects felt that an urbane, Classical style was appropriate even in London suburbs. Ricardo's house for Debenham in Kensington is Classical and the house designed by Leonard Stokes (1858–1925) for his brother by Streatham Park is in a Georgian manner. This house, Yew Tree Lodge, was built in 1898–9 and is exactly contemporary with Dixcote nearby (page 134), by Walter Cave, but in a very different style. Muthesius noted how Stokes had 'recently developed a liking for eighteenth-century English forms – which he handles with his own peculiar breadth of vision and power', although Littleshaw, Stokes's own house in the country built a few years later, is in a vernacular manner (page 152).

Yew Tree Lodge is certainly not a conventional neo-Georgian house. With its smooth elevations of two colours of brick, wide cornice and precise symmetry, it is stylish as well as formal. Stokes managed to group all the flues into central stacks, which are separated by a concave brick wall above the pitched roof – an effect of central massing reminiscent of Vanbrugh. Stokes was not constrained by his Georgian manner: the side, garden elevation is enlivened by two symmetrically placed bay windows. An equally sure architectural sense governed the placing of the carefully designed rainwater heads and down-pipes on the entrance façade. With its dignified but friendly air and low, spreading proportions, Yew Tree Lodge seems much superior to many neo-Georgian houses which came after it. Stokes managed to combine the sense of the Arts and Crafts movement with the civilised urbanity of the Classical tradition.

Yew Tree Lodge, Streatham Park / *Leonard Aloysius Stokes*

Lowther Lodge, Kensington Gore / RICHARD NORMAN SHAW

One of the largest, cleverest and most delightful of essays in the 'Queen Anne' style is now rather overwhelmed by its surroundings, but when built it was on a spacious site which was not really in the country but not, really, in London either. Lowther Lodge was built in 1873–5 for William Lowther, MP, at the top end of a large garden stretching south from Kensington Gore. In his designs, dated 1872, Lowther's architect, Richard Norman Shaw (1831–1912), felt able to treat his 'Queen Anne' style in a playful and free manner. The house is as large as Shaw's 'Old English' country houses (page 70), but on the front which faces Kensington Gore he was able to play urban architectural games. This front is symmetrical and yet not symmetrical, and enlivened with a profusion of rubbed-brick detail, gables, tall ribbed chimneys and the deep coved cornices which were a favourite of Shaw and Nesfield. Some features are inexplicable,

except from a Picturesque point of view, such as the brick 'arcade' placed above the eaves of the pitched roof on the east wing: surely it cannot be for stopping snow sliding off? Lowther Lodge differs from Shaw's country houses in that its central 'saloon' is only single-height rather than Shaw's usual double-height great halls.

When Lowther died in 1912, the house was bought by the Royal Geographical Society which, in 1928–30, added a further wing to the east designed by Kennedy and Nightingale. The impressive scale of this magnificent brick house was greatly and sadly diminished in 1880 when Albert Hall Mansions, the prototype of many late-Victorian blocks of flats, rose up to nine storeys immediately next door. It was designed by none other than Richard Norman Shaw. Lowther's reaction to his overbearing new neighbour is not recorded.

Lowther Lodge, Kensington Gore / *Richard Norman Shaw*

Bedford Park / E. W. GODWIN, R. NORMAN SHAW, E. J. MAY and others

'Angels and ministers of grace! am I dreaming!' wondered the American humanist, Moncure Daniel Conway, when he visited the site of the Battle of Turnham Green in 1882, 'Right before me is the apparition of a little red town made up of quaintest Queen Anne houses.... Surely my eyes are cheating me; they must have been gathering impressions of by-gone architecture along the riverside Malls, and are now turning them to visions, and building them by ideal mirage into this dream of old-time homesteads!'[39] Bedford Park may not have been the first housing development which can be described as a 'garden suburb' but it was very influential, not least on American visitors. A Continental like Muthesius recognised the historical importance of Bedford Park: 'There was at the time virtually no development that could compare in artistic charm with Bedford Park, least of all had the small house found anything like so satisfactory an artistic and economic solution as here. And herein lies the immense importance of Bedford Park in the history of the English house. It signifies neither more nor less than the starting point of the

smaller house, which immediately spread from there over the whole country.'

Bedford Park was the creation of the speculator Jonathan T. Carr who, in 1875 bought 24 acres near Hammersmith and next to a suburban railway station. His intention was clever: to build 'Artistic' houses which might appeal to members of the middle class with advanced taste who were repelled by the standard mid-Victorian stuccoed house of the Kensington and Bayswater type and who were interested in the fashionable cult of 'The House Beautiful'. The planning of Bedford Park is not especially remarkable but to build 'Queen Anne' houses on such a scale was. By 1883 490 houses had been built and the experiment was a success, even though Bedford Park Ltd. went bankrupt in 1886.

The 'Queen Anne' character of Bedford Park was created by Norman Shaw, both directly and indirectly. Between 1877 and 1880 he designed a number of house types as well as making what village 'centre' there is in the suburb, that is, the row of gabled shops and

the Tabard Inn (above, right), all deliberately varied in the 'Old English' style, and the 'Queen Anne' Gothic church opposite. Many other houses are versions of the Shaw style by Maurice Bingham Adams, W. Wilson, E. J. May or Coe and Robinson.

Carr's first architect, however, was E. W. Godwin (see page 186) who, in 1875, provided standard house designs. The first completed were Nos. 1 (page 206, left) and 2 The Avenue. These are in a more austere 'Queen Anne' style with a projecting bay rising three storeys to a tile-hung gable. Unfortunately, these houses were heavily criticised for their cramped plans and in 1877 Godwin resigned, to be succeeded by Shaw. Nos. 1 and 2 The Avenue were corner houses and, like all Bedford Park houses, did not have basements (a progressive omission). Godwin was therefore obliged to pack in as many rooms as possible on three floors and the staircase was very tight.

One of the most delightful houses in Bedford Park is the Vicarage to the Church of St Michael and All Angels. Although the church is by Shaw, the adjacent Vicarage (pages 208-9) was designed by Edward John May (1853–1941), who had been Decimus Burton's last pupil and who then worked for Nesfield and Shaw. In 1880 Shaw recommended May – a Bedford Park resident – to succeed him as estate architect. The Vicarage is a more disciplined essay in the 'Queen Anne' style, having no gables but a tall pitched roof surmounted by two splendid brick chimneys. The symmetrical garden front has the happy feature of two bay windows – with 'Ipswich' glazing bars – separated by a diminutive garden door under a wooden lintel and pitched roof. Also by May is the terrace in Priory Gardens (above, left).

An artfully discordant note amongst all the red brick and tile was provided in 1891 when No. 14 South Parade was built, an oddly severe white studio house by the young C.F.A. Voysey (page 206, right). By then, 'Queen Anne' was clearly becoming old-fashioned amongst the avant-garde.

Bedford Park / *E. W. Godwin, R. Norman Shaw, E. J. May* and others

Bedford Park / *E. W. Godwin, R. Norman Shaw, E. J. May* and others

Manor Farm, Hampstead / BASIL CHAMPNEYS

Basil Champneys (1842–1935) designed eclectic late-Victorian buildings of a particular charm and sympathy. He could give the 'Queen Anne' style a feminine sweetness that was lacking in the work of some of his contemporaries. This was very appropriately demonstrated in his buildings for Newnham College, Cambridge, a pioneering establishment for women. Here, the buildings erected over three decades after 1874 are delightfully varied and picturesque, very different in character from the hard, red-brick Gothic buildings of Girton College – the first college for women – designed by Waterhouse. Champneys was the son of the dean of Lichfield and was educated at Trinity College, Cambridge. He was articled as a pupil to the Gothicist Prichard of Llandaff, but after designing one Gothic church in north London, Champneys turned to the more sympathetic 'Queen Anne' style. Most of Champneys's buildings were for schools or universities, where educational buildings were humanised by his picturesque and pretty detailing. Apart from Newnham College, the Butler Museum

at Harrow School and the King Edward VII School at King's Lynn are particularly fine examples of his work. Champneys also designed middle-class houses in Hampstead and elsewhere. Champneys was a cultivated man with literary interests. He was a friend of the writer Coventry Patmore, for whom he designed a Roman Catholic church in Hastings and of whom he wrote a posthumous memoir.

Champneys designed Manor Farm, off Frognal in Hampstead, for himself in 1881. It was illustrated in Maurice B. Adams's book of 1883, *Artists' Homes*. Although the house, now called Hall Oak, has the coved cornice, the Ipswich-type windows and brick detailing typical of Shaw's 'Queen Anne' manner, it has an unusual, four-square character of its own and the principal elevations are symmetrical. Like many larger seventeenth-century houses, Manor Farm originally had a balustraded gallery on top of the roof, but the original wooden balustrades which ran between the four central chimney-stacks have disappeared.

Manor Farm, Hampstead / *Basil Champneys*

Nos. 49–51 Frognal, Hampstead / REGINALD THEODORE BLOMFIELD

Although Blomfield (1856–1942) revived the Classicism of Wren and Gibbs and eventually took up the Grand Manner, he was content to live in a house in a more traditional, vernacular style – possibly thinking it more appropriate to the village character of Hampstead. Blomfield designed this pair of semi-detached houses in Frognal in 1892. He lived in No. 51 himself and No. 49 was taken by the bookbinder and printer, T. J. Cobden-Sanderson. The houses are simple, unpretentious brick buildings but a Classical touch is given by the gables which can be read as tall pediments and the windows sport the rather un-English addition of shutters.

Blomfield lived in Hampstead until his death at the age of eighty-six. He therefore had the misfortune to have to endure the building of pioneering Modern movement houses in the 1930s nearby in Frognal and Frognal Lane, designed by Connell Ward and Lucas and by Maxwell Fry. Blomfield fulminated against these outrages, but in vain.

Nos. 49–51 Frognal, Hampstead / *Reginald Theodore Blomfield*

213

Garth House, Edgbaston / WILLIAM HENRY BIDLAKE

Born in Wolverhampton and trained in the offices of Colonel Robert Edis and Bodley and Garner, W. H. Bidlake (1862–1938) was the best Birmingham architect of his generation. His finest buildings were churches, such as St Agatha's, Sparkbrook, of 1899–1901, but he designed several good houses on the new Four Oaks suburban estate in Edgbaston. Muthesius noticed these; Bidlake, he thought, 'in his more recent houses, especially in their interiors, . . . has found a very independent, novel interpretation. But he has the same naturalness and breadth of interpretation as Lutyens . . . inside as well as outside everything is extremely natural. Yet though his means are of the simplest, he manages to create interiors of great intimacy.'

Garth House, in Edgbaston Park Road, Birmingham, was designed in 1901 for Ralph Heaton, a partner in the Birmingham Mint and a man with Arts and Crafts tastes. An odd feature of this well-composed house of red brick and roughcast is a flat-topped tower, the lower parts of which contain the staircase but the upper part of which is nothing but a box room. Inside, the hall has a clever arrangement of an inglenook fireplace separated from the staircase by an open screen of attenuated wooden columns – a feature worthy of Voysey or Baillie Scott.

Garth House, Edgbaston / *William Henry Bidlake*   215

Redhill, Headingley / FRANCIS W. BEDFORD and SYDNEY DECIMUS KITSON

Bedford and Kitson (1866–1904 and 1871–1937) were among several firms of architects mentioned by Muthesius who are little known today. The partnership was described in *Das Englische Haus* as 'a firm of very promising young architects who have already built a number of country houses which are among the best work of recent years. Their exteriors are more or less traditional in design, but inside they experiment in more independent ways, though without becoming fantastic, and create rooms which are striking for their comfort and their pleasant appointments and furniture and give an impression of quiet refinement. To judge from their work to date we can expect much of them.' Unfortunately, possibly owing to the early death of Bedford, little in fact came of the firm, whose later work in Leeds is unremarkable. Bedford was from the best possible stable: Ernest George's office; Kitson trained with E. J. May and with W. D. Caroë and was a son of the Leeds engineering magnate, James Kitson, later Lord Airedale. Bedford and Kitson practised in Leeds, near or in which are most of their houses, churches and public buildings. Their partnership commenced in 1897. Kitson later wrote a life of the painter John Sell Cotman.

Redhill, in Shireoak Road, Headingley, is one of many turn-of-the-century houses in this wealthy suburb of Leeds. It is also a good example of how the achievement of Norman Shaw and his generation was diffused throughout the country, raising the general standard of domestic architecture and making a suburban house, even in the twentieth century, a well-built, sensibly planned and recognisably traditional building. In the case of Redhill, however, it should be said that the Norman Shavian tile-hanging and half-timbering do not

make the house look indigenous to Yorkshire. 'Old English' had become a convention, what a home-owner wanted and expected.

Redhill was built in 1900–1. The interior survives unaltered, with a naturalistic plaster frieze and an art nouveau style chimney-piece.

Redhill, Headingley / *Francis W. Bedford* and *Sydney Decimus Kitson*   217

Laneside and Crabby Corner, Letchworth / BARRY PARKER and RAYMOND UNWIN

The omission of the famous firm of Parker and Unwin from *Das Englische Haus* is extraordinary. Not only had the partnership built enough to have come to Muthesius's attention before going to press, as well as having published *The Art of Building a Home* in 1901, but Parker and Unwin also sustained the simple, rational traditions in English house building which Muthesius most admired. Parker and Unwin eschewed neo-Georgian and remained faithful to a simple vernacular manner, were committed to bringing the advances made in house design to the problem of housing the working classes well, and were instrumental in the realisation of the ideas of the garden suburb and garden city. Socialists, inspired by the ideas of Ruskin and Morris and the Utopianism of Edward Carpenter, they were serious, earnest and moral.

Barry Parker (1867–1947) was born in Chesterfield, served his articles with G. Faulkner Armitage – uncle of Armitage Rigby, Baillie Scott's competitor on the Isle of Man – in Manchester, and in 1896 set up in practice in Buxton. Parker was influenced by his friend Edgar Wood and by Baillie Scott. Raymond Unwin (1863–1940) was Parker's second cousin who, in 1893, married Unwin's sister. Unwin was born in Rotherham, trained as an engineer with the Staveley Iron and Coal Company, for which he also designed miners' cottages. He joined Parker in Buxton in 1896. Both men engaged in political activity as well as designing middle-class houses. In 1902 the pair were asked by Joseph and Seebohm Rowntree to design a model village at New Earswick, near York; in 1904 their design for the new garden city at Letchworth was adopted and in 1905 they were asked

to plan Hampstead Garden Suburb by Dame Henrietta Barnett. In 1904 Parker and Unwin moved from Buxton and eventually settled in Letchworth. Unwin became more and more concerned with town planning and housing the working classes, and the partnership was dissolved in 1914.

Laneside (Colour Plate P) and Crabby Corner were a pair of semi-detached houses which is one of the most interesting Parker and Unwin buildings in Letchworth. Now called Arunside, the two houses were built in 1904–5. Unwin designed the pair for himself and for Howard Pearsall, a director of the First Garden City Ltd., the company which promoted Letchworth. In 1906 Unwin moved out of Laneside and went to live in a seventeenth-century farmhouse near Hampstead Garden Suburb; in the same year Parker moved into Crabby Corner. The asymmetrical semi-detached plan of the houses enabled a convincingly cottage-like long building to be erected, of brick and roughcast. The interiors were extremely simple and had open plans, with staircases acting as room dividers. In this austere and earthy domestic setting, the Unwins were clothed in homespun tweeds, 'Ruskin' flannel from the Isle of Man, and specially made sandals. Crabby Corner eventually became too small for Parker's growing family, so that in 1914 he added a three-storey addition in the form of a rather Germanic-looking tower. The windows of the top floor of this could be removed so as to make an open-air sleeping balcony, then a fashionable accessory to the Simple Life. The two houses are now owned by St Christopher's School, Letchworth.

Laneside and Crabby Corner, Letchworth / *Barry Parker* and *Raymond Unwin*

Letchworth in Hertfordshire was the first garden city. The Garden City Association had been formed in 1899; in 1901 and 1902 Garden City Conferences had been held in Bourneville and Port Sunlight. In 1903 the Garden City Pioneer Company was formed to find a site and 3,818 acres were purchased near Baldock. In the same year, the First Garden City Ltd. was registered and Parker and Unwin prepared a development plan which was adopted in 1904. 'The high standard of beauty which the Company desires to attain ... can only result from simple, straightforward building and from the use of good and harmonious materials. They desire as far as possible to discourage useless ornamentation and to secure that buildings shall be suitably designed for their purpose and position.' A low density of twenty-two persons per acre was planned; in the event it was even lower and the town centre was never completed according to Parker and Unwin's conception.

As it was intended that Letchworth should be a socially mixed community, a 'Cheap Cottages' exhibition was held in 1905 for which architects were invited to submit designs for cottages for agricultural workers which could be erected for £150 each. Although 114 cottages were built, Letchworth remained a predominantly middle-class community, nationally notorious for its liberal causes promoted by cranks.

102 Wilbury Road (pages 220–1) was built in 1908–9 for Parker's craftsman brother, Stanley. The house is an essay by Parker and Unwin in adapting the vernacular as cheaply as possible for simple, not to say puritanical living. The well-proportioned exterior is all white, with roughcast laid over brick and concrete; the steep and homely pitched roof is tiled. Internally the brickwork is left exposed and merely painted, the joists whitewashed. Homeliness is suggested by the inglenook fireplaces. Austere though the house is, it is a

sensible and practical design, well built, which could be a model for economical house construction today.

Tanglewood, 17 Sollershott West, Letchworth, was designed by M. H. Baillie Scott (pages 222–3) and built in 1906–7 for Mrs Branson. It remains an unaltered example of several small houses designed by Baillie Scott in the new garden city. As with some of the architect's larger houses, Tanglewood has hall, living-room and porch connecting as one space. The design makes much use of timber and, with its sweeping roofs, is calculatedly Picturesque – like all of Scott's many cottages. In places, the roof comes down to within a few feet of the ground, increasing the apparent size of the house and exaggerating its air of quaint homeliness.

Letchworth / *Parker* and *Unwin, M. H. Baillie Scott* and others 221

Letchworth / *Parker* and *Unwin, M. H. Baillie Scott* and others

Letchworth / *Parker* and *Unwin*, *M. H. Baillie Scott* and others

Port Sunlight

Port Sunlight was the creation of William Hesketh Lever, 1st Viscount Leverhulme, who purchased land in Cheshire for a new soap factory and for a new village for his employees in 1888. It was the first place in which the movement for improved working-class dwellings was united with the Romantic and Picturesque suburban tradition. The first layout plan for Port Sunlight was made by Lever himself. In 1910 a competition to revise the plan, enlarge the village and make a village centre was won by Ernest Prestwich. This plan, on more Beaux-Arts lines, and possibly influenced by American 'City Beautiful' ideas, centres upon the Lady Lever Art Gallery, a Classical building by William and Segar Owen.

The early buildings are in a red-brick and half-timbered Tudor manner, mainly by William and Segar Owen (above right, Hulme Hall; and page 225, below left), Grayson and Ould and Douglas and Fordham (above left, Dell Bridge and the Lyceum). After 1910, much was designed by J. Lomax Simpson. But Lever adopted the policy of

inviting many outside architects to contribute designs, so that many of the famous London names are represented in Port Sunlight, not least Lutyens. One curiosity is the crescent of terraced houses (page 225, right) by the side of the Lady Lever Art Gallery. These, in a consciously anti-vernacular Regency manner, are by Charles Reilly, the principal of the nearby Liverpool School of Architecture who did much to establish Beaux-Arts teaching methods and neo-Classical style into architectural schools – both anathema to the old Arts and Crafts men.

Muthesius thought that 'there is no better way for those who wish to take a quick and pertinent look at the achievements of the English architects of today than to visit the workmen's village of Port Sunlight. Certainly these are only factory workers' houses. But they contain the whole repertoire of contemporary means of expression in such accomplished form that the estate may be considered the flower of the small modern house in a small space. . . . In one sense Port

Sunlight may be regarded as the present day outcome of Norman Shaw's pioneering work at Bedford Park thirty years ago, for it is a solution of the problem of the small house and a grouping together of houses to form a residential area in a way that is modern and satisfies all practical and artistic requirements. In both places the architects drew upon early vernacular architecture, the motifs of which offered the best source for the design of the houses and the layout of the streets.'

Whether the quality of Port Sunlight, still maintained in fine condition, will survive the selling off of the village by Lever Brothers remains to be seen.

Port Sunlight

Hampstead Garden Suburb / PARKER and UNWIN, EDWIN LUTYENS and others

Hampstead Garden Suburb exemplifies both the success and the failures of the English idea of the perfect, cosy, leafy suburb as an escape from the wicked, dark and dirty city: it is very desirable, but dull. The Suburb, way beyond Hampstead, was the creation of Dame Henrietta Barnett, whose husband, Canon Barnett, was the co-founder and first warden of Toynbee Hall. As a result of their philanthropic experiences in the East End of London, the Barnetts dreamed of founding an ideal community like a traditional village, with all social classes mixed. The site chosen for this was on the edge of London just north of an extension to Hampstead Heath, the purchase of which, to preserve the land as open space, Mrs Barnett had been instrumental in securing in 1905.

Ironically, as with Bedford Park thirty years before, the establishment of this traditional, pseudo-rural village was only made possible because of the existence of a railway and because of the speculative instincts of businessmen. Charles Tyson Yerkes, a Chicago transportation tycoon and promoter of the American-backed Underground

Electric Railways Co. of London, decided to extend the Charing Cross, Euston and Hampstead Railway (now the Northern Line) to Golders Green and to encourage building there to generate more traffic. The opening of this electric tube railway in 1907 made Hampstead Garden Suburb easily accessible from central London. (Was Yerkes the 'Yankee' Dame Henrietta Barnett met on a ship in 1896 who 'talks of a proposal . . . to convey all London about in tunnels' and who said that 'the system of underground travelling he anticipated would cause the erection of a station on the western edge of Hampstead Heath'?)

The Garden Suburb Trust was formed in 1906. The first layout plan was prepared by Parker and Unwin, who envisaged a picturesque, low-density development with eight houses to the acre. In 1908, Alfred Lyttleton, as chairman of the board, brought in Lutyens to plan the central area on the highest point in the Suburb. Here he proposed greater civic formality, with a central leafy 'square' containing two churches and an institute. Lutyens's more formal ideas brought him into conflict with Mrs Barnett: 'a nice woman, but proud

226

of being a philistine – has no idea much beyond a window box full of geraniums, calceolarias and lobelias, over which you can see a goose on a green', he wrote to Herbert Baker. Lutyens was also responsible for the neo-Georgian houses, in silver-grey brick with red-brick dressings, at either end of the Central Square (left, below, with the Free Church beyond).

Other houses in the Suburb were much less classical and more vernacular in character and were designed by such architects as Parker and Unwin, Baillie Scott (page 226, right), Geoffrey Lucas, W. Curtis Green, Morley Horder and C. M. Crickmer. Highly successful are the contributions of A. J. Penty, who was responsible for the rather German-looking red-brick blocks of shops and flats on the Finchley Road and for the long brick wall (left, above) with steps and brick and timber 'gazebos', which divides the Suburb from the Heath.

The Suburb never attained the classless character envisaged by the Barnetts – it was too suburban for working men to be able to afford to live there and commute to work – and the incomplete, windswept, shop-less and pub-less nature of the Central Square (as Fabian Socialists the Barnetts were naturally anti-trade and anti-drink) fails to give any sense of cohesion or community. But it is full of good architecture and is now a place where those who can are willing to pay a great deal of money to live – for small cottages designed for working men and inspired by the old traditional vernacular of England still represent the English domestic ideal.

The Boundary Street Estate, Millbank Estate and Totterdown Fields Estate/
LONDON COUNTY COUNCIL ARCHITECTS' DEPARTMENT

The English House was, and is, a middle-class ideal. Almost all of the illustrations in *Das Englische Haus* were of private houses and most architects were content to find clients who could afford their comfortable reinterpretations of tradition. But there were some architects who adhered to the Socialism of Morris, Webb and Lethaby as well as to their architectural philosophies, and they were determined that what was good in English design should improve the lives of everybody. There was, Muthesius found, 'a demand that is heard today: that of bringing art to the life of the working-classes'. This was achieved, with conspicuous success, by the Housing of the Working Classes Branch of the LCC's Architects' Department, which was set up in 1893. Under the Housing of the Working Classes Act passed in 1890, the LCC housed 47,673 persons by 1912.

London's first municipal authority, the London County Council, had only been established in 1888, superseding the Metropolitan Board of Works. The first superintending architect was Thomas Blashill who, in 1900, was succeeded by W. E. Riley. But the design

work was carried out by a team of young architects who, largely, were inspired by Arts and Crafts and Fabian Socialist ideas: Owen Fleming, T. G. Charlton, Rob Robertson, R. Minton Taylor, William Hynam, H. R. Ward, A. M. Philips and Charles Canning Windmill. Later came J. R. Stark, J. G. Stephenson, E. H. Parkes, A. S. Soutar and E. Stone Collins.

The immediate problem was to clear the worst slums in densely populated central London areas and to rehouse the inhabitants. This had to be done without putting any charge on the rates as rents were expected to pay for the buildings, and it was thought essential not to build too high or in the form of the 'barrack-like' tenements formerly erected by charitable organisations like the Peabody Trust. The solution found was to build blocks of tenements of an urban but still picturesque character, in red rather than London stock brick, using the stylistic lessons of good, eclectic, straightforward building set by Shaw, Webb and the others. How successful this architectural solution was can be seen in the LCC's first big housing development in

The Boundary Street Estate / *London County Council Architects' Department* 229

Boundary Street, Shoreditch (page 229), of 1894–1900, which replaced the notorious Old Nichol slum described by Arthur Morrison in *A Child of the Jago*, published in 1896. This was soon followed by the Millbank Estate (left) of 1897–1902 behind the Tate Gallery. Muthesius was impressed: such estates were 'almost model developments as regards the artistic interpretation of these important problems. Obviously in this case the artistic answer cannot consist in a display of forms. Architects have searched and have happily found it in an extremely simple distribution of masses, excellently balanced proportions, pleasing groups of buildings, combined with colour in the shape of rich red brick walls and roofs, against which the window-frames stand out vividly.'

However, such estates of flats did not seem the answer to the problems of overcrowded cities and the architects in the LCC agitated for the building of low-density 'cottage estates' in the suburbs. This policy was adopted in 1898 and the first built was Totterdown Fields in Tooting (page 228). In 1900, 38½ acres were bought and the estate of 1,229 houses and four shops was built between 1903 and 1911. Rents were originally between six and twelve shillings a week. All the houses had bathrooms and gardens. What might have been an area of repetitive 'by-law' terraces was cleverly divided up into varied and attractively detailed groups of small houses. In their simple vernacular style and sensible construction, they look back to Webb and Butterfield but provide lessons for today. In contrast to the vandalism and dereliction of more recent high-rise council tower blocks, the recent sale of such council houses shows the continuing desirability of the traditional English house amongst people of all classes. The sadness is that 'home improvements' so often spoil the reticent and practical beauty of these lasting tributes to the sense and sensibility of late-Victorian and Edwardian architects.

Notes to Parts One to Four

1. John Summerson, *The Life and Work of John Nash*, 1980, p.54.
2. Quoted in Paul Thompson, *William Butterfield*, 1971, p.45.
3. W. R. Lethaby, *Philip Webb and his Work*, 1935, 1979.
4. George Jack, 'Philip Webb', *Architectural Review*, 1915, reprinted in Alastair Service (ed.), *Edwardian Architecture and its Origins*, 1975, p.17.
5. Christopher Hussey, *The Life of Sir Edwin Lutyens*, 1950, p.26.
6. Quoted in Robert Macleod, *Style and Society*, 1971, p.40.
7. W. R. Lethaby, *Philip Webb and his Work*, 1935, p.223.
8. F. M. Simpson, 'G. F. Bodley, R.A., F.S.A., D.C.L.', *RIBA Journal*, xv, 1908, pp.151–2.
9. Edward Warren, 'The Life and Work of George Frederick Bodley', *RIBA Journal*, xvii, 1910, p.308.
10. Andrew Saint, *Richard Norman Shaw*, 1976, p.51.
11. Mark Girouard, *Victorian Country Houses*, 1971, p.171.
12. *British Architect*, ix, 5 April 1878, p.156.
13. Roderick Gradidge, *Dream Houses*, 1980, p.49.
14. Andrew Saint, *Richard Norman Shaw*, 1976, p.261.
15. Gertrude Jekyll, *Home and Garden*, 1901, quoted in Roderick Gradidge, *Dream Houses*, 1980, p.116.
16. Christopher Hussey, *The Life of Sir Edwin Lutyens*, 1950, p.96.
17. *Country Life*, 20 January 1912, p.93.
18. Christopher Hussey, *The Work of Sir Robert Lorimer*, 1931, p.44.
19. Nikolaus Pevsner, 'Goodhart-Rendel's Roll-Call', *Architectural Review*, 1965, reprinted in Alastair Service, *Edwardian Architecture and its Origins*, 1975, p.479.
20. Hussey, *Lutyens*, op. cit., p.169.
21. David Ottewill, 'Robert Weir Schultz (1860–1951): An Arts and Crafts Architect', *Architectural History*, xxii, 1979, p.99.
22. Reginald Blomfield, *Richard Norman Shaw, R.A.*, 1940, p.88.
23. Said by Robert Shaw, Norman Shaw's son. In Andrew Saint, op. cit., p.186.
24. Lecture on building given in Edinburgh, 1889, quoted in Geoffrey Hoare and Geoffrey Pyne, *Prior's Barn and Gimson's Coxen. Two Arts and Crafts Houses*, 1978.
25. Victorian Society Notes, *Of The Soil Racy. A Tour of Arts and Crafts Rogues in North Norfolk*, 1971, p.15.
26. Lawrence Weaver, *Small Country Houses of Today*, vol. 2, 1922, p.20, quoted in Gradidge, op. cit., p.106.
27. C. F. A. Voysey, 'The English Home', *British Architect*, lxxv, 27 January 1911, reprinted in David Gebhard, *Charles F. A. Voysey, Architect*, 1975, pp.57–65.
28. Ibid.
29. 'A Small Country House', *The Studio*, December 1897, quoted in James Kornwolf, *M. H. Baillie-Scott and the Arts and Crafts Movement*, 1972, p.254.
30. Ernest Newton, *A Book of Country Houses*, 1903.
31. Hussey, *Lutyens*, op. cit., pp.121 and 133.
32. *Builder*, 5 May 1883.
33. F. M. Simpson, op. cit., p.152.
34. *The Recollections of Thomas Graham Jackson*, 1950, pp.153 and 163.
35. '"Architects I have known": The architectural career of S. D. Adshead', ed. Alan Powers, *Architectural History*, xxiv, 1981, p.113.
36. 'Goodhart-Rendel's Roll Call', op. cit., p.480.
37. H. S. Goodhart-Rendel, *English Architecture since The Regency*, 1953, p.198.
38. 'Goodhart-Rendel's Roll Call', op. cit., p.480.
39. Moncure Daniel Conway, *Travels in South Kensington*, 1882.

Short Biographies of the Architects

The following are summaries of the careers of the architects of the houses in this book, giving sources of further information about them. Fuller biographies of many of these architects will be found in Dora Ware's *A Short Dictionary of British Architects* (George Allen & Unwin, 1967) and in the new four-volume *Macmillan Encyclopaedia of Architects* (The Free Press, New York, 1982), while the new *Edwardian Architecture: A Biographical Dictionary* by A. Stuart Gray (Duckworth, 1985) provides all the information that could possibly be needed about most architects.

Charles Robert Ashbee (1863–1942)

Born in London, the son of the famous pornographer, C. R. Ashbee studied at Cambridge before entering the office of G. F. Bodley. Inspired by both Arts and Crafts and Socialist ideals, he founded the Guild of Handicraft in the East End of London in 1888. A printer, a designer of jewellery and silverware and an historian, instrumental in founding the Survey of London, Ashbee built comparatively little. In London, most of his work was in Cheyne Walk, Chelsea (Plates pp. 194–5), where he lived. After moving the Guild of Handicraft to Chipping Camden in 1902, he was responsible for both restorations and new buildings in Gloucestershire. He was briefly involved in the replanning of Jerusalem after the First World War. See also Colour Plate G and Plate p. 109.

Alan Crawford, 'Ten Letters from Frank Lloyd Wright to Charles Robert Ashbee', in *Architectural History*, xiii, 1970.
C. R. Ashbee and the Guild of Handicraft, Cheltenham Art Gallery and Museum exhibition catalogue, 1981.
Fiona McCarthy, *The Simple Life: C. R. Ashbee in the Cotswolds*, 1981.
Alan Crawford, *C. R. Ashbee. Architect, Designer and Romantic Socialist*, 1985.

Mackay Hugh Baillie Scott (1865–1945)

Born in Kent, M. H. Baillie Scott was articled to Charles Davis, city architect of Bath, and set up in practice on the Isle of Man in 1889. In 1901 he moved to Bedford. Baillie Scott's work was entirely domestic, characterised by an often ingenious handling of internal space and concern with decoration. His houses included Bexton Croft, Knutsford, Cheshire (1894–6), the White Lodge, Wantage, Berkshire

(1898–9), The Garth, Cobham, Surrey (1899–1900) and Waterlow Court, Hampstead Garden Suburb, London (1909). He also executed interiors in the ducal palace at Darmstadt, Germany, for the grand duke and a tree house for Queen Marie in Romania. He published *Houses and Gardens* in 1906 illustrating his own work and a second volume, with his later partner, A. E. Beresford, in 1933. See also Plates pp. 136–7, 222–3, and Plan 5, p. 37.

John Betjeman, 'M. H. Baillie Scott', *Journal of the Manx Museum*, vii, 1968, pp. 77–80.
James Kornwolf, *M. H. Baillie Scott and the Arts and Crafts Movement*, 1972.

Francis W. Bedford (1866–1904)

Bedford was a pupil of Ernest George and Peto. He practised in Leeds in partnership with S. D. Kitson (q.v.) from 1897 until his early death in 1904. See also Plates pp. 216–17.

John Francis Bentley (1839–1902)

J. F. Bentley was born in Doncaster and articled to the church architect Henry Clutton. In 1862 Bentley became a Roman Catholic and most of his work consisted of designing Roman Catholic churches, culminating in Westminster Cathedral, London (1895–1902). His domestic work was also largely ecclesiastical in character but it showed a sophisticated development of the eclecticism of the 'Queen Anne'. This included the Convent of the Sacred Heart, Hammersmith, London (1875–88), St John's School, Beaumont, Old Windsor, Berkshire (1887–8), and the Redemptorist Monastery at Clapham, London (1891–3). Bentley also designed interiors at Carlton Towers, Yorkshire. See also Plate p. 183.

W. de L'Hôpital, *Westminster Cathedral and its Architect*, 2 vols., 1919.
W. Scott-Moncreiff, *John Francis Bentley*, 1924.
A. S. G. Butler, *John Francis Bentley, the Architect of Westminster Cathedral*, 1961.
Helen Smith and others, *A Catalogue of an Exhibition of the Work of John Francis Bentley*, 1976.

William Henry Bidlake (1862–1938)

W. H. Bidlake was born in Wolverhampton, Staffordshire, the son of an architect. He studied at Cambridge and then worked for R. W. Edis and for Bodley and Garner before setting up practice in Birmingham in 1887, initially with John Cotton. He designed both churches and houses, including his own house, Woodgate, in Four Oaks, Birmingham (1897). He contributed an essay on 'The Home from Outside' in W. Shaw Sparrow, ed., *The Modern Home: A Book of British Domestic Architecture for Moderate Incomes*, 1906. See also Plates pp. 214–15.

Sutton Webster, 'W. H. Bidlake 1862–1938', in *Architecture West Midlands*, xxvi, 1976, pp. 17–25.
Alan Crawford, ed., *By Hammer and Hand: The Arts and Crafts Movement in Birmingham*, 1984.

Sir Reginald Theodore Blomfield (1856–1942)

Reginald Blomfield was born in Devon, the son of a clergyman. He was educated at Haileybury and Exeter College, Oxford, and then was articled to his uncle, Arthur Blomfield. Although beginning within the orbit of the Arts and Crafts movement and the Art Workers' Guild, Blomfield soon became a partisan of English Classicism. He was the author of *The Formal Garden in England* (1892), *A History of Renaissance Architecture in England* (1897) and *A History of French Architecture* (1911, 1920), amongst numerous published writings on architecture. He also wrote a biography of *Richard Norman Shaw* (1940) and *Modernismus* (1934), an attack on Modern architecture. Blomfield undertook large Classical structures, such as rebuilding the Quadrant in Regent Street and part of Piccadilly Circus (1920–3), and the Menin Gate, Ypres, for the Imperial War Graves Commission (1923–6). His domestic work included Caythorpe Court, Lincolnshire (1899), Moundsmere Manor, Hampshire (1908), and Salcote Place, Rye, Sussex (1905). See also Plates pp. 162–3, 213.

C. H. Reilly, *Representative British Architects of the Present Day*, 1931.
Richard A. Fellows, *Sir Reginald Blomfield. An Edwardian Architect*, 1985.

Detmar Jellings Blow (1867–1939)

Having studied at the South Kensington Schools and been articled to Wilson, Son & Aldwinkle, Detmar Blow was introduced to the world of the Arts and Crafts movement by meeting Ruskin in Abbeville Cathedral in 1888. Ruskin persuaded him to train as an architect by being apprenticed to a builder. Later he acted as clerk of works for Ernest Gimson for the Charnwood Forest Cottages and for Philip Webb on the restoration of East Knoyle church. His independent work in the country showed great care for traditional craftsmanship, but in London he exploited the Edwardian taste for French Classicism, entering into partnership with Fernand Billerey. Blow and Billerey built a certain amount on the Grosvenor Estate. He was also the architect of Government House, Salisbury, Rhodesia (now Harare, Zimbabwe). His country houses include Wilsford Manor, Wiltshire (1904–6) and Hilles House, Gloucestershire (1914), which he built for himself. He became Lord of the Manor of Painswick. See also Plates pp. 118–19.

Journal of the RIBA, 3 April 1939, p. 571.
The Grosvenor Estate in Mayfair, Survey of London, Part I, 1977, Part II, 1980.
Roderick Gradidge, *Dream Houses*, 1980.
Simon Blow, 'Blow by Blow Account of a Duke's Desertion' in *The Spectator*, 25 January 1986, p. 22.

George Frederick Bodley (1827–1907)

Born in Hull in Yorkshire, Bodley was an early pupil of George Gilbert Scott, against whose work he reacted in his first buildings. In his early churches Bodley showed himself to be one of the most original exponents of vigorous High Victorian Gothic, but after the late 1860s his work became more English, more refined and more subtle in character. This may well have been due to the influence of another Scott pupil, Thomas Garner (1839–1906), with whom he was in partnership from 1869 until 1897. Bodley was the most accomplished church architect of the late Victorian decades, his work including St John's, Tue Brook, Liverpool (1869), St Augustine's, Pendlebury, Lancashire (1870–4), the Church of the Holy Angels, Hoar Cross, Staffordshire (1872–6). He did little domestic work but some early houses were pioneering essays in the 'Queen Anne'

233

manner. Garner independently designed Hewell Grange, Worcestershire (1884–91). See also Plates pp. 64–7, 179.

F. M. Simpson, 'George Frederick Bodley', *Journal of the RIBA*, xv, 1908, pp. 145–58.
Edward Warren, 'The Life and Work of George Frederick Bodley', *Journal of the RIBA*, xvii, 1910, pp. 305–40.
John Brandon-Jones, 'Letters of Philip Webb and his Contemporaries', in *Architectural History*, viii, 1965.
David Verey, 'George Frederick Bodley: Climax of the Gothic Revival', in *Seven Victorian Architects*, ed. Jane Fawcett, 1976.

Cecil Claude Brewer (1871–1918)

Cecil Brewer was born in London and studied at the atelier run by F. T. Baggalay and Walter Millard; he was then articled to Baggalay. While working for Robert Weir Schultz in 1895 Brewer, together with A. Dunbar Smith (q.v.), won the competition for the Passmore Edwards Settlement in Tavistock Place, London. Most of Smith and Brewer's early work was domestic but after winning the competition for the National Museum of Wales in 1909 they became established as Classicists and as architects of public buildings. See also Plates pp. 150–1.

Builder, 16 August 1918, p. 260.

Walter Henry Brierley (1862–1926)

Born in York and articled to his father, Walter Brierley inherited a practice in York founded by John Carr in the eighteenth century. The firm continues today as Brierley, Leckenby, Keighley and Groom. Brierley was the most important Edwardian architect in Yorkshire, designing both houses (Plates pp. 146–7) and churches. His work included the reconstructions of Sledmere Hall (1908) and Hackness Hall (1910) after fires.

Frederick Chatterton, ed., *Who's Who in Architecture*, 1923.

Ronald Alexander Briggs (1858–1916)

R. A. Briggs was born in Essex and articled to Gilbert R. Redgrave. He then worked for G. Moreing, Isaacs & Florence, E. C. Lee and J. J. O'Callaghan of Dublin before setting up in practice in 1884. Briggs published *Bungalows and Country Residences* (1891 etc.), *Homes in the Country* and *The Essentials of a Country House*. He was principally a domestic architect and his work included The Old Mill at Aldeburgh, Suffolk (c. 1903), and four houses at Bellagio (Dormans Park), East Grinstead, Sussex. He also designed a number of hotels. See also Plates pp. 92–3.

Who's Who in Architecture, 1914.
Journal of the RIBA, 20 May 1916.

William Butterfield (1814–1900)

Born in London and in independent practice in 1840, Butterfield became closely involved with the Cambridge Camden Society and the Catholic revival within the Church of England. His work was largely ecclesiastical and he was the first to free the Gothic Revival from historical precedent by the use of structural polychromy and bold geometrical forms, notably in the Church of All Saints, Margaret Street, London (1849–59). Other notable churches included St Alban's, Holborn, London (1859–62) and All Saints, Babbacombe, Devon (1865–74). His influential domestic work consisted principally of vicarages, schools and cottages; his only large-scale house was Milton Ernest Hall, Bedfordshire (1853–6). He was the architect of Keble College, Oxford (1866–86). See also Plates pp. 54–5.

John Summerson, 'William Butterfield, or the Glory of Ugliness', in *Heavenly Mansions*, 1949.
Mark Girouard, *The Victorian Country House*, 1971.
Paul Thompson, *William Butterfield*, 1971.
Stefan Muthesius, *The High Victorian Movement in Architecture, 1850–1870*, 1972.

William Douglas Caroë (1857–1938)

Born in Liverpool where his father was Danish consul, W. D. Caroë was educated at Cambridge before being articled to the church architect J. L. Pearson. In partnership with Herbert Passmore for some years, Caroë's practice was largely ecclesiastical. He was architect to the Ecclesiastical Commissioners and consulting architect to a number of cathedrals, including Canterbury, Durham and Southwell. His domestic work included houses for Wycombe Abbey School, Marlow Hill, High Wycombe, Buckinghamshire (1898–1902), and Coleherne Court, Old Brompton Road, London (1901–3). See also Plates pp. 110–13.

Walter Frederick Cave (1863–1939)

The son of Sir Charles Daniel Cave, Bart., of Sidmouth, Walter Cave was articled to Sir Arthur Blomfield. He set up in practice in 1886. Most of his work was domestic and included Ewelme Down, Oxfordshire, Littlecourt, Northamptonshire, and The Wharf, Sutton Courtenay. In London he designed the Union Jack Club in Waterloo Road (1907). He was also architect to the Whiteley Homes. See also Plates pp. 134–5.

Builder, 13 January 1939, p. 116.

Basil Champneys (1842–1935)

Basil Champneys was born in London, the son of a clergyman, and was articled to the church architect, John Prichard of Llandaff. He set up in practice in 1867. Although he designed a number of churches, he was most successful at educational buildings in which he handled the 'Queen Anne' style with particular sympathy. He was the architect of Newnham College, Cambridge (1875 etc.), which was deliberately domestic in scale and style. Later he designed the Rylands Library, Manchester (1890–9) in a refined Gothic manner. See also Plate p. 211.

Reginald Blomfield, 'Basil Champneys', *Journal of the RIBA*, xlii, 1934–5, pp. 737–8.
Mark Girouard, *Sweetness and Light: The 'Queen Anne' Movement 1860–1900*, 1977.

Thomas Edward Collcutt (1840–1924)

T. E. Collcutt was a pupil of G. E. Street and, before establishing his reputation by winning the competition for Wakefield town hall, Yorkshire, in 1877, designed 'art furniture' for the firm of Collinson and Lock. His architecture was usually in an eclectic 'Queen Anne' manner, often employing terracotta. Most of his work consisted of public and commercial buildings. These included the Imperial Institute, South Kensington, London (1887–93), the Royal English Opera House, Cambridge Circus, London (1888–90), the Bechstein (now Wigmore) Hall, London (1890–1900), and Lloyd's Registry, Fenchurch Street, London (1903–4). See also Plates pp. 82–3 and Plan 2, p. 36.

Mark Girouard, *Sweetness and Light: The 'Queen Anne' Movement 1860–1900*, 1977.
Juliet Kinchin, 'Collinson & Lock – Manufacturers of Artistic Furniture', *Connoisseur*, cci, May 1979, pp. 46–53.

Sir Guy Dawber (1861–1938)

E. Guy Dawber was born in King's Lynn, Norfolk, and articled to Sir Thomas Deane in Dublin before working for Sir Ernest George & Peto. After 1887 when his eyesight became impaired, obliging him to leave London, Dawber acted as clerk of works at Batsford Park for George and made a study of Cotswold vernacular architecture. In 1891 he moved his practice from Bourton-on-the-Hill, Gloucestershire, back to London. Most of Dawber's work was domestic and included Swinbrook House, Oxfordshire, Stowell Court, Somerset (1925), and Tuesley Court, Godalming, Surrey (1928). See also Colour Plate L and Plates pp. 164–5.

C. H. Reilly, *Representative British Architects of the Present Day*, 1931.

George Devey (1820–86)

Born in London, Devey studied painting under J. S. Cotman and J. D. Harding and trained as an architect under Thomas Little. Exclusively a domestic architect, he designed large houses, usually in an Elizabethan manner, and convincingly picturesque small cottages, lodges and farm buildings. Works include cottages at Penshurst, Kent (1850–60), Wendover Manor, Buckinghamshire (1871–3), Denne Hill, Kent (1871–5), St Alban's Court, Kent (1874–8). See also Plates pp. 50–1.

W. H. Godfrey, 'George Devey FRIBA: A Biographical Essay', *Journal of the RIBA*, xii, 1906, pp. 501–25.

W. H. Godfrey, 'The Work of George Devey', *Architectural Review*, xxl, 1907, pp. 23–30, 83–8, 293–306.

Mark Girouard, *The Victorian Country House*, 1971, 1979.

John Douglas (1829–1911)

John Douglas was a pupil of the Lancaster church architect E. G. Paley and he worked almost exclusively in Cheshire. His early buildings are Gothic, often with a French character, but he soon became one of the principal exponents of the revival of the black and white half-timbered architecture of the county. Douglas did much work for the Duke of Westminster on the Eaton Hall estate (Plate p. 85). Other houses included Oakmere Hall (1868–70), and Dee Banks, Chester, built for himself (1896–7). See also Plates pp. 84–6.

Nikolaus Pevsner and Edward Hubbard, *The Buildings of England: Cheshire*, 1971.

William Flockhart (1854–1913)

William Flockhart was born in Glasgow and articled to the Glasgow architects Adamson and McLeod in 1870–5. He then worked for Campbell Douglas and Sellars in Glasgow and for James W. Wallace in London in 1879–81, with whom he was briefly in partnership. He set up on his own in London in 1881 and designed many buildings in Bond Street, Hill Street and elsewhere in Mayfair as well as large houses in Scotland. He also designed the interiors of the liner *Balmoral Castle*. See also Plate p. 189.

Builder, 18 April 1913.

Alan Powers, ed., '"Architects I have known": The Architectural career of S. D. Adshead', in *Architectural History*, xxiv, 1981, p. 113.

Sir Ernest George (1839–1922)

Ernest George was articled to the London architect, Samuel Hewitt, and studied at the Royal Academy Schools. He set up in practice first with Thomas Vaughan, from 1861 until 1871, and then in partnership with Harold Peto, a garden designer and member of the family of contractors, 1876–90, and finally with Alfred Yates, 1893–1919. George was principally a domestic architect, adapting northern European, early Renaissance sources with extreme picturesqueness. In the 1880s he was a serious rival to Norman Shaw and several of the most talented architects of the next generation trained in his office. His houses included Batsford Park, Gloucestershire (1888–92) and many town houses on the Grosvenor Estate in Mayfair, London. He was also the architect of Claridge's Hotel, London (1894–7) and the Ossington Coffee Tavern, Newark-on-Trent, Nottinghamshire (1882). See also Colour Plates E and N and Plates pp. 76–9, 176–7.

Architects' Journal, lvi, 1922, pp. 855–60.

Andrew Saint, *Richard Norman Shaw*, 1976.

Roderick Gradidge, *Dream Houses*, 1980.

Ernest William Gimson (1864–1919)

Ernest Gimson was the son of a Leicester engineer. He was advised by William Morris to train as an architect in the office of J. D. Sedding, where he met the Barnsley brothers, Ernest and Sydney. All three had a great interest in the craft side of architecture and in 1894 they left London for Pinbury in the Cotswolds, where a workshop for making furniture was established. In 1901 this was moved to Daneway House nearby. Apart from small houses and cottages in Leicestershire (Plates pp. 128–9) and the Cotswolds, Gimson's principal work was the Hall at Bedales School, Hampshire (1910).

W. R. Lethaby and others, *Ernest Gimson: His Life and Work*, 1924.

Leicester Museums and Art Gallery catalogue, *Ernest Gimson*, 1969.

Annette Carruthers, *Ernest Gimson and the Cotswold Group of Craftsmen*, Leicester Museums Publication, 1978.

Mary Comino, *Gimson and the Barnsleys*, 1980.

Roderick Gradidge, *Dream Houses*, 1980.

Edward William Godwin (1833–86)

E. W. Godwin was born in Bristol and was articled to William Armstrong, the city's engineer. He set up in practice in 1853 in Bristol and moved to London in 1865, following his winning of the competition for Northampton Town Hall (1861). Godwin's early work was Gothic, strongly influenced by that of William Burges. Later he became identified with the Aesthetic movement in his designs for furniture. His domestic work included several houses in the Tite Street–Chelsea Embankment area of London (1877–82, Plate p. 187), and the first houses in Bedford Park, Chiswick (1876, Plate p. 206 (*left*)). He also designed Dromore Castle, Ireland (1867–70) and Beauvale Lodge, Nottinghamshire (1871–4).

Dudley Harbron, *The Conscious Stone: The Life of Edward William Godwin*, 1949.
Elizabeth Aslin, *The Aesthetic Movement: Prelude to Art Nouveau*, 1969.
Mark Girouard, *The Victorian Country House*, 1971, 1979.
John O'Callaghan, *The Fine Art Society and E. W. Godwin*, 1976.
Mark Girouard, *Sweetness and Light: The 'Queen Anne' Movement 1860–1900*, 1977.
T. Affleck Greeves, *Bedford Park: The First Garden Suburb*, 1975.

Sir Thomas Graham Jackson (1835–1924)

T. G. Jackson was born in Hampstead and educated at Brighton and at Wadham College, Oxford. He was articled to Sir Gilbert Scott in 1858 and set up in practice in 1862. In his Examination Schools at Oxford (1877), Jackson produced an eclectic Elizabethan style as an alternative to Gothic which became highly influential in the universities. Most of Jackson's work was ecclesiastical or school and university buildings. He was also the author of many books on architecture, notably *Modern Gothic Architecture* (1873) and *Byzantine and Romanesque Architecture* (1913). See also Plates pp. 184–5.

Basil H. Jackson, ed., *The Recollections of Sir Thomas Graham Jackson*, 1950.

Sydney Decimus Kitson (1871–1937)

S. D. Kitson was the son of the Leeds engineering magnate James Kitson, later Lord Airedale. He trained with E. J. May and with W. D. Caroë before setting up in practice in Leeds. He was in partnership with F. W. Bedford (q.v.). See also Plates pp. 216–17.

William Richard Lethaby (1857–1931)

W. R. Lethaby was born in Devon and was articled to a local architect before becoming Norman Shaw's chief assistant in 1879. He was in independent practice after 1889 but built comparatively little, his great influence within the Arts and Crafts movement coming from his teaching and writing. He was a founder of the Art Workers' Guild in 1884 and of the Design and Industries Association in 1915. He was a leading member of the Society for the Protection of Ancient Buildings and was surveyor to Westminster Abbey between 1906 and 1927. Lethaby designed a number of houses but his most impressive work is All Saints Church at Brockhampton, Herefordshire (1901–2). He wrote several books on architecture and architectural history and was the biographer of Philip Webb. See also Plates pp. 90–1.

Reginald Blomfield, 'W. R. Lethaby: An Impression and a Tribute', *Journal of the RIBA*, xxxix, 1932, pp. 293–313.
John Brandon-Jones, 'W. R. Lethaby, 1857–1931', *Architectural Association Journal*, lxiv, 1949, pp. 194–7.
Robert Macleod, *Style and Society*, 1971.
Godfrey Rubens, 'William Lethaby's Buildings', in Alastair Service, ed., *Edwardian Architecture and its Origins*, 1975.
Sylvia Backmeyer and Theresa Gronberg, eds., *W. R. Lethaby 1857–1931. Architecture, Design and Education*, 1984.
Godfrey Rubens, *William Richard Lethaby and his Work*, (forthcoming).

Sir Robert Stodart Lorimer (1864–1929)

Robert Lorimer was born in Edinburgh, where he first trained with Sir Robert Rowand Anderson before going to London to work for G. F. Bodley. He returned to Scotland in 1892 and set up in practice in Edinburgh. Lorimer specialised in the restoration of old Scottish houses and the building of new ones. He was also an influential garden designer. After the First World War he acted as one of the principal architects to the Imperial War Graves Commission and designed the Scottish National War Memorial in Edinburgh Castle. His houses include Earlshall, Fife, Scotland (1892), Rowallan, Ayrshire, Scotland (1902), Barton Hartshorn, Buckinghamshire (1902–8), and High Barn, Hascombe, Surrey (1901–3). See also Colour Plate F and Plates pp. 106–7.

Christopher Hussey, *The Work of Sir Robert Lorimer*, 1931.
Peter Savage, *Lorimer and the Edinburgh Craft Designers*, 1980.

Sir Edwin Landseer Lutyens (1869–1944)

Lutyens was born in Surrey and worked for a short time in the office of Ernest George and Peto before setting up on his own at the age of twenty. Following his meeting with the landscape gardener, Gertrude Jekyll, and the building of Munstead Wood (Plates pp. 94–5), Lutyens built a series of brilliant houses in the 1890s in the English vernacular tradition which established his reputation. In the first years of the new century he took up the Renaissance manner in which he designed both houses and offices for the magazine *Country Life* (1905). His involvement in the 'High Game' of Classicism culminated in his selection as architect for the city of New Delhi in 1912. In 1917 he became one of the principal architects of the Imperial War Graves Commission and in the 1920s much of his work consisted of designing war cemeteries and memorials, notably the Memorial to the Missing of the Somme at Thiepval, France (1928–9) and the Cenotaph, London (1919–20). At the same time he was designing large commercial buildings such as the headquarters of the Midland Bank in London (1924–39). His design for the Roman Catholic Cathedral in Liverpool (1933) remained largely unexecuted. Lutyens's houses include Orchards, Godalming, Surrey (1897–9), Tigbourne Court, Surrey (1899–1901), Grey Walls, Gullane, Scotland (1900–1), Marshcourt, Hampshire (1901–4) and Castle Drogo, Devon (1910–32). See also Colour Plate M, Plates pp. 34, 97–101, 168–9, 226–7, and Plan 7, p. 37.

Lawrence Weaver, *Houses and Gardens by Edwin Lutyens*, 1913, 1981.
Christopher Hussey, *The Life of Sir Edwin Lutyens*, 1950, 1984.
A. S. G. Butler, *The Architecture of Sir Edwin Lutyens*, 3 vols., 1950, 1984.
Peter Inskip, *Edwin Lutyens*, 1979.
Daniel O'Neill, *Edwin Lutyens: Country Houses*, 1980.
Roderick Gradidge, *Edwin Lutyens: Architect Laureate*, 1981.
Mary Lutyens, *Edwin Lutyens: A Memoir by his Daughter*, 1980.
Lutyens. The Work of the English Architect Sir Edwin Lutyens (1869–1944), Arts Council of Great Britain exhibition catalogue, 1981.

Sir Mervyn Edmund Macartney (1853–1932)

Mervyn Macartney was born in Ireland and educated at Lincoln College, Oxford, before being articled to Norman Shaw. He was a founder of the Art Workers' Guild but had a particular affection for the architecture of the English Renaissance. He was the author of *English Houses and Gardens in the 17th and 18th Centuries* (1908) and, with John Belcher, of *Later Renaissance Architecture in England* (1901). He was editor of the *Architectural Review* in 1905–20 and surveyor to the fabric of St Paul's Cathedral, 1906–31. His domestic work included No. 167 Queen's Gate, London (1889), Bussock Wood, Winterbourne, Berkshire (1907), and The Court, Woolhampton, Berkshire. See also Plates pp. 160–1.

Andrew Saint, *Richard Norman Shaw*, 1976.

Charles Rennie Mackintosh (1868–1928)

C. R. Mackintosh was born in Glasgow and articled to John Hutchison. In 1889 he joined the firm of Honeyman and Keppie, under whose name many of his designs were executed. In 1904 the firm became Honeyman, Keppie and Mackintosh. One of the most remarkable designers of the turn of the century, Mackintosh designed the Glasgow School of Art. His domestic work in Scotland included Windyhill, Kilmacolm (1899–1901), and Hous'hill, Nitshill (1903–10). Mackintosh left Scotland for London in 1914, his only English works being a studio in Glebe Place, Chelsea (1920), the interior of No. 78 Derngate, Northampton (1916–20) for W. J. Bassett-Lowke, and additions to a cottage at Little Hedgecourt, East Grinstead, for the photographer E. O. Hoppé (c. 1920). See also Colour Plate J and Plate p. 139.

Thomas Howarth, *Charles Rennie Mackintosh and the Modern Movement*, 1953, 1977.
Robert MacLeod, *Charles Rennie Mackintosh*, 1968.
Roger Billicliffe, *Charles Rennie Mackintosh, Furniture and Interiors*, 1979.

Arthur Heygate Mackmurdo (1851–1942)

A. H. Mackmurdo was articled to T. Chatfield Clark of London and then worked for the church architect James Brooks. His remarkable talent as a designer was announced by the title page of his book *Wren's City Churches* (1883). Mackmurdo founded the Century Guild in 1882 and was an important figure in the Arts and Crafts movement. From 1882 until 1890 he was in partnership with Herbert P. Horne; in the 1890s he worked with George Hornblower and E. S. Walters. His domestic work included No. 6 and No. 8 Private Road, Enfield (1872–6 and 1886–7), No. 12 Hans Road, London (1891) and his own house, Great Ruffins House, Wickham Bishops, Essex (c. 1904). See also Plates pp. 192–3.

Nikolaus Pevsner, 'Arthur H. Mackmurdo', in *Studies in Art, Architecture and Design*, vol. ii, 1968.
Edward Pond, 'Mackmurdo Gleanings', in James Richards and Nikolaus Pevsner, eds., *The Anti-Rationalists*, 1973.
John Doubleday and others, *The Eccentric A. H. Mackmurdo, 1851–1942*, exhibition catalogue, Colchester, 1979.

James Marjoribanks MacLaren (1843–90)

James MacLaren was born in Stirling, Scotland and, after completing a Beaux Arts training in Paris, was articled to the Glasgow architects Campbell Douglas. After working briefly for E. W. Godwin, MacLaren set up in practice in 1886. Most of his work was in Scotland, notably the Stirling High School (1887–8), and in Perthshire for his patron, Donald Currie of Glenyon Glenlyon (1889–90). Despite his early death, MacLaren's work had great influence on architects like C. F. A. Voysey and C. R. Mackintosh. See also Plates pp. 190–1.

H. S. Goodhart-Rendel, 'Rogue Architects of the Victorian Era', *Journal of the RIBA*, 1949, p. 258.
Duncan McAra, 'An Architect for Connoisseurs', *The Scottish Art Review*, xii, no. 4, 1970.
Alastair Service, 'James MacLaren and the Godwin Legacy', *Architectural Review*, cliv, 1973, pp. 111–18.
Alastair Service, ed., *Edwardian Architecture and its Origins*, 1975.

Charles Edward Mallows (1864–1915)

Charles Mallows was born in Bedford and was articled to the Bedford architect F. T. Mercer in 1879. Subsequently he worked for H. H. Bridgeman, Salamans and Wornum and for Wallace and Flockhart. He set up in practice in 1886 at first with F. W. Lacey. Subsequently he worked with the Bedford architect G. Grocock. His talents as a draughtsman were in great demand and he often worked with other architects on different projects, including Russell, Cooper and Davis, A. W. S. Cross, and T. H. Mawson, the landscape architect. See Colour Plate K and Plates pp. 144–5.

Builder, 11 June 1915.
Journal of the RIBA, 1915, p. 417.

Edward Brantwood Maufe (1883–1974)

Edward Maufe, born Muff, was educated at St John's College, Oxford, before being articled to W. A. Pite. He was principally a church architect, winning the competition of Guildford Cathedral in 1932. His houses included Yaffle Hill, Broadstone, Dorset (1929), and Shepherd's Hill, Buxted, Sussex (1926), which he altered and enlarged for himself. See also Plates pp. 126–7.

Architects' Journal, clxi, 1975, pp. 67–8.

Edward John May (1853–1941)

E. J. May was the last pupil of Decimus Burton. He worked for W. E. Nesfield and for Norman Shaw and set up in practice in 1881. He built a number of houses in Bedford Park (Plates pp. 207 (*left*), 208–9), where he lived, and also designed Ballindune, Haslemere, Surrey (1905), and the Waifs and Strays Home at Pyrford, Surrey (1907).

Frederick Chatterton, ed., *Who's Who in Architecture*, 1923.
Andrew Saint, *Richard Norman Shaw*, 1976.

Short Biographies of the Architects

Arnold Bidlake Mitchell (1863–1944)

Arnold Mitchell was a pupil of Ernest George and Peto and set up in practice in 1886. He had a large practice, building many houses in Harrow, Middlesex, including his own house, The Orchard (1900). He was the architect of Old Walls, Milford-on-Sea, Lymington, Hampshire, built for Siemens (1897), and he also worked abroad, in Ostend for the King of the Belgians and in Argentina where he designed railway stations. He invented Lott's Bricks, the building toy for children. He retired to Lyme Regis, Dorset, in the 1920s where he built himself a house facing the sea. See also Plates pp. 166–7.

Architect and Building News, 10 November 1944, p. 89.
Builder, 10 November 1944, p. 375.

John Nash (1752–1835)

Born in London and apprenticed to Sir Robert Taylor, Nash set up in London in 1774 but went bankrupt in 1783 and retreated to Wales. He returned to London in 1798. Best known as the planner and architect of Regent's Park and Regent Street and architect to George IV at Buckingham Palace (1824–30) and the Brighton Pavilion (1815–21), Nash also had a large country-house practice. His houses included Luscombe, Devonshire (1800–4), Killymoon, Ireland (1801–3), Lough Cutra, Ireland (1811), Cronkhill, Shropshire (1802), Sandridge Park, Devonshire (1805), Southgate Grove, Middlesex (1797). See also Plates pp. 46–7.

Terence Davis, *John Nash, the Prince Regent's Architect*, 1966.
Nigel Temple, *John Nash and the Village Picturesque*, 1979.
John Summerson, *The Life and Work of John Nash*, 1980.

William Eden Nesfield (1835–88)

Nesfield was the son of the landscape gardener, William A. Nesfield, to whose friend, the architect William Burn, he was articled. He then worked for Anthony Salvin. After Continental travel, Nesfield set up practice in 1863 with Norman Shaw, whom he had met in Burn's office and with whom he was in formal partnership between 1866 and 1869. Nesfield, with Shaw, created the 'Old English' and 'Queen Anne' styles but in the 1870s the two drew apart. Before his premature retirement in 1880, Nesfield was principally a domestic architect but, owing to both diffidence and personal circumstances, he built comparatively little. His houses included Cloverley Hall, Shropshire (1866–74), Kinmel Park, Wales (1866), Bodrhyddan, Wales (1872–4). He also designed the lodge at Kew Gardens (1867, Plate p. 18). See also Plates pp. 33, 69.

J. M. Brydon, 'William Eden Nesfield', *Architectural Review*, i, pp. 235–47 and 283–95, 1897, reprinted in Alastair Service, ed., *Edwardian Architecture and its Origins*, 1975.
H. B. Creswell, 'William Eden Nesfield, 1835–1888: An Impression and a Contrast', *Architectural Review*, ii, 1897, pp. 23–32.
Andrew Saint, *Richard Norman Shaw*, 1976.
Clive Aslet, 'The Country Houses of W. E. Nesfield', *Country Life*, 16 and 23 March 1978, pp. 678–81 and 766–9.

Ernest Newton (1856–1922)

Newton was born in London and was articled to Norman Shaw, whose chief assistant he became. He set up in practice in 1879. Along with other Shaw pupils, Newton founded the Art Workers' Guild in 1884. He was primarily a domestic architect, interpreting English vernacular traditions in a reticent, solid manner. Newton published several books of his work: *Sketches for Country Residences* (1883); *A Book of Houses* (1890), and *A Book of Country Houses* (1903). His houses included Redcourt, Haslemere, Surrey (1894–5, Plates pp. 158–9 and Plan 3, p. 36), Steep Hill, Jersey, Channel Islands (1899–1900) and Luckley, Wokingham, Berkshire (1907). See also Plates pp. 88–9.

W. G. Newton, *The Work of Ernest Newton, RA*, 1925.
Roderick Gradidge, *Dream Houses*, 1980.
Richard Morrice, 'Ernest Newton, 1856–1922. Grace Without Style', in Roderick Brown, ed., *The Architectural Outsiders*, 1985.

Barry Parker (1867–1947)

Barry Parker was born in Chesterfield, Derbyshire, and was articled to G. Faulkner Armitage of Manchester. He set up in practice in 1896 in Buxton, Derbyshire, where he was joined the following year by his second cousin and brother-in-law Raymond Unwin (q.v.). Both Parker and Unwin were Christian Socialists with a deep commitment to town planning and the garden city movement. They prepared plans for New Earswick, York (1901), Letchworth Garden City (1903, Colour Plate P and Plates pp. 219–21) and for Hampstead Garden Suburb (1905–7, Plates pp. 226–7), in each of which they designed small-scale housing. In 1901 Parker and Unwin published *The Art of Building a Home*. In 1906 the Buxton office was closed; Parker moved to Letchworth, Unwin to Hampstead. The partnership was formally dissolved in 1914.

Walter Creese, 'Parker and Unwin: Architects of Totality', *Journal of the Society of Architectural Historians*, xxii, 1963, pp. 161–70.
Walter Creese, *The Search for Environment: The Garden City Before and After*, 1966.
Dean Hawkes, 'The Architectural Partnership of Barry Parker and Raymond Unwin: 1896–1914', *Architectural Review*, clxiii, 1978, pp. 327–32.
Dean Hawkes and Nicholas Taylor, *Barry Parker and Raymond Unwin, Architects*, 1978.
Mark Swenarton, *Homes fit for Heroes*, 1981.

Andrew Noble Prentice (1866–1941)

Andrew Prentice was born in Scotland and articled to William Leiper of Glasgow before coming to London to work for T. E. Collcutt. In 1893 he published *Renaissance Architecture and Ornament in Spain*. Prentice's work was largely domestic and included Chapelwood Manor, Sussex (1905), Stinsgot Manor, Lincolnshire (1911), and Notgrove Manor, Gloucestershire (1908), as well as several houses in Broadway, Worcestershire. He also designed interiors for steamships. See also Plates pp. 35, 154–5.

Frederick Chatterton, ed., *Who's Who in Architecture*, 1923.

Edward Schroeder Prior (1852–1932)

E. S. Prior was educated at Harrow School and Cambridge before entering the office of Norman Shaw. He was a founder of the Art Workers' Guild and secretary of the Arts and Crafts Exhibition Society from 1902 until 1917. His work was characterised by a degree of eccentricity and by the careful use of materials. He was the author of several books on medieval architecture, notably *A History of Gothic Art in England* (1900), and was Slade Professor of Fine Art in Cambridge from 1912 until his death. He built at Harrow School and Winchester College and his St Andrew's, Roker, Sunderland, Co. Durham (1906–7) was one of the finest Arts and Crafts churches. See also Colour Plate H and Plates pp. 120–5.

Christophe Grillet, 'Edward Prior', in Alastair Service, ed., *Edwardian Architecture and its Origins*, 1976.
Geoffrey Hoare and Geoffrey Pyne, *Prior's Barn and Gimson's Coxen*, 1978.

Augustus Welby Northmore Pugin (1812–52)

The son of the French émigré architectural draughtsman, Augustus Charles Pugin, who worked for John Nash, Pugin was born in London and first established himself as a stage designer, furniture designer and draughtsman before taking up architecture. He became a fanatical apostle of the Gothic Revival, which he justified on both moral and functional grounds, through a stream of books, notably *Contrasts* (1836), *The True Principles of Pointed or Christian Architecture* (1841) and *The Present State of Ecclesiastical Architecture in England* (1843). Apart from his collaboration with Charles Barry on the new Palace of Westminster, most of his architectural work consisted of Roman Catholic churches. His simplified Gothic domestic work was also influential, notably the Bishop's House at Birmingham (1839–41, Plates p. 23) and two houses for himself: St Marie's Grange near

Salisbury (1835–6) and The Grange, Ramsgate, Kent (1843–4). See also Plates pp. 19, 53.

Benjamin Ferrey, *Recollections of A. N. Welby Pugin and his Father, Augustus Pugin*, 1861.
Kenneth Clark, *The Gothic Revival*, 1928.
Michael Trappes-Lomax, *Pugin: A Mediaeval Victorian*, 1932.
Phoebe B. Stanton, *Pugin*, 1971.
Alexandra Wedgwood, *A. W. N. Pugin and the Pugin Family* (Catalogues of Architectural Drawings in the Victoria and Albert Museum), 1985.

Halsey Ralph Ricardo (1854–1928)

Halsey Ricardo was educated at Rugby School and worked for Basil Champneys. He became particularly interested in the use of washable coloured external materials in urban buildings and published 'Colour in the Architecture of Cities' in *Art and Life, and the Building and Decoration of Cities*, a series of lectures by members of the Arts and Crafts Exhibition Society in 1896. He also wrote about William Butterfield in the *Architectural Review* in 1900. Ricardo was for a time in partnership with the potter William de Morgan. He was the architect of the Howrah Railway Station in Calcutta (1900–8). His domestic work included his own house, Woodside, Graffam (1905). See also Colour Plate O and Plates pp. 198–9.

H. S. Goodhart-Rendel, 'The Work of Beresford Pite and Halsey Ricardo', *Journal of the RIBA*, xliii, 1935, p. 118.

Anthony Salvin (1799–1881)

Born in Worthing, Anthony Salvin trained in Edinburgh and possibly worked for John Nash. He was primarily a country-house architect, usually working in the Tudor and Elizabethan styles. His works include Harlaxton Manor, Lincolnshire (1831–8), Mamhead, Devon (1826–38), Peckforton Castle, Cheshire (1844–50), Thoresby Hall, Nottinghamshire (1864–75). See also Colour Plate A and Plates pp. 48–9.

Obituary in the *Builder*, xl, 1881, pp. 809–10.
Christopher Hussey, *English Country Houses: Late Georgian 1800–1840*, 1958, 1984.
Mark Girouard, *The Victorian Country House*, 1971, 1979.

Robert Weir Schultz (1860–1951)

Robert Weir Schultz was born in Scotland and articled to Robert Rowand Anderson in Edinburgh before going to London in 1884 to work in the office of Norman Shaw. Between 1887 and 1891 he travelled in the Near East and Greece, partly with Sydney Barnsley, and became an authority on Byzantine architecture. A close friend of W. R. Lethaby, Schultz was strongly influenced by Arts and Crafts ideals. Much of his work was carried out for the 3rd and 4th Marquesses of Bute. In 1915 he changed his name to R. W. S. Weir. His houses include West Green House, Hartley Wintney, Hampshire (1899–1900), and Pickenham Hall, Norfolk (1903–5). See also Plates pp. 114–17 and Plan 6, p. 37.

David Ottewill, 'Robert Weir Schultz: An Arts and Crafts Architect', in *Architectural History*, xxii, 1979.
Gavin Stamp, *Robert Weir Schultz, Architect, and his Work for the Marquesses of Bute*, 1981.

Adrian Gilbert Scott (1882–1963)

Adrian Gilbert Scott was the younger brother of Giles Gilbert Scott (q.v.). Articled to Temple Moore and strongly influenced by his brother, most of his work was for the Roman Catholic Church. His domestic work included cottages in Bushey, Hertfordshire (1907), and his own house, Shepherd's Well, Frognal, Hampstead, London (1930). See also Plates pp. 156–7.

George Gilbert Scott, Junior (1839–97)

Scott was the eldest son of Sir Gilbert Scott, the leading mid-Victorian Gothicist, in whose office he trained. He reacted against his father by designing in late Gothic styles in his church of St Agnes, Kennington, London (1874–91) and by adopting the 'Queen Anne' style in a handful of vicarages and houses (Plate p. 27). These included Garboldisham Manor, Norfolk (1868–74), St Mark's Vicarage, Leamington, Warwickshire (1873–6), Pevensey Vicarage, Sussex (1876–9), and houses in Park Street, Hull, Yorkshire (1876–7, Plate p. 27).

Scott became a Roman Catholic and died insane in the Midland Grand Hotel at St Pancras Station. See also Plates pp. 80–1.

Walter Millard, 'Notes on Some Works of the Late George Gilbert Scott, MA, FSA', *Architectural Review*, v, 1898–9, pp. 58–67 and 124–32.
Francis A. Bown, 'The Ideals of George Gilbert Scott Junior', *Leicester Cathedral Quarterly*, viii, 1972, pp. 8–12.
Geoffrey Fisher, Gavin Stamp and others, *Catalogue of the Drawings Collection of the Royal Institute of British Architects: The Scott Family*, 1981.

Sir Giles Gilbert Scott (1880–1960)

Giles Gilbert Scott was the son of George Gilbert Scott junior and was articled to his father's pupil, Temple Moore. In 1903 he won the competition for the Anglican Cathedral in Liverpool. At first his work was largely ecclesiastical but in the 1920s and 1930s he designed a wider range of building types including Cambridge University Library (1930–4), Battersea Power Station, London (1929–33), and the standard GPO telephone kiosk (1924 and 1935). His small domestic practice included No. 129 Grosvenor Road, London (with Adrian Scott, 1913–15), and his own house, Chester House, Clarendon Place, London (1924–5). See also Plates pp. 26, 156–7.

Geoffrey Fisher, Gavin Stamp and others, *Catalogue of the Drawings Collection of the Royal Institute of British Architects: The Scott Family*, 1981.

John Dando Sedding (1838–91)

J. D. Sedding was born at Eton and articled to G. E. Street. He practised first in Cornwall with his brother Edmund Sedding, who died in 1868. He then moved to Bristol and in 1874 to London. Sedding's work was largely ecclesiastical. His Holy Trinity Church, Sloane Street, London (1888–90) showed the application of Arts and Crafts ideals to church design executed by many artists and craftsmen. He designed few houses but became interested in garden design, publishing *Gardencraft Old and New* in 1891. After his comparatively early death, his projects were completed by Henry Wilson. See also Plates pp. 24, 180–1.

Henry Wilson and others, *A Memorial to the Late J. D. Sedding*, 1892.
J. P. Cooper, 'The Work of John D. Sedding', *Architectural Review*, i, 1897, reprinted in Alastair Service, ed., *Edwardian Architecture and its Origins*, 1975.

Richard Norman Shaw (1831–1912)

Norman Shaw was born in Edinburgh and, like his friend and sometime partner, W. E. Nesfield, trained with both William Burn and Anthony Salvin. Shaw began practice in 1862 as a Gothicist but he soon, with Nesfield, invented the 'Queen Anne' and 'Old English' styles and became renowned as a domestic architect of great versatility and enterprise. He was the most representative late Victorian architect, his work reflecting the changing styles and aspirations of the period. In his one complete public building, New Scotland Yard, London, for the Metropolitan Police (1887–90), a picturesque manner was mixed with a more formal Classicism and in the 1890s Shaw became a pioneer of revived Renaissance Classicism. His last works, such as the Piccadilly Hotel, London (1905–8), are full-blown Edwardian Baroque. His houses include Glen Andred, Sussex (1866–8), Cragside, Northumberland (1870–4), Swan House, Chelsea, London (1876–80), Adcote, Shropshire (1876–80), Bryanston, Dorset (1889–94, Plate p. 41). See also Colour Plate C, Plates pp. 70–3, 174–5, 205, 207 (*right*) and Plan 1, p. 36.

Reginald Blomfield, *Richard Norman Shaw, RA, Architect. 1831–1912*, 1940.
Nikolaus Pevsner, 'Richard Norman Shaw', in Peter Ferriday, ed., *Victorian Architecture*, 1963.
Andrew Saint, *Richard Norman Shaw*, 1976.

Arnold Dunbar Smith (1866–1933)

Dunbar Smith was articled to J. G. Gibbins of Brighton and then worked for Walter Millard in London when, presumably, he met his partner Cecil Brewer (q.v.). Smith and Brewer won the competition for the Passmore Edwards (now Mary Ward) Settlement in Tavistock Place in 1895. In 1909 they won the competition for the National Museum of Wales in Cardiff with a design in the American Beaux

Arts manner. In 1912 they designed the shop in Tottenham Court Road for Ambrose Heal. After Brewer's death, Smith designed the extensions to the Fitzwilliam Museum in Cambridge. Domestic work by Smith and Brewer included Rushymead, Coleshill, Buckinghamhire, and Ditton's Place, Balcombe, Sussex (1904). See also Plates pp. 150–1.

The Times, 11 December 1933.
Builder, 15 December 1933.

John James Stevenson (1831–1908)

J. J. Stevenson was born in Glasgow and articled to David Bryce before moving to London and working for Sir Gilbert Scott. He became an influential advocate of the 'Queen Anne' style of domestic architecture both in his own work and in his writings, notably the two volume *House Architecture* (1880). Between 1871 and 1876 Stevenson was in partnership with E. R. Robson working on designs for buildings for the London School Board. His houses included his own, Red House, Bayswater (1871–3), Munstead House, Godalming, Surrey (1878) and Ken Hill, Norfolk (1880). See also Plates p. 173.

F. W. Troup and Harry Redfern, 'The Late J. J. Stevenson, FSA', *Journal of the RIBA*, xv, 1907–8, pp. 482–3.
Mark Girouard, *The Victorian Country House*, 1971, 1979.
Mark Girouard, *Sweetness and Light: The 'Queen Anne' Movement 1860–1900*, 1977.

Leonard Aloysius Stokes (1858–1925)

Leonard Stokes was articled to S. J. Nichol in 1874 and then worked successively for G. E. Street, J. P. St Aubyn, T. E. Collcutt, and Bodley and Garner. He set up in practice in 1882 and specialised in work for the Roman Catholic Church. Stokes was a refined and sophisticated architect who applied his talents to such buildings as telephone exchanges as well as houses. His domestic work included All Saints Convent, London Colney, Hertfordshire (1900–1), North Court, Emmanuel College, Cambridge (1913–15), and Minterne Manor, Cerne

Abbas, Dorset (1904–7) for Lord Digby. See also Plates pp. 152–3, 203 and Plan 8, p. 37.

H. V. Molesworth Roberts, 'Leonard Aloysius Stokes', *Architectural Review*, c. 1946, pp. 173–7, reprinted in Alastair Service, ed., *Edwardian Architecture and its Origins*, 1975.

George Edmund Street (1824–81)

George Street was born in Essex and was a pupil of George Gilbert Scott in the 1840s before setting up in practice, first in Cornwall and then Berkshire and Oxford. He moved to London in 1856 and was soon established as one of the leading Gothic Revivalists. He was arguably the greatest High Victorian Gothicist, for his work demonstrated remarkable originality and formal strength. Street was strongly influenced by Italian Gothic and his buildings show an impressive attention to detail. His work was principally ecclesiastical and his churches include All Saints, Boyne Hill, Berkshire (1854–65), St James the Less, London (1859–66), St Philip and St James, Oxford (1858–65), All Saints, Denstone, Staffordshire (1860–2). In 1867 he won the commission for the new Royal Courts of Justice in the Strand in London, a job which preoccupied him throughout the 1870s. His domestic work consisted principally of vicarages and schools. St Margaret's Convent, East Grinstead, Sussex (1864–90) is one of the finest essays in secular and domestic Gothic. He built a house for himself at Holmbury St Mary, Surrey, in 1873–6. See also Plates pp. 58–9.

Arthur Edmund Street, *Memoir of George Edmund Street, RA, 1824–1881*, 1888, 1972.
Henry-Russell Hitchcock, 'G. E. Street in the 1850s', *Journal of the Society of Architectural Historians*, 1960.
John Summerson, 'Two London Churches', in *Victorian Architecture: Four Studies in Evaluation*, 1970.
Stefan Muthesius, *The High Victorian Movement in Architecture, 1850–1870*, 1972.
David B. Brownlee, *The Law Courts. The Architecture of George Edmund Street*, 1984.

Francis William Troup (1859–1941)

F. W. Troup was born in Aberdeenshire and articled to the Glasgow firm of Campbell Douglas and Sellars. In 1883 he moved to London to enter the office of J. J. Stevenson, and he set up in practice in 1889. Steeped in the Arts and Crafts movement, he designed an impressive range of building types, including both small houses and office buildings. His reputation has been tarnished by his assisting Herbert Baker in the rebuilding of the Bank of England in the 1920s. See also Plates pp. 148–9.

Neil Jackson, *F. W. Troup, Architect. 1859–1941*, 1985.

Hugh Thackeray Turner (1853–1937)

Thackeray Turner was a pupil of Sir Gilbert Scott and chief assistant to George Gilbert Scott junior. In 1885 he entered into partnership with Colonel Eustace J. A. Balfour (1854–1911), brother of A. J. Balfour the future prime minister and a pupil of Basil Champneys. In 1890 Balfour became surveyor to the Grosvenor Estate in London, where Balfour and Turner designed town houses and flats in an urbane 'Queen Anne' manner. In the country, Turner demonstrated his Arts and Crafts ideals in his reticent, traditional houses. From 1885 until 1911 he was secretary of the Society for the Protection of Ancient Buildings. His domestic works include Nos. 1–6 Balfour Place, London (1891–4), York Street Ladies Chambers, London (1892), Wycliffe Buildings, Guildford, Surrey (1894), Lygon Place, Ebury Street, London (1910). See also Plates pp. 103–5.

RIBA Journal, 1 January 1938, p. 258.
Annual Report of the SPAB, 1938, pp. 9–11.
The Grosvenor Estate in Mayfair, Survey of London, Part I, 1977, Part II, 1980.

Sir Raymond Unwin (1863–1940)

Raymond Unwin was born near Rotherham, Yorkshire, and was trained both as an engineer and an architect. He was in partnership with his second cousin and brother-in-law Barry Parker (q.v.) from 1896 until 1914, after which date he concentrated on his work as a town planner. He wrote extensively on both town planning and architecture. See also Colour Plate P and Plates pp. 219–21, 226–7.

Charles Francis Annesley Voysey (1857–1941)

Born in Yorkshire, the son of an Anglican clergyman who later founded his own Theistic Church, Voysey was articled to J. P. Seddon and then worked in the office of George Devey. He set up in practice in 1881 but began by designing fabrics, wallpapers and rugs. Most of Voysey's work consisted of medium-sized houses, characterised by his somewhat puritanical aesthetic. He also designed a wallpaper factory for Sanderson and Sons (1902) and much furniture. His houses include New Place, Haslemere, Surrey (1897), Lowicks, Frensham, Surrey (1894), the Orchard, Chorleywood, Middlesex (1899) for himself, and a house for H. G. Wells at Sandgate, Kent (1902). See also Colour Plate I, Plates pp. 130–3, 206 (*right*), and Plan 4, p. 36.

John Betjeman, 'C. F. A. Voysey: the Architect of Individualism', *Architectural Review*, lxx, 1931, pp. 93–6.
John Brandon-Jones, *C. F. A. Voysey: a Memoir*, 1957.
John Brandon-Jones, 'C. F. A. Voysey', in Peter Ferriday, ed., *Victorian Architecture*, 1963.
Nikolaus Pevsner, 'C. F. A. Voysey', in *Studies in Art, Architecture and Design*, vol. ii, 1968.
David Gebhard, *Charles F. A. Voysey, Architect*, 1975.
Joanna Symonds, *Catalogue of Drawings by C. F. A. Voysey in the Drawings Collection of the Royal Institute of British Architects*, 1976.
John Brandon-Jones and others, *C. F. A. Voysey, Architect and Designer, 1857–1941*, 1978.
Duncan Simpson, *C. F. A. Voysey and the Architecture of Individuality*, 1979.

Fairfax Blomfield Wade (1851–1919)

Fairfax B. Wade was the brother of the sculptor George Wade, for whom he designed one of a pair of houses, Nos. 63 and 64 Sloane Street, London (1894–6). He later changed his name to Fairfax B. Wade-Palmer. See also Plate p. 197.

Nikolaus Pevsner, 'Goodhart-Rendel's Roll-call', *Architectural Review*, 1965, reprinted in Alastair Service, ed., *Edwardian Architecture and its Origins*, 1975, p. 480.

George Walton (1867–1933)

George Walton was born in Glasgow and first trained as a bank clerk. In 1888 he opened a firm for interior decoration and designed tearooms in Glasgow for Miss Cranston, as did C. R. Mackintosh. Walton moved to London in 1897. Like his friend C. F. A. Voysey, Walton also designed wallpapers and furniture. During the First World War he worked for the Central Liquor Traffic Control Board, redesigning nationalised public houses in the Carlisle area. His houses included the White House, Shiplake, Berkshire (1908) and Wern Fawr, Harlech, Wales (1907–10). See also Plates pp. 140–1.

Nikolaus Pevsner, 'George Walton', *Journal of the RIBA*, xlvi, 1939, reprinted in *Studies in Art, Architecture and Design*, 1968, vol. ii.

Philip Speakman Webb (1831–1915)

Born in Oxford, Webb first trained with the Reading architect, John Billing, and then worked with George Edmund Street. His first independent work was the Red House at Bexleyheath, Kent (1859–60, Plates pp. 60–1) for his friend William Morris, whom he had met in Street's office. This house and other early buildings show the influence of Street's Gothic manner but soon Webb became more eclectic in style, combining influences ranging from the 'Queen Anne' to the Byzantine. His work was almost entirely domestic and was conspicuous for sound construction and painstaking attention to detail and the careful use of traditional materials. Few of his houses survive intact. His important works included Arisaig, Inverness-shire (1863), Rounton Grange, Yorkshire (1872), Smeaton Manor, Yorkshire (1876–9) and Clouds House, East Knoyle, Wiltshire (1876–86). See also Colour Plate D and Plates pp. 62–3, 74–5.

George Jack, 'An Appreciation of Philip Webb', *Architectural Review*, xxxviii, 1915, pp. 1–6.
W. R. Lethaby, *Philip Webb and his Work*, 1935, 1979.
John Brandon-Jones, 'Philip Webb', in Peter Ferriday, ed., *Victorian Architecture*, 1964.
Robert Macleod, 'William Morris and Philip Webb', in *Style and Society: Architectural Ideology in Britain, 1835–1914*, 1971.

William White (1825–1900)

William White was a pupil of George Gilbert Scott and set up in practice in Cornwall in 1847. Like his friend G. E. Street, White was one of the most original Gothic Revivalists of the 1850s. His work was largely ecclesiastical but he designed a number of vicarages and a few larger houses, notably Quy Hall, Cambridgeshire (1868), and Humewood, Ireland (1866–70). See also Colour Plate B and Plates pp. 56–7.

'The Late William White, FSA', *Journal of the RIBA*, vii, 1900, pp. 145–6.
Paul Thompson, 'The Writings of William White', in John Summerson, ed., *Concerning Architecture*, 1968.
Mark Girouard, *The Victorian Country House*, 1971, 1979.
Stefan Muthesius, *The High Victorian Movement in Architecture, 1850–1870*, 1972.

Edgar Wood (1860–1935)

Born near Manchester and articled to James Murgatroyd of Manchester, Edgar Wood was the most important Arts and Crafts architect in the north of England. He was in partnership with J. H. Sellars after 1904. He designed the Methodist church and school in Middleton, Lancashire (1899) and the First Church of Christ Scientist in Manchester (1903). With Sellars he designed Upmeads, Stafford (1908), a house with a flat concrete roof. See also Plates pp. 142–3.

John Archer, 'Edgar Wood and J. Henry Sellars', in Alastair Service, ed., *Edwardian Architecture and its Origins*, 1975.
Julian Treuherz, ed., *Partnership in Style: Edgar Wood and J. Henry Sellars*, Manchester City Art Gallery exhibition catalogue, 1975.

Bibliography

All the quotations from *Das Englische Haus* by Hermann Muthesius have been taken from *The English House*, translated by Janet Seligman and edited by Dennis Sharp (Crosby Lockwood Staples 1979). Contemporary books on domestic architecture, let alone relevant articles in *Country Life*, *The Builder* and other journals, are far too many to be listed here as a flood of well-illustrated books on modern houses by such authors as Lawrence Weaver and W. Shaw Sparrow appeared in the years after 1900. These books alone testify to the importance of domestic architecture in England at the time. A very comprehensive bibliography of these publications and of modern writings is given by Roderick Gradidge in his *Dream Houses: The Edwardian Ideal* (Constable 1980), which is essentially concerned with the 1890s.

In the preparation of the exhibition catalogue, *The English House 1860–1914* (International Architect and The Building Centre Trust 1980), and this present work, the following modern books were of particular assistance: Susan Beattie, *A Revolution in London Housing: LCC Housing Architects and their Work 1893–1914* (GLC, Architectural Press 1980); John Brandon-Jones and others, *C. F. A. Voysey: Architect and Designer 1857–1941* (Lund Humphries 1978); Mark Girouard, *The Victorian Country House* (Clarendon 1971, and Yale 1981); Mark Girouard, *Sweetness and Light: The 'Queen Anne' Movement 1860–1900* (Clarendon 1977); Peter Inskip, *Edwin Lutyens* (Academy Editions 1979); Andrew Saint, *Richard Norman Shaw* (Yale 1976); Alastair Service, Ed., *Edwardian Architecture and its Origins* (Architectural Press 1975); Alastair Service, *Edwardian Architecture* (Thames and Hudson 1977); in addition to the volumes of Nikolaus Pevsner's *Buildings of England* series (Penguin) and the printed *Catalogue of the Drawings Collection of the Royal Institute of British Architects*.

The following are more recent additions to the field: Peter Davey, *Arts and Crafts Architecture* (Architectural Press 1980); Mary Comino, *Gimson and the Barnsleys* (Evans Brothers 1980); Jill Franklin, *The Gentleman's Country House and its Plan 1835–1914* (Routledge & Kegan Paul 1981), which contains plans of many houses illustrated in this book and also a comprehensive list of houses giving documentary source material; Roderick Gradidge, *Edwin Lutyens: Architect Laureate* (George Allen & Unwin 1981); various authors, *Lutyens: The Work of the English Architect Sir Edwin Lutyens (1869–1944)* (Arts Council of Great Britain 1981); Gavin Stamp, *Robert Weir Schultz and his Work for the Marquesses of Bute* (Mount Stuart 1981); Clive Aslet, *The Last Country Houses* (Yale 1982); Margaret Richardson, *Architects of the Arts and Crafts Movement* (Trefoil 1983); while Stefan Muthesius – great nephew of Hermann – provides a welcome and necessary antidote to the theme of this present and all these books in *The English Terraced House* (Yale 1982).

Some of the material in this present work, together with a longer essay on Lutyens's Deanery Garden and one on the strange history of Norman Shaw's Grims Dyke by Andrew Saint was published in *International Architect*, vol. i, no.6, 1981.

It should be noted that the 1980 Exhibition Catalogue, *The English House, 1860–1914*, although much shorter than this book, contained illustrations of several original drawings and plans of almost every house which it has not been possible to include here.

Index

Locations are given under the main entry for each property (for London properties, see also the entry for London). Page numbers in *italic* refer to the illustrations in the text

Index

Index

Index